Other Kinds of Families:

Embracing Diversity in Schools

Other Kinds of Families:

Embracing Diversity in Schools

Edited by

TAMMY TURNER-VORBECK
MONICA MILLER MARSH

Teachers College, Columbia University
New York and London

Published by Teachers College Press, 1234 Amsterdam Avenue, New York, NY 10027

Portions of Chapter 7 previously appeared in J. Kroeger (2006), "Stretching performances in education: The impact of gay parenting and activism on identity and school change," *The Journal of Educational Change*. Reprinted with permission from *The Journal of Educational Change*.

Chapter 9: "Been no crystal ball" first appeared in *Homeless in America, Part One: A Children's Story*. Copyright ©1999 by the Insitute for Children and Poverty.

Library of Congress Cataloging-in-Publication Data

Other kinds of families: embracing diversity in schools / edited by Tammy Turner-Vorbeck and Monica Miller Marsh.
    p. cm.
  Includes index.
  ISBN 978-0-8077-4839-8 (hardcover) — ISBN 978-0-8077-4838-1 (pbk.)
  1. Home and school—United States. 2. Parent-teacher relationships—United States. 3. Multicultural education—United States. I. Turner-Vorbeck, Tammy. II. Miller Marsh, Monica 1965–
  LC225.3.085 2007
  371.19'2—dc22

                                                                          2007024416

ISBN: 978-0-8077-4838-1 (paper)
ISBN: 978-0-8077- 4839-8 (hardcover)

Printed on acid-free paper
Manufactured in the United States of America
15 14 13 12 11 10 09 08   8 7 6 5 4 3 2 1

To all members of the human family,
who form their own unique familial bonds
and then, together,
bravely face the ontological questions
of the human condition.

And to our own children,
Kristen, Cassandra, Justin, Paul, Adam, and Angelika
who continue to bravely face obstacles unfairly
put before them long ago.

They are our inspiration.

Contents

Introduction

Tammy A. Turner-Vorbeck
Monica Miller Marsh

When we each enrolled our newly adopted older children in our respective public school systems, state university campus preschool/kindergarten program, and Catholic school (in the states of Indiana and New York), our professional experience did not prepare us for the multitude of biases and obstacles we encountered and continue to encounter today as members of families labeled "nontraditional." From trying to complete forms that were ignorant, if not insensitive, to the complicated dimensions of our families to the frustrated and often tearful reactions of our children to their teachers' assignments to bring in nonexistent baby photographs and to write about the origin of first names, we each found ourselves actively educating school personnel and advocating for more inclusive definitions and representations of family in school and curriculum. Our personal circumstances and experiences necessitated a championing of a relatively unrecognized form of diversity, and through that, our individual passions for family diversity were born.

We first met at a National Association of Multicultural Education (NAME) conference in 2002 in Washington, D.C., in a small session on commercial curriculum materials available for teachers wanting to present diverse definitions of family to their students, one of the only two sessions among hundreds that year that had anything to do with family diversity. After a somewhat lively discussion among participants, the session ended, and we wandered outside the meeting room and struck up a conversation in the hallway. It was there that the seeds were planted for this book, though we didn't yet realize it. We shared stories of our personal and professional interests in the topic of family diversity, having both recently adopted older children and both being teacher educators. We exchanged business cards and vowed to stay in touch. We met again at the 2004 NAME conference in Kansas City to cultivate our ideas for this book.

Although educational and social issues surrounding family diversity are of critical importance as the demographics of families in both the United

States and the world change, they are an ignored part of broader diversity discussions. Family structure remains a neglected focus within diversity studies and education. We contend that the vast diversity of families found in schools and society today suggests an urgent need for a reconsideration of the ways in which families are currently and have come to be represented in school curriculum and culture.

Along with critical analyses, an examination of the school experiences of members of diverse families is needed to illuminate what it means to live as a member of an "other kind of family." To begin this discussion, the construct of the *other* needs to be clarified. Constructions of "otherness" occur through various discourses, wherever *we* are *it* and *they* are *the other*, in the definition of the *essential* versus the *inessential*, when *one* is *the absolute* and *the other* is *the subject*, and when we define *the other* relative to *ourselves* (Madrid, 2001). We find this construct, this phenomenon of the "othering" of peoples, to be under investigation in many related fields of study including, but certainly not limited to, curriculum studies, multiculturalism, ethnic studies, feminism, gay and lesbian studies, cultural studies, and family studies. Scholars tend to want to speak analytically of "the other" in a manner that indicates simply a lack of inclusion. There are deeper implications, however. *There is a highly personal cost to be paid for othering.* A writer in critical multiculturalism, Arturo Madrid (2001), has provided a glimpse at the personal dimensions of "othering" in this brief passage:

> Being *the other* means feeling different; is awareness of being distinct; is consciousness of being dissimilar. It means being outside the game, outside the circle, outside the set. It means being on the edges, on the margins, on the periphery. Otherness means feeling excluded, closed out, precluded, even disdained and scorned. It produces a sense of isolation, of apartness, of disconnectedness, of alienation. (p. 25)

Traditional discourses on the family have served to create teachable and researchable typologies of families on dimensions such as family structure, psychological soundness, ethnicity, and morality, among others. These discourses have constructed a normative conception of what defines a family as well as what constitutes a normal, healthy and, thus, valued family. Forms of family that diverge from these so-called standards often go unrecognized and unappreciated, and are even pathologized by labels such as *dysfunctional* or *morally wrong*. Discourses of family in education include overt, hidden, and null curricula in both formal and informal forms. Representations of family in popular culture circulate additional discourses through informal forms of curriculum. The chapters in this book consider and critique the view of the family and the experience of family as being absolute states. The authors not only advocate for opening spaces for a reconsideration of the multiple, interconnected, and complex ways in which families are formed, viewed, and function, but also for creating pedagogical opportunities to explore this complexity meaningfully.

In addition to providing critical and theoretical analyses of conceptions of family in school and culture, the chapters in this book offer narrative experiences of family to complement and bring deeper meaning to the more abstract discussions of family diversity. A comprehensive collection such as this sheds much-needed light on the topic of family diversity and on the very nature of life in a variety of families. We believe that neither the theoretical analyses nor the narratives of experience could alone produce so powerful an understanding as the combination. Instead of drawing exclusively from research in education, sociology, or psychology, this book creates a highly nuanced portrait of family diversity by drawing on a range of research methodology and writing styles spanning narrative, cultural studies, sociology/anthropology, education, social psychology, and policy studies. With its collection of analytical and experiential scholarship, this book offers a unique exploration of the phenomenon of family diversity.

The book is divided into two distinct parts. In Part I, the chapter authors contribute personal narratives, case studies, and stories highlighting "othered" forms of family and their schooling experiences. Chapters 1 through 5 are written from the multiple perspectives of parent, teacher, principal, school counselor, and scholar. These chapters address issues of single-parent, biracial, foster, and immigrant families through both personal and professional lenses.

Part II of this book features empirical and theoretical analyses that examine representations of the family in American school curriculum and culture. Drawing on sociocultural, critical, sociological, and interpretive theories, Chapters 6 through 10 further explore the representations of family that have been presented in Part I. In particular, these chapters discuss the forms and functions of three examples of colonial American families, which are juxtaposed with the families of today; the necessary changes in ethical and philosophical dimensions of practice to address the needs of gay and lesbian families; the representations of adoption in children's literature; the experiences and representation of homeless families in school and culture; and the overt, hidden, and null curricula of family in schools.

At the end of each chapter in the book are Questions for Reflection to help readers deepen their engagement with family diversity.

REFERENCE

Madrid, A. (2001). Missing people and others: Joining together to expand the circle. In M. Andersen & P. Hill-Collins (Eds.), *Race, class, and gender*. Belmont, CA: Wadsworth.

DIVERSE FAMILIES: NARRATIVES OF EXPERIENCE

The chapters in Part I feature personal narratives, case studies, and stories highlighting *other kinds of family* and their schooling experiences.

In Chapter 1, Elizabeth Heilman opens the collection by offering definitions of *family* and explaining the concept of family hegemony. This chapter weaves Heilman's personal narrative with the theoretical as she details her family's multiple transgressions from the hegemonic family mold. Heilman focuses particularly upon consequences for family-school interactions and offers suggestions for teachers.

In Chapter 2, A. Y. "Fred" Ramirez considers the involvement of immigrant families in their children's schooling. Data were gathered through interviews with parents, prospective teachers, practicing teachers, and other school personnel, in an attempt to understand how schools can better support the cultures of all families. The chapter concludes with examples of successful school programs and offers strategies for working with immigrant families.

In Chapter 3, Teresa Rishel, a former elementary school principal, elucidates how school climate and culture affect the daily lives of students and parents. She brings to light both the subtle and obvious ways and the extent to which parents are often disallowed participation in their child's education. She shares her insights on how the seemingly simplistic traditions and activities of schooling (field trips, committees, sports, PTO, school lunches) surface as potentially disparaging and alienating methods of prohibiting the inclusion of all family types and structures as participants in the school community.

As a first-grade teacher, Lisa Rieger uses her perspective in Chapter 4 to explore how to effectively dialogue with and include all kinds of families in the school culture. She believes that as young children enter the world of school, they bring an incredible wealth of life experience with them. Much of this experience centers upon developing students' individual identities and their relationships with the people who love and care for them. She examines the value in genuinely celebrating the growth, learning, and rich diversity within the classroom with students and their families, and she provides the reader with specific classroom activities that invite students and their families to tell their unique stories.

The focus of Chapter 5 is on foster youth who are underrepresented in higher education and overrepresented in state prisons. Ilyana Marks argues that professional school counselors (PSCs), such as herself, are aptly positioned to provide the transitional supports and academic guidance to enable foster youth to develop the strengths and resilience necessary for college preparedness. She offers a systemic approach for PSCs to draw upon federal, state, and community support to effectively service former wards of the court in their efforts to obtain advanced degrees.

Chapter 1

Hegemonies and "Transgressions" of Family: Tales of Pride and Prejudice

Elizabeth Heilman

This book describes variations on families that are clearly different from what exists in the popular imagination as the dominant or ideal family. These include biracial families, adoptive families, stepfamilies, gay families, and immigrant families, for example. Each of these families experiences social stresses and complex challenges in dealing with institutions ranging from schools and social services to medical providers and real estate agencies. This chapter, however, addresses more subtle and sometimes complex forms of family hegemony. These include the number of children, the age range of children and partners, how family members look in relation to each other, the type of mother and couple in the family, multistage families, and whether the family appears to have just too many, although perhaps subtle, markers of difference. Each of these transgressions departs from a hegemonic cultural ideal of family. In writing this chapter, I am arguing that the familiar ways to think about not only families but also about family diversity hides the complexity of experience and discrimination. Families have many, many characteristics, and each one of them is subject to both idealization and stereotyping and discrimination.

THE NORMAL AND IDEAL FAMILY

To begin, "family" itself is a loose concept with many definitions, alternatively emphasizing residence, rules, legal status, genetics, and emotionalties.

7

From the U.S. Census Bureau (2004):

> A family is a group of two people or more (one of whom is the householder) related by birth, marriage, or adoption and residing together; all such people (including related subfamily members) are considered as members of one family.

From a historian:

> It is worth noting that the word *family* originally meant a band of slaves. Even after the word came to apply to people affiliated by blood and marriage, for many centuries the notion of family referred to authority relations rather than loved ones. (Coontz, 1992, pp. 43–44)

From the *Archives of General Psychiatry*:

> A family is a social group organized or governed by a repeatable set of rules. (Jackson, 1965, p. 590)

From the American Academy of Family Physicians (2003):

> The family is a group of individuals with a continuing legal, genetic and/or emotional relationship. Society relies on the family group to provide for the economic and protective needs of individuals, especially children and the elderly.

From a second grade student:

> A family is people who live together who help and love each other. (Fuller & Olsen, 1997, p. 3)

Although these definitions of family seem vague, the commonly held conceptions of the "ideal" family and the "normal" family are less vague and easier to capture. The fields of psychology, sociology, and law all have explicit definitions of both the normal and the ideal. As Walsh (2003) describes, "a family is viewed as normal if it fits patterns that are common or expectable in ordinary families. . . by definition families deviating from the norm are abnormal" (p. 6). "Normal" is actually a mathematically relevant concept, and in psychology it means approximately average in any psychological trait. A normal family is thus simply a statistically typical family. These days, a never-divorced, two-parent family with two children is still often called "normal" in colloquial use, even though fewer than one-fourth of households conform to this family model and this includes families that will experience divorce or some other form of family restructuring in the future. According to the U.S. Census Bureau (2000), the average household size was 2.59 in 2000, and nuclear families, made up of married couples with children, fell to 23.5% of all households in 2000, down from 45% in 1960.

About half of today's children will spend some portion of childhood in a single-parent family, and more than a third will live with a stepparent. Over half of marriages end in divorce, and two-thirds of divorced women and three-quarters of divorced men will remarry. These increasing rates of divorce and separation, repartnering, and formation of stepfamilies mean that many children may now have full siblings (sharing both biological parents), half siblings (sharing one biological parent), and stepsiblings (who are not biologically related but who each has a biological parent in a partner relationship). According to recent census data, when children lived with only one parent, other adults were present 41% of the time when the parent was a mother and 60% of the time when the parent was a father, and these adults are not counted as stepparents, although many fulfill that role. An opposite-sex unmarried partner was in the household for 1 in 8 children living with a single mother and 1 in 3 of those living with a single father. About half of children without either parent had at least one grandparent in the household (U.S. Census, 2003).

As this brief review suggests, there is so much family diversity that a statistical norm is no longer meaningful. Yet the *normal* family remains a powerful image in our collective imagination, as does the *ideal* family. While the *normal* family is statistically the most *average* or least statistically deviant, the *ideal* family is simply the one that seems to be the *best*. The ideal family in American culture seems to feature married heterosexuals, preferably a tastefully blond mother and a dark-haired father, who have easily and naturally conceived and birthed their two children. The children are spaced about three years apart, and the boy is older. The cultural association between a particular type of family and an ideal family has long roots and received a boost from 1950s social science research. As Walsh (2003) explains, there was a conflating move from statistical normality to ideal made by Talcott Parsons in the 1950s in his influential studies of the "normal family" in which the White, middle-class, suburban, nuclear family came to be defined as "universal and essential for human development" (Parsons & Bales, 1955, p. 6). How did this happen?

WHAT IS FAMILY HEGEMONY?

The ideal has a powerful influence when a certain type of family "naturally" seems better. When one group or type seems to be implicitly better than another, it is what sociologists call a *hegemonic* construction. Hegemonic constructions and cultural practices are those to which most people give "spontaneous consent" to the "general direction imposed on social life by the dominant fundamental group" (Gramsci, 1978, p. 12). Family hegemony is the cultural power of the "ideal" family construct. This two-child nuclear family is commonly seen on television and in magazine stories, and in advertisements for vacations, new cars, and cereal among other products. The boy is often about 10 years old, his sister 7. As a university professor, I have frequently asked American preservice teacher college students to "draw a typical family," and this is what is most commonly depicted, often along with a medium-sized dog. About a third of my students draw three children or also depict grandparents. This is consistent with research on conceptions of family among college students (Etaugh & Malstrom, 1981; Fine, 1986) and school teachers (Fry & Addington, 1984; Santrock & Tracy, 1978), which suggests that normal family concepts exist and that people are stereotyped according to family status and family composition.

In her book *Life's America,* Wendy Kozol (1994) describes how *Life* magazine helped create the hegemonic image of the White, nuclear, middle-class American family with traditional gender roles. As Shank (1996) points out, when other families were represented in *Life* magazine, "they were used to represent the social and political problems that threatened the happy ideal" (p. 530). Relying on "the powerful rhetoric of domesticity and the equally persuasive capabilities of the news photograph," the photo essays in the section called "The Week's Events" translated "social and political issues into narratives about representative families." The effect was that in *Life* magazine, "pictures of families promoted ideals about home and private life, public issues, social identities, and ultimately, the nation itself" (Kozol, 1994, pp. viii–ix). The ideal family then became not just a statement about normalcy, but, much more powerfully, a symbol of safety, success, happiness, and patriotism, and a wide range of publications and popular media has helped create the image (Coontz, 1992; Olson & Douglas, 1997).

While family diversity is increasing, as is awareness of this diversity, it is worth noting that "there is no political support for policies or programs aimed at buttressing variants (Mason, Skolnick, & Sugarman, 1998), and there remains vast governmental policy support for the hegemonic ideal. For example, the 1996 Welfare Reform Act, referred to as the "Personal Responsibility and Work Opportunity Reconciliation Act of 1996" (PRWORA), stated, "The Congress makes the following findings: (1) Marriage is the foundation of a successful society. (2) Marriage is an essential institution of a successful society which promotes the interests of children." In 2003, Congress reaffirmed this. President George W. Bush declared October 12–18, 2003, to be "Marriage Protection Week," during which he called for the "protection" of the "sacred institution" of heterosexual marriage by the funding of the "Healthy Marriage Initiative," which Congress passed in 2006. The goals include "increasing the percentage of children who are raised by two parents in a healthy marriage" (Administration for Families and Children, 2006), leaving no question that the hegemony of the ideal family structure is alive and well, even if not the "ideal family." When these sorts of views are so dominant in the culture and even in legislation, it can be hard to realize the extent to which such ideas are culturally created and the extent to which we attribute positive qualities to the typical or ideal family and negative qualities to a wide range of departures from the ideal. Connell (2000) explains how hegemony works. The hegemonic form "need not be the most common form" (p. 11); it is simply the most valued.

Historian Gillis (1996) argues that we all live in two families. One is our actual family that we live *with* and the other is this ideal hegemonic family that Gillis says we live *by*, or in comparison with. The family we live *by* is a set of ideals and images that shape our expectations of how our families should be, and these myths are so basic to our experiences that we are often unaware of just how important they are. In reviewing Gillis's work, Skolnick (1998) points out that since the 1970s the ideology of "The Family" and the sociology of the Parsonsian model have been critiqued, and even implicitly critiqued in popular culture in programs such as *Roseanne* and *The Simpsons*. Yet, she observes:

> Images of "the family we live by" continue to exercise power over American hearts, minds, and politics. This power should puzzle the alarmists who warn that family values have declined, that we live in a postmarital or postnuclear family culture. Indeed, how can the alarmists explain the emotional appeal of their own jeremiads if family values are obsolete? (p. 233)

Hegemonies of family can create negative self-judgments in the same way that other stereotypes do. Thus, it is not just others who make these judgments but the family members themselves. As Ganong, Coleman, and Mapes wrote in 1990, "Negative evaluation of one's family structure may lead to lowered self-esteem" (p. 293). Family structure stereotypes may also influence how members of different family forms perceive and value themselves. There is evidence that this is so for stepfamily members (Coleman & Ganong, 1987; Visher & Visher, 1988), divorced people (Gerstel, 1987), and single adults (Cargan, 1986).

In the following two sections, I address particular constructs of the hegemony of family with vignettes contextualized within the research on the aspect of family under discussion. The research is highly uneven, since some aspects have been explored in a significant body of research, while others remain largely ignored. I use only stories from my own experience and that of my immediate friends and colleagues, and I recognize that these narratives are highly subjective. Yet I find the range of experiences from a case study of one compelling. And I used to think I was pretty normal.

The Construct of Family Size and Composition

For 10 years, I was the parent of an only child. I'd always wanted more children, but I divorced when my son was young, and I preferred to have more children with a spouse. This took time. There is a 10-year gap between my first two children and only 19 months between my second child and the twins who are my third and fourth children. When I had one child, it was not enough per the ideal family construct; now that I have four, it is just too many. "How many children do you have?" I used to be asked. "Just one." I'd reply. (Why did I say "just"?) My perception of the response was that having only one child was stingy and reflected that I was perhaps a bit cold or maybe infertile. There was often a silence in which the hanging question seemed to be "Why just one?" Such inquiries and corresponding prejudice can be especially painful for families who wish to have more children but can't, and for families who have lost a child or children through death.

In contrast, when my three youngest children (all girls) were babies and toddlers under age 3, over and over again, strangers would comment with responses ranging from concern to distaste. "You've got your hands full!" they would exclaim, and "I'm glad it is you and not me!" I was unable to go out of the house with my three young children without eliciting public commentary. The general public response to my family of four still seems be that I am unruly and perhaps don't know about birth control. There is also the implicit, or even direct, suggestion that I cannot provide good care for so many children and, especially, as a professional woman, that I am surely shirking in some realm. In my current job, a small group of colleagues, without any knowledge of my family and private life at all but with knowledge of the number of publications I have written and the number of children I have birthed, apparently decided that I must be out of balance and they have made frequent patronizing remarks about the need to be with my family, take up hobbies, or work less.

While mothers with many children are seen as out of control or, at least, distracted, disorganized, and somewhat neglecting, children from large families are stereotyped as unattended and overly competitive with siblings and other children. In contrast, an only child is stereotyped as spoiled, lonely, self-centered, and noncooperative, with self-centered or overly indulgent parents. As Mancillas (2006) has discovered in a review of the literature, "negative stereotypes of only children are pervasive despite a growing trend toward single-child families and evidence of the only child's strengths. People maintain definite beliefs about the characteristics of each ordinal position in a family, typically viewing only children as lonely, spoiled, and maladjusted" (p. 270). Falbo's (1984) seminal research and review of the literature on the actual experience of only children suggested that only children tend to have higher self-esteem and achieve more, and subsequent research supports this. Yet this prejudice remains. According to the U.S. Census Bureau (2003), the percentage of American mothers who have only one child rose from about 10% to 23% between 1980 and 2000. About 20% of children under age 18 are singletons. Now it is as common for a woman to have no child or one child as it was to have four or five children 30 years ago. In 2002, 52% of families with children had just one or two children. In 1840, the average American woman had borne nearly *seven* children; a century later, the average had fallen to about two. Family size rose from a little over two children in 1940 to nearly four children in 1957, and by 2006, this had declined to 2.13.

In 1960, the average devout Catholic family had 4.83 children (Westoff & Jones, 1979), while today they contain only slightly more children than any other family. When I was a child and living in the New York metropolitan area in the late 1960s, my neighborhood included the Dooleys with eight children, the Fitzgeralds with five, and the Fitapauldis with 14. My own family contained four children. Two families, the Arthurs and the Walters, were Protestants with two children, and to me these families seemed quite odd. They had carpeting, air-conditioning, evenly green grass in their yard, and took part in a range of activities such as piano and dance class. Currently, in larger cities like New York and San Francisco, almost 30% of families have a single child (Newman, 2001).

The Construct of Homogeneity Among Family Members

Another way in which many families and family members experience prejudicial treatment occurs when a member doesn't seem to fit with the group. The hegemonic family, the ideal, is a biological unit of people who appear to be significantly alike because of looks, age, and size or because of similar religion and beliefs. The hegemonic family, the ideal, is a biological unit of people who are significantly homogeneous and who progress along predictable pathways. A dominant myth of family has to do with the natural stages of family life, such as the stage before having children, the preschool stage, or the empty nest stage. Families with members in multiple stages violate the hegemonic ideal. My son is now in college and his sisters are in elementary school, so we are also way out of line in terms of stages, and it is made worse by the fact that my partner has two grandchildren. We are a tri-stage family, simultaneously elementary school parents, empty nesters, and grandparents.

One morning, a few years ago, as I got ready for work, I realized that I had two parent teacher conferences that day, one in the morning and one much later at night. The first was for preschool, the second for high school. But I needed to pick one outfit for both, and I wanted the teachers in each place to view me as favorably as possible and to subject me and my family to as little prejudice as possible. "What signifiers should I wear today?" I had to ask myself. The ideal preschool mother doesn't work full-time, so she should wear a simple skirt or slacks, while the high school mother in my town does work full-time and she is successful, so she should wear a cool suit. What sort of information should I share? I just found a great math tutor for my son (good high school mother, cool). I was working on making each kid a scrapbook (good preschool mother). Oh, the discourses and signifiers to negotiate! This made me realize that since the ideal family spaces children three years apart and the ideal preschool mother is very different from the ideal high school mother, it was impossible, by definition, for me to be the ideal mother and for us to be the ideal family.

For 19 months, I had the right *number* of children—two—but we were still in violation of the ideal family since my children were so far apart in age and stage. As reported by Harris, Raley, and Rindfuss (2002), data from June Current Population surveys from 1985 and 1990 show that the median age difference between siblings is less than 3 years and two-thirds of sibling pairs have an age difference of 4 years or less. The Census Bureau does not calculate and report this data; instead, it reports overall family size correlated with race, income, and martial status. My family fits these statistics, but hidden in the average is my son's 10-year gap. I searched heartily for statistics on the percentage of families with larger gaps between siblings and came up with nothing comprehensive. Jann Blackstone-Ford (2007), author of *Midlife Motherhood* (2004), writes, "Most child rearing experts will agree that a three year age difference between siblings is ideal, but when divorce and remarriage are so prevalent in our society, it is not uncommon to find a ten, fifteen, or even twenty year difference between the oldest and the youngest sibling." I'm not sure how common or uncommon it is, but I do know that my children's 10-year gap makes people uncomfortable. Many simply ask, "So what happened?" The valued 3-year gap is supported as well by the U.S. Centers for Disease Control and Prevention (CDC), whose study on the topic recommended conceiving a child 18 to 23 months after the birth of a previous baby as the ideal spacing for the infant's health. The longer gap between children seems unnatural and unhealthy, and feeds into the same sort of cultural worries about family and sibling socialization that creates anxiety about only children. Increasing rates of divorce and separation, repartnering, and stepfamilies may mean that many "only" children acquire half siblings and stepsiblings (who are not biologically related but who each have a biological parent in a partner relationship). Children do not necessarily live in the same household as any of these siblings, but they may.

There is great variety in who counts as a sibling and who counts as something else—for example, "my stepdad's son." The definition of who is a sibling is also constructed differently between ethnic and cultural groups and societies (Cicirelli, 1994). For example, African-Caribbean and African people may view a range of biologically and nonbiologically related family members as siblings (Chamberlain, 1992; Graham 1999; Prevatt-Goldstein, 1999), and research in the United States focuses on the long-standing practice of "going for kin" among African-American communities wherein nonbiologically related people refer to, and act toward, each other as brother, sister, mother, father, and so on (Liebow, 1969; Stack, 1974). This raises the issue of the importance of culture, language, interpretation, and subjectivity to constructing definitions, and the importance of the social and emotional experiences of who is a sibling, rather than a self-evident, biological, or legal state. Being a sibling is a socially constructed relationship, not just a technical fact.

Highlighting half- and stepsibling distinctions is common. One of my older daughters' teachers insisted on the usage "half brother" in reference to my son, her brother, even though we have never made that distinction and it made my daughter uneasy. One of my neighbors has had physical custody and parenting duties for a stepdaughter for 10 years. Her three girls are 9, 11, and 12. Each parent brought a child from a previous marriage, and they had one together, and this mother is often asked which ones are "really hers," which, of course, makes both mother and daughters feel terrible. This happens often to families with adopted and nonadopted children as well. Although "they are all ours" or "we don't make that distinction" is a common response, the hegemony of blood relations as defining of family seems to create these inquiries. Conversely, among the more painful forms of family discrimination is the delegitimizing of any uglier, darker, less athletic, fatter, or in other way less desirably *different* child. Even when they are full genetic kin, such children are commonly asked if they are stepsiblings or adopted if their lighter, prettier, leaner siblings seem significantly different. Plain Jessica was teased by her uncle, "Are you sure you are Samantha's sister?" Thin, dark, and clumsy Christopher is asked by his P.E. teacher, "Do you and [blond, athletic] Tyler have different fathers?"

Even within families there can be confusion and inconsistency about who counts as a family member. Using panel data on approximately 9,400 individuals in the 1987–1988 and 1992–1994 waves of the National Survey of Families and Households, White (1998) examined discrepancies in reported sibling number. She found that 15% of the sample reported fewer siblings in the second wave than in the first wave, and 16% also reported more siblings. Although some may have died and been born, or departed or arrived due to marriage and divorce, there is clearly some shifting definition of *sibling* occurring in the minds of respondents as well.

My daughter and son were further delegitimized as "half siblings" because racial boundaries were crossed and they couldn't "pass" as full-blood siblings as many half and stepsiblings can. Always small for his age, my son is a dark-haired, biracial, half-Chinese kid, while my daughter is a tall, round-faced blond. According to the U.S. Census of 2000, nearly 7 million Americans identified themselves as members of one or more races (U.S. Census, 2001). Our family is Chinese, Irish-Catholic, Jewish, Eastern European, and Scottish. We are also a tri-religion family. My partner is Jewish, my son a sort of agnostic Buddhist, and my daughters participate in some aspects of both Catholic and Jewish life. When getting stitches for one daughter, we were asked to state our religion at the clinic admissions desk. While I paused, my daughter said, "It depends on what day." This seemed to be the right answer but it was utterly uncapturable, since the clerk needed to click one religion box. Are we secular humanists with ethnic commitments to several religions? While waiting for the doctor, we engaged in an inconclusive review of what we were and what we weren't. I wasn't able to locate a statistic on how many half and stepsiblings cross ethnic boundaries, but there must be a lot of parents and brothers and sisters who don't look like each other and who participate in different ethnic and religious traditions. And the number will increase. Interracial partnerships are rising, as are transracial adoptions. In 1990, about 14% of 18-to-19-year-olds, 12% of 20-to-21-year-olds, and 7% of 34-to-35-year-olds were involved in interracial relationships (Rosenfeld & Kim, 2005).

More than once, when strangers observe my son with his sisters, the relationship is misread, and the strangers comment on what a good babysitter he is. His identity and brotherly relationship is unseen and invalidated. This happened with me and my son, too, even though I am in my mid-forties because of my small, blond appearance, I am often thought to be in my mid-thirties. Sometimes when I am in public with my ethnic-looking, grown-up looking, college-age son, and I do something that shows we are close, like pay for his clothes or call him "dear," it is read as dating rather than motherly behavior. Apparently we don't *look like* mother and son, and so we are not treated that way in encounters with those who don't know us well. Worse, when my son was in high school, during parent-teacher conferences, teachers often used the phrase "parents *and guardians*," with an emphasis on *guardians* in what seemed to be an attempt to be inclusive of my obviously nonparental status. At his school, I sometimes found myself making allusions to his birth or my pregnancy with him so the teachers would get it. "Gee, when I was pregnant with Alex, I sure never imagined him learning trigonometry!"

This makes us self-conscious, to say the least. I wonder about the effects on my son of never seeming to belong in his own family.

The misreading of relationships also happens with my gray-bearded mate, whom I suspect is sometimes believed to be my father, or too old for me, although this is rarely blatant. In the hegemonic ideal family, the man is no more than 3 years older than the woman. The irritating stereotype here is that I am valued for my youth (this is incredibly tiresome for me in my middle age), instead of for my sharp mind, my professional vigor, and/or our solid compatibility. Any couple with an older-looking man and a younger-looking woman risks being seen through economic and physical reproduction lenses. In the stereotype, the man is supposedly attracted to the woman's functioning ovaries, and she, to his cash flow and manly accomplishment. In our case, my own cash flow and manly accomplishment are just fine, and we both fear my ovaries. But he is clearly older and, thus, we violate the life-stage norm of families, so the May-December trope is located to interpret our relationship.

Just as contemporary couples are more likely to cross boundaries of ethnicity, religion, and gender than they were in earlier years, there is also a significant increase in age differences among couples, including younger men with older women. In 2000, men were 6 or more years older than women in 24.7% of cohabiting unmarried couples and in 19.6% of married couples. As Johnson (2005) points out, "although the U.S. Census Bureau tracked these pairings differently between 1997 and 2003, there's clearly a rise." In 1997, at least 117,000 of 1.1 million unmarried couples nationwide were women with men at least 10 years younger, while at least 262,000 of 53 million married couples were women married to men at least 10 years younger. There are increasing examples and stories in the media of a widening age range in couple partnerships—for example, an *Oprah Magazine* story announcing "Now, more than ever, women are marrying men a quarter of a century older or a dozen years younger than themselves" (Brady, 2007). Yet, there is no question that families with such couples are still stigmatized. Johnson (2005) reports one couple's experience.

> "As if love crosses all boundaries and all things except for age," said Ms. Lutz, 53, who met her husband of 16 years, John, when she was 34 and he was 22. "It just couldn't possibly be that two people love each other and found mutual ground, could it? People just either assume that there's something provocative about our relationship or there's something wrong with John."

Stereotyping or misreading of the relationships never happens with my blond daughters. Not only are they seen as just fine and obviously mine, but up to four other additional children have been considered mine, too, because they all looked like me and were standing nearby. On a beach excursion with two friends and our kids, I took seven blond children between the ages of 6 and 8 over to a food stand. Like me, one of my friends has a set of twins. Surely nobody could think they were all mine. But they did. The sheer numerical improbability didn't stop two different people from commenting. One said, "You have a nice-looking family," and another asked, "Are they all yours?" The answer should have been, "Are you crazy? Are you completely out of your mind? Of course they are not all mine!" But the kids did *look like* siblings, and they did *look like* me. They looked more like me than their mothers, so they were assumed to be mine. This happens to me often when I have one or two extra blond children with me. The fact that it happened with a total of seven same-aged children reflects the power of the "families-look-alike" construct to overwhelm sheer reason.

THE EXPERIENCE OF STIGMA AND PREJUDICE RELATED TO FAMILY

What is most important to emphasize is that families that depart from hegemonic ideals are stigmatized and will experience the social stress of prejudice. As Ganong, Coleman, and Mapes wrote in 1990, most research on stereotypes has focused on categories of race, gender, physical attractiveness, religion, ethnicity, and occupations. Family structure, they argue, "is another social category and a potentially salient cue for stereotyping as are family positions related to different family structures (e.g., divorced mother, stepfather)" (p. 287). Yet, as they point out, and as remains true today, surprisingly little research has been done on stigma, stereotypes, and prejudice related to family.

Prejudice essentially means prejudgment, and although the term is most commonly associated with perceptions of racial and cultural groups, this type of thinking and response occurs across a wide range of categories in which power operates and in which ideals and symbolic types are frequently manifested in popular culture and in family and school socialization. Since family hegemonies are produced from local discourses and experiences as well as from broader cultural ideals, they are necessarily shot through with power, which means that some people benefit and others are disadvantaged. These experiences are embedded in cultural, material, institutional, and bodily relations. A simple set of questions to ask about whether a cultural hegemony exists for a dimension of family centers upon the notions of *consensus* and *consequence*: Is there loose consensus about what a typical family is, such as typical number or appearance of siblings? Does the image exclude many? Are there consequences for this exclusion?

Harvard psychologist Gordon Allport's classic work, *The Nature of Prejudice* (1954), provides this definition: "Prejudice is an antipathy based on faulty and inflexible generalization. It may be felt or expressed. It may be directed toward a group or an individual of that group" (p. 10). The experience of prejudice is one in which an external marker or sign becomes a stand-in for a characteristic that the holder is presumed to have or not have. The result is to be both unseen—to have one's actual qualities become invisible—and also to be mis-seen—to have qualities attributed that one does not have. These can be both positive and negative judgments. With prejudicial positive thinking, it is harder to imagine and see when the ideally signifying family transgresses; for example, when an attractive, upper-middle-class, two-child family inflicts child abuse. It is harder to imagine and see when a stigmatized family is healthy; for example, when an immigrant, single-parent, Mexican family with six children provides a sustaining and nurturing environment.

Not only are the objects and levels of expression of prejudice complex, but the origins of prejudice are complex as well. In fact, prejudice in any one person may arise from a mixture of cognitive and psychological processes. One of the most simplistic explanations for prejudice has been considered to be misinformation or faulty thinking. For example, a person might have inaccurate ideas about family composition and functioning. Since the nineteenth century, religion and social science have emphasized the value of the nuclear family described in this chapter. The idea that significantly different families (e.g. single-parent, step-, and multiracial families) represent less healthy types of family has been widely accepted as science, even though more recent researchers have provided substantial evidence to the contrary. Correcting misinformation, however, rarely has any significant impact on prejudices. Misperception, then, is a separate phenomenon from prejudice. As Morland (1963) points out, "We need to realize that, although sound knowledge is necessary to combat false information, it is not sufficient to change attitude. Facts do not speak for themselves; rather they are interpreted through the experiences and biases of those hearing them" (p. 125). Psychology tends to offer explanations for prejudice that are rooted in individual experience and emotional health or dysfunction, while sociologists consider social and economic structures and the distribution and experience of power, asking who benefits from dominant discourses and who is excluded. Most institutions construct family through class, cultural, and heterosexual privilege, and their policies, often overtly, aim to preserve dominant norms of femininity, masculinity, sexuality, and family life.

Erving Goffman (1986) described stigma as a disjunction between one's virtual social identity and one's actual social identity. This is very much like what Gillis (1996) described as the family one lives in versus the family one lives *by*. In *Stigma: Notes on the Management of Spoiled Identity* (1963/1986), Goffman explains stigma as "an attribute that is deeply discrediting within a particular social interaction" (p. 3). Stigma focuses on the public's attitude toward a person who possesses an attribute that falls short of societal expectations. The person with the attribute is "reduced in our minds from a whole and usual person to a tainted, discounted one" (p. 3).

Because of the dominance of family hegemonies, family members may find themselves trying to "pass." Passing occurs whenever an individual and/or his or her family is misread and when this misreading is allowed to go uncorrected. Internalizing hegemonies, unmarried couples may in some circumstances choose not to correct assumptions that they are married. This can occur with contentious divorced parents and with those who are happily living together. A family member, in sometimes highly subtle ways, may be willing not to correct an assumption that a child or a parent who is much older, poorer, less attractive, or of another race, is not connected to them. Children may allow peers to believe that their older mom is their grandmother, that their stepsiblings are biological siblings, and so on. This can become a burdensome misreading or white lie to maintain in school settings, and it intensifies the divide between public and private, and between home and school. Teachers might have no problems with an unmarried couple, but their students may not know this, since they correctly assess the wider social stigma about their family's transgression. Individuals adopt different guises in different situations as a way of coping with depersonalized and judgmental experience. These situational "false selves" may be contradictory and difficult to resolve, and may lead to feelings of guilt. Research on prejudice and cultural difference shows what an enormous impact stigmatization and doubles lives can have on children. Yet family hegemonies and stigma are not part of the mainstream discussion in education.

THE COMPLEXITIES OF MULTIPLE MYTHS AND MULTIPLE HEGEMONIES OF FAMILY

The hegemony of family is real, but I argue that my examples demonstrate that there are multiple myths and multiple hegemonies. The idea of family and the nature of family roles such as "mother of siblings" are always the site of *conflicting* forms of subjectivity. What are conflicting forms of subjectivity? The nature of the ideal family and the force of the hegemonic judgment changes to some extent depending on the aspect of family that is focused upon in specific contexts and communities. In 2004, the U.S. Census reported that Utah had the highest percentage of coupled households—67% (including unmarried and same sex couples)—while New York state had 52% and the District of Columbia had only 29%. These places, Mormon Utah and cosmopolitan New York, no doubt provide very different experiences of family. Clearly, some communities are more stigmatizing of departures from the mythic ideal and more supportive of expressions of family diversity. While a family of four children, for example, may be seen as large in some places, in others places it will not seem as large. For example, I'm the only parent of a family as large as four children among the professors where I work, but not in my neighborhood, which is full of big houses, many with three and four children. This means that my family seems smaller and less trangressive when I go home. My neighbor feels her family is more transgressive in her neighborhood than at work. Her family is more differently ethnic and immigrant when she comes home to the relatively homogeneous neighborhood from her more diverse work setting. In a neighborhood with a lot of immigrant families, she and others would probably experience her family differently.

Any given family presents and enacts their family in multiple settings, and these settings will be more and less stigmatizing. Where family is enacted and interpreted is not just in these broad regional places such as Utah, but in settings close to home—the shopping mall, grocery store, doctor's office, school, park, and the food stand at the beach. Any particular place will also be more and less stigmatizing of *different aspects* of the family that depart from the hegemonic ideal. So, for example, my neighbor's family, which includes international adoptees, may be seen as more odd when this mother takes her children to a doctor's office than when she takes them to church. In her church, she feels there is more of a global ideal or awareness and an approval of the ethical nature of this choice. Her doctor, by contrast, sees this family as having abnormal fertility. In a doctor's office, a subconscious preference for biological similarity may be more dominant. So, although the "ideal family" (and even the "normal family") has real cultural power, it must be understood as a loose construct, a flexible and sometimes conflicting hegemony, that operates with variation and operates to greater and lesser degrees in particular contexts.

Families, therefore, are different constructs and experiences in different places. The same family is different if they are in different neighborhoods, or different schools, or in their neighborhood and not their school. From the perspective of critical geography, space itself elicits or at least suggests certain expressions of family. Spatiality theories of critical geography are characterized by the fact that they don't accept the naturalness of physical space as simply a matter-of-fact product of human creation or influence.

Instead, these theories provide a means to examine how and why groups create spaces and how interpretations of space shape social, cultural, and political practices and, thus, also the formation of identity and meaning. When I enter into the preschool space, I am a different mother from when I enter into the high school space. Thus, from the perspective of critical geography, another way to think about it is that identity and family roles are always *performed,* and we all perform family roles in context and in place, and context and place and what they mean to us change.

Many geography theories draw a distinction between material spaces and mental or imagined spaces. Often, human geographers refer to this as *space* (referring to the material) and *place* (referring to the human-constructed meanings attached to specific spaces). This notion of "place" is an idea, a mental construct, or a meaning. Thus, it can be imagined and narrated. Place as a social construct is intimately connected to the social construction of identity and groups, and geographers with concern for identity often argue that place and identity are recursively constructed. Places and constructs such as "ideal family" are also recursively constructed.

The neighborhood as a cultural concept and, as a place, is created in part by the cultural concept of family. According to this view, the neighborhood as a place owes as much to *Leave It to Beaver* and *Desperate Housewives* as to the actual trees and homes. At the same time, ideas of family might be understood to be influenced by ideas of neighborhood, and the experience of family might be shaped by the experience of neighborhood. What should also be clear is that what we often have are multiply transgressing families, families that depart from the idea in many ways. Family diversity is itself diverse.

IMPLICATIONS FOR RESEARCHERS AND EDUCATORS

Multicultural research has documented how school policy, as well as culturally biased curricula and research paradigms and methods, can ignore marginalized people and their voices and their realities, while failing to serve the basic educational needs of many students. Conversely, culturally sensitive research has identified collaborative political action strategies and stakeholder research methods that lead to systems change and help diverse groups and communities gain recognition and enhanced capacities. Such research has implications for shifting the understanding of families and their experiences.

As preservice and inservice teachers, we first must understand that it is our job to teach all students, and that as a professional, it is our duty to recognize ways in which some students are valued and seen as more normal and wholesome while others are devalued. When teachers think critically about their own backgrounds and values, they have a better capacity to recognize and address preconceived and prejudicial notions about families they may have that could make it difficult for them to accept, understand, and effectively teach their students. Schools reflect their values not only in their curricula and materials, but in policies, hiring practices, governance procedures, and communications, sometimes referred to as the "hidden" curriculum—"the kinds of learnings children derive from the very nature and organizational design of the public school, as well as from the behaviors and attitudes of teachers and administrators" (Longstreet & Shane, 1993, p. 46) Are teachers comfortable talking about their own family diversity?

CONCLUSION

Teachers must gain interpersonal competence, that is, the ability to function comfortably with people who live in ways that seem different. Based on the research on effective intercultural communication, culturally competent individuals (1) cope effectively with the psychological and emotional stress of dealing with the unfamiliar, (2) quickly establish rapport with others, (3) sense other people's feelings, (4) communicate effectively with people from varying backgrounds, and (5) respond adequately to miscommunication (Giles, Coupland, Williams, & Leets, 1991). These complex skills are just as relevant for family diversity as they are for cultural diversity.

Families are present in a wide range of subject matter, and it is up to teachers to make sure the teaching is accurate and inclusive (Turner-Vorbeck, 2005). Family diversity is the norm, not the exception in American history (see Chapter 10, this volume). The use of narratives and children's literature can also be powerful ways for schools to explore family diversity and foster understanding, and improve student self-esteem and academic performance (see Chapter 8, this volume). When students can relate to the information being presented, they are more likely to understand academic concepts and experience success in school. As with all students, students from diverse families are most successful when schools honor and value them. The family as a hegemonic ideal and source of stigma and prejudice needs to be taken very seriously. The lenses of research need to expand to include a much wider consideration of multiple myths and multiple hegemonies of family. The strategies developed to address other forms of diversity can serve as a resource and starting point for more awareness and sensitivity, for challenging assumptions and warrants of privilege, for more research and for better practice in relation to family diversity. When diverse families can flourish without prejudice, our children will be healthier and we will have a more democratic and more just society.

QUESTIONS FOR REFLECTION

1. Do I believe that some family types are inherently better than others? Do I have different expectations of only children? Single-parent-family children? Adoptees?
2. Identify and analyze the key differences between the terms *ideal family*, *normal family,* and *hegemonic family*.
3. In your own words, explain *family hegemony*. How does family hegemony affect what happens in public school classrooms? Give examples from your own experiences.
4. Why do some critics feel that families are in decline? In what ways are families changing according to the U.S. Census?
5. Refer to the definition and discussion of *prejudice* in the chapter. Discuss what it means when mistakenly positive judgments are made. To whom does this happen? What assumptions are made? Whom might this harm? In what ways?
6. Explain how psychology, popular culture, law and policy, and school practice sometimes contribute to reinforcing family hegemony.

REFERENCES

Administration for Families and Children. (2006). *Healthy marriage initiative.* Retrieved October 3, 2006, from http://www.acf.hhs.gov/healthymarriage/.

Allport, G. (1954). *The nature of prejudice.* Boston: Beacon Press.

American Academy of Family Physicians. (2003). *Definition of family.* Retrieved October 3, 2006, from http://www.aafp.org/online/en/home/policy/policies/f/familydefinitionof.html.

Blackstone-Ford, J. (2004). *Midlife motherhood: A woman-to-woman guide to pregnancy and parenting.* New York: St. Martin's Press.

Blackstone-Ford, J. (2007). *Midlife mother. The huge age difference between siblings.* Retrieved March 3, 2007, from http://www.midlifemother.com/The%20New%20Normal/huge_age_differences .htm.

Brady, L. (2007). Love: What's age got to do with it?" *Oprah Magazine 8* (2), 131–138.

Bryan, L. R., Coleman, M., Ganong, L. H., & Bryan, H. (1986, February). Person perception; Family structure as a cue for stereotyping. *Journal of Marriage and the Family, 48*, 169–174.

Cargan, L. (1986). Stereotypes of singles: A cross-cultural comparison. *International Journal of Comparative Sociology*, 27, 200–208.

Chamberlain, M. (1992). Brothers and sisters, uncles and aunts: A lateral perspective on Caribbean families. In E.B. Silva & C. Smart (Eds.), *The new family?* (pp. 31– 45). London: Sage.

Cicirelli, V. G. (1994). Sibling relationship in cross-cultural perspective. *Journal of Marriage and the Family*, 56, 7–20.

Coleman, M., & Ganong, L. H. (1987). The cultural stereotyping of stepfamilies. In K. Pasley & M. Inger-Tallman, *Remarriage and stepparenting: Current research and theory* (pp. 19–41). New York: Gilford Press.

Connell, R. W. (2000). *The men and the boys*. Sydney: Allen & Unwin.

Coontz, S. (1992). *The way we never were: American families and the nostalgia trap*. New York: Basic Books.

Etaugh, C., & Malstrom, J. (1981). The effect of marital status on person perception. *Journal of Marriage and the Family*, 43, 801-805.

Falbo, T. (1984). *The single-child family*. New York: Guilford Press.

Fine, M. A. (1986). Perceptions of stepparents: Variation in stereotypes as a function of current family structure. *Journal of Marriage and the Family*, 48, 537–543.

Fry, P. S., & Addington, J. (1984). Professionals' negative expectations of boys from father-headed single-parent families: Implications for the training of child-care professionals. *British Journal of Developmental Psychology*, 2, 337-346.

Fuller, M. L., & Olsen, G. (1997). *Home-school relations: working successfully with parents and families*. Boston: Allyn and Bacon.

Ganong, L. H., Coleman, M., & Mapes, D. (1990). A meta-analytic review of family structure stereotypes. *Journal of Marriage and the Family*, 52, 287–297.

Gerstel, N. (1987). Divorce and stigma. *Social Problems*, 34, 172 186.

Giles, H., Coupland, N., Williams, A., & Leets, L. (1991). Integrating theory in the study of minority languages. In R. L. Cooper & B. Spolsky (Eds.), *The influence of language on culture and thought: Essays in honor of Joshua A. Fishman's sixty-fifth birthday* (pp. 113–136). New York: Mouton de Gruyter.

Gillis, J. R. (1996). *A world of their own making: Myth, ritual, and the quest for family values*. New York: Basic Books.

Goffman, E. (1986). *Stigma: Notes on the management of spoiled identity*. New York: Simon & Schuster. (Original published 1963)

Graham, M. J. (1999). The African-centred world view: Developing a paradigm for social work. *British Journal of Social Work*, 29 (2), 251–267.

Gramsci, A. (1978). *Selections from the prison notebooks of Antonio Gramsci*. (Q. Hoare & N. Smith, Trans. and Ed.). New York: International Publishers.

Harris, K., Raley R. K., and Rindfuss, R. R. (2002). Family configurations and child care patterns: Families with two or more preschool age children. *Social Science Quarterly 83* (2), 455–471.

Jackson, D. D. (1965). Family rules: Marital grid pro quo. *Archives of General Psychiatry*, 12, 589–594.

Johnson, L. (2005, October 9). It's not so unusual for women to be on the older end of May-December matches. *Post Gazette*. Retrieved October 3, 2006, from http://www.postgazette.com/pg/05282/583984.stm.

Kozol, W. (1994). *Life's America: Family and nation in postwar photojournalism.* Philadelphia: Temple University Press.

Liebow, E. (1969). *Tally's corner.* Boston: Little Brown.

Longstreet, W. S., & Shane, H. (1993). *Curriculum for a new millennium.* Boston: Allyn and Bacon.

Mancillas, A. (2006). Challenging the stereotypes about only children: A review of the literature and implications for practice. *Journal of Counseling and Development, 84* (3), 268–274.

Mason, M. A., Skolnick, S., & Sugarman, D. (1998). *All our families: New policies for a new century (A report of the Berkeley family forum).* New York: Oxford University Press.

Morland, K. (1963). The development of racial bias in young children. *Theory into Practice, 2* (3), 120–127.

Newman, S. (2001). *Parenting an only child.* New York: Broadway Books.

Olson, B., & Douglas, W. (1997, March). The family on television: Evaluation of gender roles in situation comedy. *Sex Roles, 36,* 409–427.

Parsons, T., & Bales, R. F. (1955). *Family, socialization, and interaction process.* Glencoe, IL: Free Press.

Personal Responsibility and Work Opportunity Reconciliation Act of 1996. Pub.L. 104-193, 110 Stat. 2105 (PRWORA). Retrieved October 6, 2006, from http://www.publicpolicy.umd.edu/puaf650-Fullinwider/handouts-Responsibility-Welfare%20Reform%20Act.htm.

Prevatt-Goldstein, B. (1999). Black siblings: A relationship for life. In A. Mullender (Ed.), *We are family: Sibling relationships in placement and beyond* (pp. 75–92). London: British Agencies for Adoption and Fostering.

Rosenfeld, M., & Kim, B. (2005). Independence of young adults and the rise of inter-racial and same-sex unions. *American Sociological Review 70*(4), 541–562

Santrock, J., & Tracy, R. (1978). Effects of children's family structure status on the development of stereotypes by teachers. *Journal of Educational Psychology, 70,* 754–757.

Shank, B. (1996). We're happy family: Me, my mom and daddy. *American Quarterly, 48*(3), 530–534.

Skolnick, A. (1998). Public dreams, private lives. *Contemporary Sociology, 27* (3), 233–235.

Stack, C. (1974). *All our kin.* New York: Harper & Row.

Turner-Vorbeck, T. (2005). Expanding multicultural education to include family diversity. *Multicultural Education, 13*(2), 6–10

U.S. Census Bureau. (2000). *Profile of General Demographic Characteristics for the United States: 2000.* Retrieved February 18, 2007, from http://www.census.gov/Press-Release/www/2001/tables/dp_us_2000.pdf.

U.S. Census Bureau. (2001). *Two or more races: Population 2000.* Retrieved October 3, 2006, from www.census.gov/prod/2001pubs/c2kbr01-6.pdf.

U.S. Census Bureau. (2003). *Living arrangements of children in 2003.* Retrieved October 3, 2006, from www.census.gov/population/ pop-profile/dynamic/LivArrChildren.pdf.

U.S. Census Bureau. (2004). *America's families and living arrangements: 2003.* Current Population Reports, P20-553. Retrieved October 3, 2006, from http://www.census.gov/prod/2004pubs/p20-553.pdf.

Visher, E. B., & Visher, J. S. (1988). *Old loyalties, new ties: Therapeutic strategies with stepfamilies.* New York: Brunner/Mazel.

Walsh, F. (2003). *Normal family processes: Growing diversity and complexity.* New York: Guilford Press.

Westoff, C. F., & Jones, E. F. (1979). The end of "Catholic" Fertility. *Demography, 16,* 209–217.

White, L. (1998). Who's counting? Quasi-facts and stepfamilies in reports of number of siblings. *Journal of Marriage and the Family, 60* (3), 725–733.

Chapter 2

Immigrant Families and Schools:
The Need for a Better Relationship

A. Y. "Fred" Ramirez

The subject of immigrant families and their relationship with schools is a vital topic for today's educators. Although there is an abundance of research on immigrant families, my contribution is that I write from my experiences as a son, student, teacher, *and* researcher. I am the product of immigrant grandparents; therefore, I am a third-generation, U.S.-born citizen. Many educators and academics in my life believed that partly due to my ethnicity, it would be difficult for me to succeed in education. I knew, though, that my grandparents came to this country to build a life of opportunity for themselves, as well as their children and their children's children. When I fulfilled the academic obligations for my degrees, I felt as if I were fulfilling the desires of my grandparents, which were to gain an education and to contribute to society. Contrary to my educational experiences, my parents and their friends experienced schools filled with animosity, prejudice, and racism. Although they were part of the K–12 educational system over 50 years ago, many of their experiences as U.S. citizens are still being faced by immigrant families today.

BRIEF HISTORY OF POLICIES ON IMMIGRATION IN THE UNITED STATES

As a former high school history teacher, I enjoy reading stories about people and the stories of cultures. I developed this passion from my father, who taught me much about the history of the United States, as well as the histories of other nations. As a teacher, I found that the textbooks used in schools often exalted the stories of people coming from Europe to escape religious persecution to form a new land. Today, Americans travel to Ellis Island to remember their ancestors who crossed the Atlantic to arrive at a country wherein they believed they could give a better life to their children and their children's children. Although these stories are fascinating and we generally still believe there is opportunity to build a better life for oneself here, we tend to forget, or perhaps we have not learned, that once the immigrants arrived here, many of these people were persecuted because of their ethnicity or their faith. What seems to get lost in the messages and images of our history textbooks is that people who immigrated to the United States often became those who implemented policies forbidding others to arrive, in the belief that others coming to the United States would be a negative influence on those already here. This nativism, or policy of favoring assimilated ethnic groups in a country over immigrants (Gollnick & Chinn, 2006) has continually fueled prejudice within communities. The very stories that often get lost in the pages of history textbooks can help us begin to understand why the United States has a history of contributing to anti-immigrant sentiment.

This history of anti-immigrant feelings can be directly traced to economic fluctuations in this country. When the economy was bright in the United States, nativism died down; however, during the Great Depression, post–World War I and post–World War II McCarthy eras, anti-immigrant sentiment escalated. My father, who was born in southern California, has shared with me many of the obstacles that immigrant and Latino American citizens faced due to the color of their skin during the 1940s in the school and work environments (Ygnacio Ramirez, Jr., personal conversation, September 12, 2006). This historical consideration is important due to the fact that we are still seeing anti-immigrant sentiment within California and the nation today. From the 1990s to the present, the United States has seen much anti-immigrant sentiment based on political expansion, a prolonged recession, and companies turning their attention overseas to secure their workforce. Along with anti-immigrant feelings come anti-immigrant policies, which our nation has had for many years. In 1994, California passed Proposition 187, which banned undocumented immigrants from public schools, medical assistance, and other government services. The experience of the September 11, 2001, terrorist attacks has led to tighter restrictions on immigration and pressure at the national level to pass new immigration legislation. Figure 2.1 highlights some of these policies through the 1970s.

A review of policies does not show the many local atrocities that have been inflicted upon many ethnic groups by local magistrates and citizens because of prejudice. What emerges from our history is a portrait of how national and state policies affect local legal and illegal immigrant families

FIGURE 2.1. Examples of Anti-immigrant Policies in the United States

1800–1850s	• Boat captains were required to post bond to the state of New York due to expenses incurred by the state for destitute immigrants. Later, a $1.00 head charge was implemented on new arrivals so new immigrant hospitals could be built. • American Republican Party proposes strict immigrant policies. • Irish potato famine, increase in Irish immigrants to the United States.
1850–1900s	• With the Gold Rush in California weakening, Blacks, Asians, and American Indians are banned from public schools for two decades. • 14th Amendment is ratified, granting citizenship to anyone born on U.S. soil. (http://www.loc.gov/index.html) • Chinese Exclusion Act. (http://www.cetel.org/1882_exclusion.html) • Depression and Congress passes a literacy test that President Grover Cleveland vetoes.
1900–1950s	• President Theodore Roosevelt calls for immigrant restrictions. • A call to segregate Asian students is rescinded. • New literacy test for new immigrants. • Immigration Act of 1924. • Lemon Grove case, first separate but equal case before the courts (Alvarez, 1986). • Visa restrictions on European Jews and others during the beginnings of World War II. • Deportation of more than 400,000 Mexicans (60% legal U.S. citizens) to Mexico. Also interned are some German and Italian Americans. • 110,000 Japanese Americans interned in detention camps. • Chinese Exclusion Act suspended. • McCarran-Walter immigration acts suspend Asian immigration and citizenship quotas, renews quotas for total immigration. • Labor unions and NAACP favor Operation Wetback, which forces close to one million Mexicans to go to Mexico.
1960–1970s	• Supreme Court rules in favor of language-minority students being taught in a language they understand. • Hostility toward new Southeast Asian immigrants rises.

and the education of their children. As educators, we need to address the immigrant population in terms that show we understand the possible conflicts they may be feeling regarding education. This can be done by understanding and honoring the culture, customs, and language of immigrant populations that are in our schools.

CULTURAL UNDERSTANDING, COMMUNICATION, AND LANGUAGE

Consider time spent in the classroom with your child's teacher, observing instructional methods that do not allow for student-teacher interaction. Now imagine yourself as an immigrant parent attending a back-to-school night or open house at your child's school. Think of the anxiety you would feel about speaking or asking questions. For many nonimmigrant parents, this may not seem problematic, for we have either been teachers or in positions of power and the school's administration wants us to be present for these events; however, even many English-speaking families are apprehensive about attending functions such as these (Ramirez, 1999a). Immigrant parents may have many questions, but may not attend school events due to cultural and language barriers, or issues of transportation and child care.

In the United States, we have seen an influx of immigrants arriving from Mexico, China, India, Eastern Europe, Latin America, Vietnam, and elsewhere in the Pacific Rim. Schools that are prepared for such diversity and appreciate the nature of acculturation, or the adoption of the dominant groups' cultural patterns by a new or oppressed group (Gollnick & Chinn, 2006), will allow immigrant families to create avenues for sharing their culture with the schools. Such schools can educate parents about the culture of the American educational system, while educators can learn about immigrant communities, their families, and their cultures. This situation differs from schools that practice assimilation or diffuses the culture of immigrants by insisting that families adhere to American practices and norms. By incorporating the families' cultures and offering language translational services for parents and teachers, schools will help families become stronger advocates for the school, teachers, and, most of all, their children.

Cultural Understanding

Research by Moll and his colleagues promotes the idea of working with teachers to conduct field studies on those who teach language to minority students (Moll, 1992; Moll & Diaz, 1993; Moll & Gonzalez, 1997; Moll, Velez-Ibanez, Greenberg, & Rivera, 1990). These researchers found that when classroom teachers conduct field research on their own students (perhaps in their students' homes), they become learners themselves and not just the facilitators of knowledge, as they are accustomed to being. Moll and Gonzales (1997) state:

> Once teachers entered households as "learners," as researchers seeking to construct a template for understanding and tapping into the concrete life experiences of their students, the conventional model of home visits was turned on its head. No attempt would be made to "teach" parents or to visit for other school-related reasons. (p. 101)

The authors demonstrate that teachers develop a different perspective when they are in the field researching families.

Delpit (1995) speaks of educators' "ignorance of community norms" as being devastating to the development of children. When teachers desire to institute parent education courses for their students' families, Delpit suggests that teachers need to understand the plight of parents before instituting parent policies or parent programs. In Boston, Delpit found that Latino parents and their children's teachers were involved in "yelling matches" concerning the bringing of children to their classrooms before the school day officially began. What looked like apparent disregard by the parents for the teachers' requests (that all children remain in the playground before school) was actually a misinterpretation on the teachers' part regarding how these Latino women viewed the school and its teachers. The women felt that the school was an extension of their own home, and the teachers served as surrogate mothers. If the children were left outside, the parents viewed this as parallel to child abuse and not caring for the children's welfare. Solutions could have been suggested, such as the school inviting parents in to discuss the issue to better understand the viewpoints of the children's families or surveying the parents to find out what items they like and dislike about the school.

Language Development

Language policies and language use by teachers and students is a volatile topic, especially in the state of California, where bilingual instruction is permitted only with a parent's written permission. Latino and other second-language parents are often not told by schools and school districts that they have the right to bilingual education for their children. Curriculum standardization, assessments, and standardized testing have contributed to some teachers feeling the need to teach toward the test and assisting second-language learners by translating testing materials for the students. Many teachers, principals, and superintendents fear for their jobs if test scores are low. In some Spanish-speaking communities, parents have been asked by schools to teach their children more English skills within the home. This is problematic because many Spanish-speaking families do not have the resources or skills to assist in the development of the English language for their children (personal communication with Title I program advisor within a large urban district, January 2000) or the skills to assess whether their children are learning the "academic" English sanctioned within schools. Although schools may want parents to teach their children English, many teachers also lack the training to assess student fluency in academic English (personal communication with Title I program advisor within a large urban district, January 2000), thus making it difficult for children to succeed in schools. My personal conversations with district officials encouraged me to research what teachers are doing in schools with regard to family involvement for immigrant and nonimmigrant populations. Research in the school community found teachers and parents willing to address the topic of limited English proficiency (LEP) students, while some of the information gathered was positive regarding working with second-language learners; however, other information obtained was negative.

STORIES FROM THE FIELD

I have been working with families for quite some time. Through my experience, I have noticed that the teachers, and their views on families, were important factors when it came to the issue of whether parent involvement practices within schools would be met. The comments below come from several teachers located throughout the United States.

Amy, a first-year high school math teacher on the West Coast, commented that as a preservice educator she had no desire to teach second-language learners, had negative views toward bilingual education, and felt that she was "ignorant" as to what "this" community (Latinos) wanted from education. This young teacher was asked to teach a sheltered education course (traditionally, sheltered education is teaching strategies for students who enter an English-only course after being enrolled in English as a Second Language courses). She was reluctant at first, but soon witnessed a transformation within herself, for she noticed that her sheltered students were generally more motivated to learn than her English-speaking students were. Amy became more involved in her students' lives and grew to become an advocate for second-language learners. She began to recruit parents to assist her in translation, met with families off campus to discuss student progress, and generated grant monies to assist parents with furthering their own education.

Contrary to Amy's experience is that of an elementary school teacher within the same district. Grace, a fifth-grade tenured teacher from the Midwest (who had worked 6 years as a teacher), commented that she demanded that her students only speak English while they were in school, because she was "curious as to what her students were saying about her." Her attitude toward second-language students sparked a negative reaction from parents.

Because Grace felt that parents needed to work with their children on English at home and were "not doing their part," she concluded that the parents did not want their children to learn English and, therefore, did not care about them. Grace reported that many parents transferred their children to another school where the administration "catered" to the desires of the Spanish-speaking community. When Grace identified the principal at the school site to which parents were transferring their children, I decided to make a call and find out something more from this particular administrator. It turned out that the school administrator, whom Grace stated was "catering" to the parents, was a bilingual educator who worked with students to have them become academically fluent in both English and Spanish. When I asked the parents in this school about their reasons for transferring their children, they were eager to tell their stories. Parents believed that if their children could speak Spanish during recess and lunch, and then learn English during their classes, their children would become bilingual, giving them more opportunities later in life. What had been a stigmatized group of parents who were perceived by a teacher as only wanting an "easy out" for their children, turned out, in reality, to be parents who were advocates for their children and their children's education.

Mary, a Latina woman from Guatemala, told me that teachers "persuaded" her younger daughter to forgo bilingual education, and to be immersed in English-only classrooms. Although the woman's two older sons went through bilingual education and succeeded at major universities, the daughter struggled to learn both English and Spanish by the time she was a sophomore in high school. Due to Mary's insistence that the school provide bilingual education for her daughter, she felt that the school and district had labeled her as "troublesome." She didn't feel welcome to speak to any school administrators or officials. When asked about this, teachers and administrators from the school and district made comments that ranged from "Mary was a pushy parent" to "She doesn't know what she is getting herself into, since she never went to school in the United States." Why is it, we must ask ourselves, that a parent who wishes to enhance her child's educational career is labeled "troublesome" and "pushy"? There seems to be a "catch-22" in that parents who want to play a role in the education of their children are ostracized and thought of as uncaring if they are not involved. Parents who are actively involved, however, may be looked upon as having a "secret agenda." Up for our consideration here is the question of what measure we are allowing parents to be involved in their children's education.

Greg, who has taught for 11 years at an elementary school with a large number of second-language families, while discussing how he communicated with parents stated, "Yes, I write letters home in Spanish so my parents will have all the information regarding the school and my classroom." Upon further conversation, Greg confirmed that he was not fluent in Spanish, nor did he obtain a translator to assist in his letter writing. When asked what level of Spanish he had mastered, he commented, "Oh, I just do my best. I mean, they can't read anyway." Greg had just 2 years of high school Spanish. Other teachers in this particular school in southern California commented that although they were willing to work in districts with large populations of Spanish speakers, most did not want to obtain a credential in second-language learning, nor did they wish to learn any phrases in a second language.

Baker (1996) has found that, for K–12 students from bilingual homes, there are overall cognitive advantages to learning two languages. Should teachers acquire a second language, their ability to communicate with immigrant students and their families would create stronger school-home partnerships. Teachers would also be better able to assist students if they learned strategies on how to teach students with limited English proficiency.

CULTURAL CONFLICTS AND SCHOOLING

For immigrant students to succeed, either by way of attending a trade school or postsecondary education, immigrant parents need to develop knowledge about the opportunities that are available. The Tomas Rivera Center on Policy (Tornatzky, Cutler, & Lee, 2002) reported that families from immigrant, low-socioeconomic backgrounds lacked "college knowledge" that would enable their children to know about postsecondary education opportunities. The center also reported that language deficits created barriers for families to gain this knowledge.

Due to the miscommunication occurring between the school and home, both families and schools are unaware of one other's expectations (Pardini, 1995). One such expectation from schools throughout the nation is for parents to attend open house or back-to-school nights; however, as pointed out earlier, the idea of stepping foot onto school grounds is foreign to many immigrant families. Although teachers may claim that they want parents to attend open house, consider this example: Robert, a ninth-grade teacher, wishes to work in a predominantly Latino community, 30 miles from his home. His reason for working so far from his home is simple: "I love working in the city of Santa Lucia. The parents never show up for anything, and they never question my teaching." As stated previously, there is a "catch-22" for parents in this community. If a parent never shows up for events such as open house, then he or she is seen as "uncaring." If parents do show up and start to ask questions, then they are looked upon with suspicion. When parents from different ethnicities were interviewed regarding why they did not attend functions such as open house, these reasons emerged:

- The inability to get off work because most school functions are held on weeknights
- The inability to find child care
- Transportation difficulties
- Teachers not showing up for school functions
- Lack of respect from the teachers and school officials
- Children working to supplement family income and the parent(s) wanting to be home in case of any accidents
- Language barriers
- No knowledge of when functions were scheduled
- A feeling that their attendance would indicate disrespect for the teachers and school

This last issue is compelling because many immigrant parents are unaware of the cultural educational differences between their former country and the United States. In many countries, teachers are regarded as the experts in the education of children; therefore, parents feel that the teachers are in charge and are not to be questioned. Schools need to take this phenomenon into consideration when working with immigrant families. The importance of communicating with immigrant populations with regard to American education practices as well as personally welcoming the families would assist in improved school-home relations. Research has indicated, however, that there is a lack of school-home communication, which contributes to the limited number of schools creating positive school relationships (National PTA, 2000).

I concluded from the communication patterns among teachers from one school that only 5% of the students' families were contacted during the school year (Ramirez, 1999a). Since this study was conducted in a population with a large number of immigrants, I decided to interview Sheneekra Williams (name changed for confidentiality), who is the Title I coordinator for a large urban school district. During the course of the interview, Ms. Williams confided that many Title I schools were out of compliance regarding yearly parent surveys and communicating with immigrant families. When asked about urban ethnic communities, she reiterated that immigrant families often have a more difficult time trying to resolve problems that their children have in schools because if they do speak out against the teacher or request more information, they are labeled as "difficult parents."

Excellent teachers have to be excellent communicators. One difficulty here is that teacher education programs do not always demand that students take public-speaking or other communication courses. What results is what Leary (1957) calls a *dominance-submission interaction pattern*, where one person is controlling the communication. Often, the teacher is the person who is controlling the communication between the school and the home. Although Wubbels, Levy, and Brekelmans (1997) found that good teachers are dominant, which contributes to student achievement, Ramirez (1999a, 1999b) found that schools control the level and amount of communication between the school and the home. Unfortunately, this develops into misunderstood or ineffective communication between parents and the school. Wubbels, Levy, & Brekelmans (1997) found that good teachers need to have both dominant and cooperative understandings of their students, and I would suggest that teachers need to have the same qualities for working with families. Teachers need to set standards, yet be able to understand the needs of their students and families in a controlled environment that allows for measures of freedom for the student and family.

Effective school-home communication is vital for the health of a school. Unfortunately, traditional communication between schools and parents has been limited to open house, teacher-parent conferences, and sporting events. Often, when communication is delivered, the communication is ineffective and deals exclusively with disciplinary circumstances (Ramirez, 1999a). To facilitate better communication between the school and immigrant families, schools need to recognize that there may be a problem with communication. Suggestions for resolving the issue include pursuing a personal connection of involvement with the parents; communicating with them by using positive phone calls to the home, sending notes and letters in the families' native language, not speaking in verbose or condescending language to parents, and having a person on site who can translate for the parents and teachers. This demonstration of respect and support by school personnel would not only empower parents, but would also improve communication.

Alvarez, Hofstetter, Donovan, and Huie (1994) suggest strategies for improving communication:

- Any assessment of problems or issues must seek input from the spectrum of racial-ethnic groups attending a school, recognizing that none of the groups is internally homogeneous, and that perceptions affecting communication vary widely within and between groups.
- Differences in perceptions of constraints demand a varied approach to programs designed to involve parents in schools. A blanket strategy will not be effective in most urban schools.
- Unbalanced participation among groups of parents should trigger a reassessment of a school's communication strategy, not a suggestion

that one or more groups of parents are merely apathetic and
therefore may be disregarded.
• University or communication facilitators, community opinion
  leaders, or teacher linkages to organize parents for securing more
  active, reflective public involvement should be considered.

Building upon these strategies, I suggest that schools have a translator at
open house or other school-related functions for second-language speakers.
This would allow parents to feel free to express themselves and to become
more active in their children's school. Also, if parent volunteers were asking
to translate school documents, parents would feel as if they are being empowered. Schools also need to recognize that computer translators, which
are sometimes used instead of live persons, often do not translate documentation or colloquialisms properly.

Thus far we have been examining issues regarding immigrant families
and schools. Unfortunately, most of the information has been negative. Although there are problems for immigrant parents regarding positive school-
home connections in the areas that have been mentioned so far in this
chapter, there are many schools throughout our country that are making
efforts to create a stronger school-home community by reaching out to recent immigrant and nonimmigrant populations.

SCHOOLS MAKING A DIFFERENCE

For many teachers and administrators, parental involvement is centered
on those parents who are "able to attend," and those who do not attend
are seen as "uncaring" (Jones & Valez, 1997; Ramirez, 1996, 1999a). Some
schools, however, have taken the initiative to actively involve parents. These
schools seek out parents who may be considered "unable to attend."

The Anaheim Union High School District in California, has been de-
signing family involvement programs to increase parent awareness and participation in academic development by combining research and practice. One
such program was the development of a school bus that was transformed
into a mobile technology laboratory that would be driven into communities
to serve the needs of families. Other programs that the school district offers
are parent education programs for helping children succeed in school and
nights when parents may come and learn about topical information. All of
the district's programs are offered in English, Spanish, and Korean. By doing
this and providing child-care at every event, the district has seen an increase
in family involvement (Kim Bauerele, personal communication, October
2006).

In Whittier, California, due to my experience in parent education, a middle school asked me to implement an 8-week program on teaching parents how to assist their children with study skills at home. Before the program was initiated with the parents, their children's grades were recorded and evaluated throughout the duration of the parent education program. After the parents completed their training and implemented their strategies, all of the children saw an increase in academic success (Ramirez, 2004).

In the Hillsborough County Schools in Florida, a website is dedicated to instruction that helps parents and teachers better communicate with one another. However, the site also includes information for parents to access their school's School Improvement Plans and gives detailed information about the school's goals, mission, and strategies for that particular year (http://www.sdhc.k12.fl.us/INVOLVEMENT/index.asp). Such information would prove beneficial in keeping parents up to date with school issues. However, some schools and teachers may not wish to be involved in such work, and teachers often state that such demands are not part of a teacher's workload (Ramirez, 1999a).

To reduce demands placed on teachers or school personnel for directing parental involvement programs, De La Salle Institute, an all-male Catholic high school in Chicago, began the "Proud Parents Group" for the parents of incoming freshmen. At De La Salle, senior parents act as mentors for incoming freshman parents to address concerns that the new parents might have. In comparison to years before the program was established, there have been increases in parental attendance at school activities, freshman student attendance, and an increase in freshman grades. Parents and teachers who were asked to explain the increases responded that the parents and teachers now act as partners in the students' life and homework (Colletti, 1993). This program shows that parents can act as mentors for immigrant parents and "show them the ropes" of the school. Mentors can also come from local sports organizations, after-school clubs, or any other place where the parents' children interact with other students.

Lucas, Henze, and Donato (1990) have conducted research in six Southwest schools to identify the needs of their language-minority (LM) populations. The schools that were investigated showed similar traits regarding the promotion of LM students through valuing students' language and culture, high expectations, knowledge of LM methods, staff development, a variety of courses for LM students, counseling programs, staff member commitment, and parental involvement.

One LM program that has an active parental involvement component is *El Instituto Familiar* in Santa Ana, California. The institute, which is located within an urban middle school, initially involved 10 to 15 parents, but over 5 years has grown to include more than 100 parents. At first, the organizers of the program found that parents were lukewarm regarding the classes that were being offered. It wasn't until the program designers asked the parents what they wanted to learn and implemented these learning opportunities that the parents became more excited. Some of the class offerings involved learning about schools and how to help their children at home. Other courses, such as fundamental plumbing, were also offered. The parents then became active in policymaking, teaching classes for parents, and mobilizing parents for school matters. Programs such as this create opportunities for parents to become more empowered, because they are involved in the day-to-day operations of education.

As the success of these programs suggests, some schools have made parental involvement an important part of their students' education. Individually, teachers have developed ways for students and parents to interact with one another at home and in the classroom (Adenika-Morrow, 1996; Bradley, 1997; VanSciver, 1995). By creating opportunities for parents from immigrant and nonimmigrant communities, we as educators are better able to assist in creating avenues for more student success. With this in mind, let's investigate some of the strategies used by schools to create stronger relationships with families.

STRATEGIES FOR WORKING WITH IMMIGRANT POPULATIONS

In a master's-level course on families and schools, teachers are asked to research parental involvement, attitudes toward families, and school and district policies regarding families. These teachers are also asked to implement strategies that enable families to become better informed about the school and the teachers' classrooms. When first approached with this assignment, the teachers are often concerned about how they would "look" to their colleagues. When prompted further, teachers are worried that their colleagues would start to question them about "why" they want to communicate with families. Teachers fear that such questions might turn to outright indignation on the part of their colleagues. When the teachers begin to communicate with the families of their students, they find that the families enjoy hearing about the classroom and school activities, and show a genuine concern and interest in the education of their children. Teachers also find that when they work closely with immigrant families and learn some phrases in the families' native languages, the parents are more willing to consider the teachers' professional opinion about their child. This revelation on the part of the teachers is either accepted or rejected by their colleagues, depending on the individual's personality. Colleagues who "just wanted to do their time" in teaching wanted no part in communicating with families. What the teachers have found is that these were the same colleagues who were never recommended to be master teachers for student teachers, who complained about students, who were often criticized by parents, and who were most likely to have parents requesting to have their children transferred out of their classrooms.

The strategies that schools and teachers can implement to create an environment of education that allows immigrant parents to feel welcomed include the following:

- Learning a couple of phrases in the families' native language
- Making positive phone calls during the first few weeks of school to each family
- Creating a classroom newsletter with items in the families' native language
- Making personal invitations for each parent to attend a back-to-school night
- Providing other days and times for parents to meet with teachers and administrators
- Providing a translator on campus
- Providing child care for parents' children
- Adhering to Title I policies and surveying families about what they think of the school
- Allowing parents to participate in school functions, and personally inviting parents to do so
- Empowering parents and families through a PTA or PTO and staffing this organization with teachers and staff who do wish to include parents
- Having a one-day in-service for administrators, teachers, and staff to learn how to communicate and include families in positive ways

In addition to teachers, one of the most influential people when it comes to the implementation of change is the principal of the school. If the principal is an advocate for immigrant parents and is willing to communicate in ways that allow these populations to feel welcomed, then teachers are more likely to follow suit. If the principal is not an advocate for immigrant parents, then any endeavor that a teacher may undertake to improve school-home relations may be met with opposition and resentment from colleagues. This is an important measure to consider when implementing change. Administration must be supportive to effect lasting and systemic change.

Fuller and Olsen (1998) argue that if schools are to enrich parental involvement programs, the school "must consider cultural and economic differences among families." By creating a network of site-specific programs, teachers would be able to recognize differences that may contribute to the knowledge base of each student. One recommendation that Fuller and Olsen support is having bilingual advocacy groups to monitor schools' decisions. Other suggestions include learning about the families' belief systems and asking parents what they are interested in for their children's education before developing long-range goals for the school or making changes in curriculum. By taking a closer look at students' families, teachers would gain a better understanding of the needs and development of their students.

CONCLUSION

The research being conducted within the United States has contributed to an increased awareness of immigrant families in schools. Although much of this chapter supports increasing levels of parental involvement, future research specifically needs to look at how schools interact with immigrant families and the issue of parental involvement. As a researcher and former high school teacher, however, I realize that the story does not end there.

As a teacher educator, I am finding more and more preservice teachers who are uninterested in working with families, let alone recent immigrant families. Until teacher education programs instill strategies for working with families, all the research on families and schools will be relegated to conference proposals and speeches throughout the nation. Additionally, education administration courses need to develop courses that draw from the experience of former and active K–12 administrators who have worked successfully with diverse families. As pointed out earlier, within K–12 schools, the principal is the person with the most power to make or break parent/ family involvement programs. If the principal wishes to promote family and school programs, the teachers will follow suit. If the principal plays "lip service" to family and schools, then we will continue to see schools keeping parents away and not wishing to involve parents in positive ways.

We have seen in the beginning of this chapter that we are a society of immigrants, arriving at different times in our nation's history. We also saw that groups of immigrants have been systematically held accountable for the nation's woes at various times in our past. At present, the issue of immigration has again become a hot political topic. What we need to understand is that we will continue to see immigrant children in our schools whose parents need to be communicated with in ways that help them understand the educational culture, how they can become more involved in schools, and what it feels like to be empowered to help make decisions that are best for their child. What we as educators need to understand is that we can and should learn from our school community. One comment I offer to my preservice and master's students is "show me a teacher who doesn't learn from his or her students and their families, and I'll show you a teacher who shouldn't be teaching." We have the greatest task a person can ask for: to influence lives daily! On a personal side, my children love to watch the movie *Spider-Man*. In the movie, after Peter Parker is involved in a fight, Uncle Ben tells him that "with great power comes great responsibility." Whether they realize it or not, administrators, teachers, teacher educators, and administrative educators have great power to teach and learn about immigrant families and to work with them in developing strategies that benefit students. As a researcher, former teacher, and parent, I do understand the pressure that is placed on today's teachers by standardized testing and the goal of making sure "no child is left behind." I also understand, however, the stories of the parents who desire nothing more than for their children's teachers to listen and invite them to learn about our educational system. As immigrants, many parents respect teachers so much that they willingly give their child over to us as educators. Unfortunately, many of us have failed as teachers in working with families because of our political views on bilingual education or immigration, or because we are simply prejudiced. We as educators need to start to listen to other teachers and researchers who have succeeded in working with families, so we do not leave any child behind.

QUESTIONS FOR REFLECTION

1. Compare and contrast how immigrants were viewed at the turn of the 20th century with the way immigrants are viewed today. What are the similarities? What are the differences?
2. Reflect upon your own ethnic background(s). Consider how this relates to how you prefer to be taught in an educational setting. Discuss similarities and differences with others.
3. As a parent, how do you want your children's teachers to communicate with you? As a teacher, how will you communicate with families so that everyone can be included in the conversation?

Acknowledgment. The author wishes to thank Kathryn Roper, M.S., for her assistance in this project.

REFERENCES

Adenika-Morrow, T. J. (1996). A lifeline to science careers for African-American females. *Educational Leadership 53*(8), 80–83.

Alvarez, D. S., Hofstetter, C. R., Donovan, M. C., & Huie, C. (1994). Patterns of communication in racial/ethnic context: The case of an urban public high school. *Urban Education, 29*(2), 134–149.

Baker, C. (1996). *Foundations of bilingual education and bilingualism.* Bristol, PA: Multilingual Matters.

Bradley, D. (1997, March 5). The recipes of Dorothy Rich. *Education Week, 35–* 39.

Colletti, N. A. (1993). *Would a parent group for parents of high school freshman foster an increase in school-parent communication and involvement?* Paper for an action research project for Lewis University, Educational Organization and Administration.

Delpit, L. (1995). *Other people's children: Cultural conflict in the classroom.* New York: New Press.

Fuller, M. L., & Olsen, G. (1998). *Home-school relations.* Boston: Allyn & Bacon.

Gollnick, D. M., & Chinn, P. C. (2006). *Multicultural education in a pluaristic society.* Upper Saddle River, NJ: Prentice-Hall.

Jones, T. G., & Valez, W. (1997). *Effects of Latino parent involvement on academic achievement.* Paper presented at the annual meeting of the American Educational Research Association at Chicago.

Leary, T. (1957). *An interpersonal diagnosis of personality.* New York: Ronald Press.

Lucas, T., Henze, R., & Donato, R. (1990). Promoting the success of Latino language-minority students: An exploratory study of six high schools. *Harvard Educational Review, 60*(3), 315–340.

Moll, L. C. (1992). Bilingual classroom studies and community analysis: Some recent trends. *Educational Researcher, 21*(2), 20–24.

Moll, L. C., & Diaz, S. (1993). Change as the goal of educational research. In E. Jacob & C. Jordan (Eds.), *Minority education: Anthropological perspectives* (pp. 67–79). Norwood, NJ: Ablex.

Moll, L. C., & Gonzalez, N. (1997). Teachers as social scientists: Learning about culture from household research. In P. M. Hall (Ed.), *Race, ethnicity and multiculturalism* (Vol. 1, pp. 89–114). New York: Garland.

Moll, L. C., Velez-Ibanez, C., Greenberg, J., & Rivera, C. (1990). *Community knowledge and classroom practice: Combining resources for literacy instruction.* Arlington, VA: Development Associates.

National PTA (2000). *Building successful partnerships: A guide for developing parent and family involvement programs.* Bloomington, IN: National Educational Service.

Pardini, P. (1995, February). Legislating parental involvement: School officials trying to penalize parents for the aberrant children. *The School Administrator, 28–* 33.

Ramirez, A. Y. (1996, October). *Parent involvement is like apple pie: A study of a Midwestern school.* Paper presented at Journal of Curriculum Theorizing Conference, Monteagle, TN.

Ramirez, A.Y. (1999a). Survey on teachers' attitudes regarding parents and parental involvement. *The School Community Journal,9*(2), 21–39.

Ramirez, A. Y. (1999b). Teachers' attitudes toward parents and parental involvement in high school (Doctoral dissertation, Indiana University, 1999). *Dissertation Abstracts International, 60–06A,* AAG9932692.

Ramirez, A. Y. (2004). Passport to success: An examination of a parent involvement program. *The School-Community Journal, 14*(2), 131–152.

Tornatzky, L., Cutler, R., & Lee, J. (2002). *College knowledge: What Latino parents need to know and why they don't know it.* Claremont, CA: Tomas Rivera Policy Institute.

VanSciver, J. H. (1995, March). From intimidation to participation: Making parents feel welcome at special ed proceedings. *The High School Magazine,* 19–23.

Wubbels, T., Levy, J., & Brekelmans, M. (1997). Paying attention to relationships. *Educational Leadership, 54*(7), 82–86.

Chapter 3

From the Principal's Desk: Making the School Environment More Inclusive

Teresa J. Rishel

In this chapter, I discuss families within the context of school and schooling, focusing on the difficulties faced by students and parents whose views, behaviors, and life experiences do not conform to those of the American mainstream. As a former elementary school principal and educator, I learned firsthand the difficulties and frustrations many families endured as they interacted with school personnel and attempted to comply with the formal and informal rules and expectations of educational institutions. What some families did not have—their lack of the specific qualities, characteristics, and social position associated with the middle and upper-middle classes—often pushed them outside the parameters that educators accept as defining "good parents." This misperception further compromised the possibility of meaningful school-family connections, as the real-life examples I provide here show. Focusing on what parents and students lack rather than what they possess hobbles our efforts to create a more inclusive school environment. This chapter begins by reviewing some of the ways in which the ideology and culture of schools define our expectations and lead us to perceive some individuals as lacking key attributes, then provides examples of how these often-unconscious perceptions alienate and silence those who are deemed "lacking." Finally, it offers suggestions for changes in daily practices that could help make schools and schooling a more positive and equitable experience for all.

POWER AND SCHOOLING

Ideology and Schooling

An ideology—a system of beliefs and philosophical views—provides the basis on which a society or group functions by systematically determining what is considered valuable, acceptable, and important. A "dominant ideology" is a system of ideas and cultural practices that legitimate the position of the most powerful group(s) in a society by making the status quo seem both natural and neutral through the "legitimizing of certain forms of knowledge, ways of speaking, and ways of relating to the world" (Aronowitz & Giroux, 1993, p. 76). This results in the widespread acceptance of "the way things are" and makes alternative ideas and practices seem wrong. Ayers (2001) claims that democracy is not practiced in schools, but instead mimics society's inequalities by reproducing a social order of dominance and subordination. Until what *is* becomes equal or nearly equal to what *should be*, the dominant ideology is considered *hegemonic,* a term used to express domination and power, where "legitimate knowledge is the result of complex power relations" (Apple, 1993, p. 46) over which teachers have little control.

Schools, along with churches, families, and popular culture (newspapers, movies, books, and music), promote a society's key ideas and values. But schools are also themselves social communities (Jackson, Boostrom, & Hansen, 1993). In addition to explicitly teaching elements of the dominant ideology, they also implicitly reinforce it by uncritically incorporating the status quo into the rules, customs, and procedures that form school structure and shape school climate. In other words, the dominant ideology influences the school curriculum (by determining what is important and necessary for students to learn in order to function in society at large), and it permeates the everyday experiences and practices within schools through the largely unspoken yet recognizable representation of what is valued. Embedded in the taken-for-granted rules, interactions, and activities that occur in classrooms and schools, this "hidden curriculum" creates a subculture of learning and knowing that some argue has a greater impact upon students than the overt curriculum (Aronowitz & Giroux, 1993; Beane, 1990; Jackson, 1990). This unacknowledged affirmation of values and ideas that reinforce existing patterns of power and subordination between social groups makes schools complicit in sustaining inequality. By failing to examine the ideas and values that underpin our judgments concerning how others look, act, talk, or think, we validate the notion that what is, is what should be, and we teach our students to do the same. The result is an ongoing exclusion of those whose appearance, actions, or attitudes fall outside "the norm." The barriers to communication and understanding raised by an uncritical acceptance of the status quo can be virtually insurmountable for some families.

The Tyranny of Dominant Values

Schools are arranged in terms of how students are grouped and labeled, how rewards and punishments are distributed, and how grades are assigned and weighted to complement what the dominant culture values (Apple, 1995; Aronowitz & Giroux, 1993). The importance attached to academic success, for example, shapes tracking decisions. Students whose family backgrounds and social class position make them good candidates for "dominance and leadership" are placed on academic tracks, while others are channeled onto tracks that prepare them for "following and serving" (Connelly & Clandinin, 1988, p. 155). A less obvious but no less important way in which schools reinforce dominant cultural values involves the standards that educators set for family involvement in education.

Expectations for parents include demonstrating that they value and prioritize education and are actively involved in their child's schooling. The problem for many parents is that the school not only sets the expectations but also determines what constitutes a valid demonstration of their fulfillment, namely ensuring that children's homework is completed, responding to teachers' notes, attending parent-teacher conferences, and serving on school committees. Parents, no less than their children, are expected to respect and support administrators and teachers as authority figures and to abide by school practices, rules, and routines. Questioning or challenging school authority typically results in a swift rebuff from school personnel that discourages any further involvement, voice, or interest on the parents' part.

One reason teachers play a significant role in setting the expectations and boundaries for familial input and involvement is that this is an area in which they *can* act. Apple (1993) has pointed out that knowledge is the "result of complex power relations" (p. 46) that limit teachers in their professional practice. Henderson and Kesson (2003) describe educators as "caught up in the refinement of craft knowledge, the day-to-day business of teaching, and the pressures of the profession." These responsibilities, they say, often take priority over asking and answering "the more meaningful 'why' questions" (p. 49). As a result, educators need to be concerned about their role in how their actions and beliefs serve to alienate and exclude some families. We cannot realistically expect to make sweeping changes in the dominant ideology, but we can and should critically review the effects of our actions and question the assumptions underlying our everyday practices. Why are the children of working-class parents assumed to be destined for the same type of jobs as their parents? Why are they in a caste system of repetitive and boring schooling, while their more affluent peers are allowed to pursue creative and challenging courses? Why are some parents demeaned for avoiding school activities such as parent-teacher conferences, while teachers are free to select only certain parents to chaperone field trips and parties? We might ask which came first—the decision to avoid or the decision to exclude. Asking hard questions and providing honest answers could help bring about a more dynamic educational system, and certainly one that is more beneficial for all families.

The Bigger Picture of Educational Leadership and Decision Making

Educational leadership, both within a particular school district and the field as a whole, has the capacity to enhance or diminish the fragile dynamics between families and schools. Although much is written about successful home-school partnerships, digging into the still-hidden issues surrounding the alienation and exclusion of certain families must remain a key concern. The stories and situations presented in this chapter were accumulated by one principal, who is also a parent, in one school district— and could be shrugged off as anecdotally insignificant. The larger picture, though, suggests that these stories represent a recurring theme at any random school location, which would indicate that they are indeed not so unique. Framing her work using critical race theory to document Latino parent narratives about the discrimination they face as families and how it impacts their children, Auerbach (2002) adds another dimension to understanding the alienating effects of schooling. In parents' attempts— and often failure— to navigate school culture, she uses the term *rebuff* (p. 1,379) to describe the harsh and uncaring attitude of the school staff. Such rebuffing occurs as a result of the social exclusion of parents based on "perceived differences in cultural capital [which] are used to deny access to educational opportunity" (p. 1,381). The issue becomes the need for school leaders to provide better—and certainly deeper and more meaningful— ways to understand, accept, and act upon the denial of even the most basic opportunities for students and families who "lack" the needed capital.

LACK OF FINANCIAL CLOUT

Schools mirror the value that the larger society places on individuals' socioeconomic status. A low socioeconomic status negatively shapes the educational experience for many families by limiting the degree to which they are accepted and valued in the school community. Children from financially strained, low-status families find it difficult to gain full access to the school culture because it so closely resembles the broader social and cultural world of their more affluent schoolmates. Aronowitz and Giroux (1993), in discussing Bourdieu's cultural capital theory (see also Schwartz, 1997), make this overlap clear:

> The culture of the elite is so near that of the school that children from the lower middle class can acquire only with great effort something which is given to the children of the cultivated class—style, taste, wit—in short, those aptitudes which seem natural in members of the cultivated classes and naturally expected of them precisely because they are the culture of that class. (p. 76)

The idea of cultural capital became illuminated for me as I transitioned from teacher into principal and moved to a new school district. Formerly, I only had to consider my role in the classroom and to treat my students with respect, compassion, and dignity, avoiding any demarcations in regard to class, ability, or otherwise. My students were simply children who needed a variety of support at different times. In the community where I was principal, most families were solidly middle-class, not "elites." Still, the disparities between the elites and the poorer families were clear-cut in the classroom and school. Children whose parents lacked financial clout faced serious roadblocks to educational success. They lacked school materials and supplies, had no access to technology, and were unable to participate in and benefit from extracurricular clubs and activities. Their clothes were not trendy or name-brand; typically, they wore hand-me-downs from older siblings.

For many families, school was a place where debts were owed. Parents spent the entire school year paying debts owed for book rental, only to face another set of fees due in the fall. Breakfast, lunch, and milk expenses drained their finances as well. The isolation brought on by lack of funds was heightened when low-income parents visited the school, clad in mundane, secondhand clothing. Despite their and their children's attempts to "fit in," these families' lack of financial clout visibly separated them, making even simple interactions with school personnel difficult.

Lunch Count

During the first week of school, I noticed the lunch count forms left outside each classroom. This was a routine practice that helped cafeteria staff determine how many lunches to prepare. One form caught my attention because it identified the *names* of the students receiving a free or reduced-cost lunch, not just the total number of meals needed. In checking other forms, I found that student names were consistently noted, with those receiving "free" or "reduced" lunches grouped separately from the names of those who paid for lunch. At the next faculty meeting, I questioned this practice. The teachers' faces reflected confusion and apprehension. They saw it as natural, acceptable, and even necessary to distinguish between students who paid and those who did not, and I doubted that their conscious intent was to embarrass students or their families. Yet, separating the students in this public and pejorative way was both unnecessary and alienating.

As a solution, I requested that teachers report only the total number of lunches needed. The new approach resulted in less work for the teachers and no inconvenience for the cooks. Lunches were served as usual. More important, the change in practice meant one less opportunity for using the students' and parents' financial status as a sorting device. Although this was a small detail compared to some other challenges facing schools, a change in practice that removes financial clout as a potential wedge between students creates a better environment both for those who have and those who do not.

Sports Teams

Extracurricular sports were another source of alienation for students with limited finances. During my first year as principal, I was aware that students who wanted to participate in the school's basketball program were required to pay a $10 fee. The amount seemed modest to me and thus reasonable; moreover, I knew the participation fee was customary. When I was working on my budget for the following year, however, my perspective changed. I discovered not only that the basketball program's operating costs were minimal, but also that monies from other sources defrayed the coaches' salaries and referees' fees. The scorekeepers were volunteers, and the program's few equipment needs were almost all supplied by the physical education fund. Since approximately 40 students were involved in the two teams (boys and girls), the money collected exceeded the actual costs. Decisions concerning sports programs (costs, schedules, transportation) were made for the entire school district by other administrators, thus requiring that all schools remain consistent. As principal, I was not able to drop the required fee. For poor families, the participation fee was an extravagance, particularly if they had more than one child who wanted to join a team. To disallow these children's involvement because they lacked sufficient funds struck me as both a disservice and as another unnecessary, unexamined practice that isolated certain "types" of children.

Transportation to and from games and practices created problems for students whose families had no vehicle and those whose parents' work hours included late-afternoon or evening shifts. These youngsters generally did not have friends among the affluent students who were their fellow players, so they could not ask a teammate for a ride, nor could their parents offer to share the responsibility for transportation. Finally, parents who were unavailable to pick up children from practice also were unlikely to be able to attend games. For some children, simply knowing that their parents would never see them play was enough to keep them from joining a team.

One afternoon, an incident occurred that sharpened my awareness of how family finances wedged their way into students' school lives. I noticed Dalton, a junior high student, walking along the highway that led from the school to the town where he lived (3 miles away). It was nearly evening and the sun, slowly dipping behind the corn stalks, silhouetted him. I was surprised to see Dalton because I knew he normally rode the bus home. I learned that he had joined the football team. Since he did not have transportation after practice, he walked home. My initial reaction was "Good for him!" Then I had second thoughts. Dalton's family was very poor. His mother was a single parent of three boys; she had only a grade-school education and she worked for minimum wage. His mother typically did not attend school activities or events, and certainly would be unlikely to go to football games. She also would not likely have encouraged her son's participation in a sport. I realized that Dalton, who was not part of the dominant culture of the school, was going to great lengths to "belong" to a group that was held in high status. Although he was quite intelligent, Dalton had few school friends. The fact that none of the 30 or more junior high students participating in the football program offered him a ride home spoke clearly of both his reputation among his peers and the isolating effects of low socioeconomic status.

Football practice was physically demanding, especially following a long day at school. Dalton's willingness to add the burden of a 3-mile walk home after practice reinforced my sense that he would endure a great deal in order to fit in. It saddened me that some students, in their longing to belong and be like others, had to shoulder such heavy burdens. Three weeks after I saw him walking home, and just prior to the first football game, I heard that Dalton quit the team. I was left wondering what had prompted his decision—the daily walk home, the continued failure to fit in, the realization that his family probably would not watch him play, or some combination of these. The bottom line was that the structure of schooling did not serve Dalton well. Once again, we find that those who have a lack of the attributes most valued in school settings suffer the most (Rishel, 2004).

LACK OF EDUCATIONAL-EXPERIENTIAL CLOUT

Educational or experiential clout is another area where families differed. Parents who lack this kind of clout can best be described as having little knowledge or understanding of how schools operate, and/or a lack of experience in dealing with educational issues. These parents' unfamiliarity with the culture of schools may be based on their socioeconomic level, educational level, community reputation, cultural background, or other factors that separate them from the dominant cultural group. This outsider status may also limit the amount of experience and skill they have in dealing with authority figures (such as principals), thus further reducing the likelihood that they will be able to establish a connection between themselves and the school. For example, in my school, parents who belonged to the parent teacher organization (PTO) were accepted and respected *because of* their participation in this student-centered organization. Their involvement increased their awareness of what went on in the school, how it operated, and what was expected. This involvement and awareness provided sufficient clout so that, regardless of their income, education, or reputation, these parents were accepted. They were recognized by school personnel as doing what "good parents" do. In short, they "fit in."

Because I was new to the school and community, my knowledge of most of the families was limited. I considered it advantageous that I could not base my interactions with them on what I knew of their backgrounds, histories, and reputations. My goal was to maintain consistency and integrity in making decisions and to avoid being influenced by parents' varying levels of educational-experiential clout.

Textbook Selection Committee

The process of formally selecting textbooks offers a glimpse of how power is used to maintain school stability and promote the dominant ideology. Textbooks, in part because they are so common, ordinary, and familiar, are a powerful vehicle for passing on cultural beliefs, values, and attitudes (Apple, 1993). For example, critical studies of culture, gender, law, and race *could* be included as part of school curriculum, but typically they are not. Instead, the power of dominant ideological and cultural views ensures a preference for maintaining the status quo.

I witnessed the hidden agenda of hegemony when I participated in my school's annual textbook selection process. Traditionally, 12 to 15 parents, representing grades K–6, were selected to assist a faculty committee in choosing reading textbooks. Prior to my arrival, teachers chose these parent representatives, intentionally omitting adults whose input they did not want. Because I had served on book adoption committees as a teacher, I was aware that parents were selected whose beliefs and ideologies aligned with the mainstream. These parents also had significant experiential-educational clout; often, they were active PTO participants, members of the school board (or spouses of members), or parents who were highly visible in the community. A change in procedure the year I arrived made parent selection the principal's responsibility.

I was torn between following the comfortable, traditional routine of picking those considered to be "the best parents" because of status, income, or involvement, or acting on my own deep-seated beliefs about avoiding the systematic exclusion and alienation of parents. I felt that the committee should represent a variety of viewpoints and that the standard selection procedure was unfair and biased. So, although I knew that, ultimately, the choice of textbook would be decided by the teachers (another hypocrisy of the system), I wanted to try to reach and interest a broader range of parents. As a first step, parents were notified through the school's monthly newsletter to submit their names if they were interested in being on the committee, from which I would randomly select representation for each grade level. Many parents submitted their names, and although the pool still represented only a limited set of families, there were more candidates than there would have been otherwise.

I wish I could say that all went well from there, but in fact, the new procedure met with resistance from some teachers and parents. Questions surfaced in regard to the parents I had chosen for the committee: Why had certain parents been selected? Why were "unqualified" individuals placed on the committee? Did I realize how much more difficult I was making this task? To reduce some of the disparity in the parents' experience levels, I met with the group twice before it convened as a committee and provided information about the materials and the basic needs that a reading series must satisfy. After these two sessions, all of the parents had a good grasp on the task ahead.

The selection committee met several times throughout the year. I steered clear of any further involvement. One afternoon, a teacher on the committee stopped by my office to discuss its progress. She conceded that the parents were "doing pretty good," but added that it was not right to keep certain parents off the committee so that "others" could be on it. Acknowledging her comment (and reading between the lines), I noted that all parents should have the opportunity to be involved in their child's education, and that I hoped we would continue to meet that objective.

In the end, both the parents and the teachers on the selection committee chose the same text. This consensus was in some ways irrelevant, since by design, the teachers' vote was decisive. The selection process was important, though, because it now included parents who otherwise might not have participated, and, at least theoretically, it provided all parents with an opportunity to take part in collaborative and informed decision making in a school environment. All of the previewed textbooks were similar—all had the components of a comprehensive reading program and were based on "best practice" research. So, the task was less about identifying the text that was better than the others and more about forging and improving relationships between school and home. The new procedure, in changing one small piece of the hegemonic practices that promoted alienation and seclusion, helped nurture diversity, equity, and inclusion in school culture.

Daniel's Dad

Schools are social institutions and, as such, they provide students with opportunities to resist authority, rules, and routines. As Aronowitz and Giroux (1993) point out, "oppositional behavior may not be simply a reaction to powerlessness, but might be an expression of power that is fueled by and reproduces the most powerful grammar of domination" (p. 94). Showing resistance by violating school rules is a way to rebel against the dominant ideology. The following story about a fifth-grader named Daniel Thomas describes not only his rebelliousness, but the "why" behind it. His behavior—repeatedly breaking school rules and resisting authority—was rarely spontaneous. He appeared to be able to control himself, if he chose to do so. Daniel was the type of student who was not easily ignored or forgotten. He was a mouthy, arrogant, and confident boy who often intimidated his peers by taunting and harassing them. His "don't mess with me" demeanor, once provoked, was explosive. But Daniel also could be sweet and kind, using his charms to dissipate any ill feelings that his aggressive behavior evoked in others. His wit and charm, combined with his toughness, made him a unique force in the classroom and the school. Daniel managed the boundaries of schooling as best he could, yet was regularly sent to my office to be disciplined. However, over time, visits to the principal's office were less and less effective, and his physical aggression increased.

During recess one day, Daniel dealt a severe blow to another student, who suffered a knocked-out tooth and a bloody nose. When Daniel arrived at my office, clearly aggravated, he explained that his father had told him to "defend" himself. Moreover, his father would "deal with" the principal or anyone else who tried to punish him. Finally, Daniel assured me that his father would not allow him to be kicked out of school. As mandated by the district in the wake of the Columbine shootings[1] (Building Blocks for Youth, 2006; Ferrandino & Tirozzi, 2000), I suspended Daniel for two days. His parents were notified to pick him up immediately. The school secretary, still eager to provide me with details of students' family backgrounds, asked if I knew "who Daniel's dad was." Clearly signaling that such information had an important bearing on this child's discipline, she ignored my automatic "I don't care" response. She said that Mr. Thomas was the community bully, known for his explosive temper and willingness to fight anyone who crossed him, a behavior pattern that had begun when he was in junior high. She reported that he was feared by most people, and she warned me that he would seize any opportunity to retaliate against me. She begged me to let the matter drop. Taking this information into consideration, I invited Mr. Thomas to sit down in my office when he arrived at school to pick up Daniel. He refused, stating that he would not be there long. I summarized the recess incident and repeated what Daniel had said about his father endorsing fighting.

Interrupting me, Mr. Thomas pounded his fist on my desk and yelled that *his son* would not be kicked out of school, would not act like a "wimp," and had the right to defend himself. He stated flatly that if Daniel did not defend himself, he would punish him. Pacing the office, Mr. Thomas suggested that I reconsider the suspension. I willed myself to remain calm and vowed to allow the man to continue, as long as his aggression was not physical. He finally sat down and stared angrily at me. Trying not to ignite the situation further, I remained silent. After a few moments, I said something about his apparent love for Daniel and his obvious discomfort with school situations. Slowly, he explained that his father had expected him to be a bully, and because of that, he was never accepted at school, nor did he like school. He said he wished he could do it over and thought he could do a good job the second time around. To my surprise, he started sobbing. After regaining his self-control, he apologized and agreed that he and Daniel would support the school rules. At the beginning of our meeting, I had been disturbed, seeing all too clearly how Daniel had come to be the way he was. By the end, I also saw glimpses of the same wit and charm that Daniel possessed, the same ability to smooth over damage. But more than that, I saw a long chain of ill feelings about school and school authorities, passed down from generation to generation. Daniel, pushed by his father to rebel against school ideology, had limited options. Like his father before him, for as long as this boy was a student, Daniel had to operate within a system whose culture he rejected, and felt rejected by; neither father nor son knew how to break through the barriers, or possibly, whether they even wanted to do so.

As this incident illustrates, parents' reactions to school policy are shaped by their own histories as students. As a school administrator, it was my responsibility to ask the "why" questions to understand parental actions and reactions instead of holding on to expectations, judgments, ideologies, and tradition. The measures I used in communicating with Mr. Thomas were not extraordinary, but they regarded the nature of human dignity, which is often missing as we become entwined in day-to-day tasks and rely unthinkingly on the status quo to guide our expectations.

LACK OF SOCIAL-CULTURAL CLOUT

Part of the distancing between families and schools occurs due to the perceived lack of parental social-cultural clout. Parents differ in their financial status, level of education, occupation, and position in the community, among other things. Those with greater wealth, more education, and higher-status jobs have greater social-cultural clout because the dominant ideology defines those personal attributes as signs of success, and thus power. In family-school relationships, those who have social-cultural clout are more likely to have their opinions validated and their decisions accepted than those who lack such clout. The narratives reported below, based on my experiences as a parent, illustrate this dynamic.

As a teacher in the same school district where my two distinctly different sons attended school, I approached every parent-teacher conference with a sense of trepidation. On one hand, I regularly received positive feedback about my older son, who was a good student, with age-appropriate social and emotional development. On the other hand, teachers regularly described my younger son as "immature." Although he, too, was academically gifted, he struggled with social and emotional development. His kindergarten teacher recommended retaining him to allow his emotional development to "catch up" with that of his peers. Disagreeing, yet apprehensive, I refused to allow retention.

The teacher warned me that I would regret my decision, but I felt her recommendation disregarded my son's individual "life situation," and I believed retention would be as likely to decrease as increase his maturity. How could emotional maturity be enhanced by repeating academic work? A year later, my son's maturity level would be what it was, regardless of what *grade* he had attended. As for his life circumstances, he had recently experienced his parents' divorce, his father's move to another city, and his mother's return to work.

During the next 7 years, I attended parent-teacher conferences and continued to hear that my son was immature for his age, although he was academically successful. In high school, parent-teacher conferences were by request only. With the usual feeling of trepidation, I met with his six teachers. After the meetings, I walked to my car, elated. At last, the focus of the conference was not my son's immaturity. He graduated at the top of his high school class and received his college degree from West Point Military Academy, where his professors described him as "very mature."

Hidden within this narrative are examples of how the social-cultural clout I possessed made it possible for me to override the kindergarten teacher's recommendation that my son be retained in grade and to take no action in response to subsequent teachers' judgments that my son was immature. Because I was a district colleague and a professional with expertise in education, my son's teachers accepted my decisions, although they did not agree with them, and they continued to treat both me and my son in a positive manner. These personal experiences directly influenced my professional perspective. I vowed not to describe a child as immature when conferencing with parents, because I do not believe that educators can alter a child's level of maturity. I am not persuaded that retention is a viable method of encouraging, promoting, and teaching maturity. If maturity were dependent on grade retention, I suspect that my son would have had to repeat many grades, perhaps graduating from high school around age 28. The assumption that retention promotes maturity is questionable, at best. Research clearly supports the idea that grade retention does little to bolster a child's self-esteem, efficacy, or academic achievement, and substantial evidence specifically warns that retention in kindergarten is harmful (Darling-Hammond, 1998; Jimerson, Pletcher, & Kerr, 2005; Nagaoka & Roderick, 2004). Yet teachers exercise great power in this area, strongly influencing parents' decisions.

Over the years, I witnessed scenarios similar to the one I described above, as my colleagues promoted retention for maturity to some parents who would not listen. I began to appreciate the value of social-cultural clout. Parents who lacked this clout were demeaned and thought of as difficult and not sufficiently interested in their child's education if they seemed reluctant to follow a teacher's professional advice. In teachers' lounges, hallway conversations, and informal gatherings of educators, these parents were maligned, rejected by teachers who dismissed them as ill-informed and lacking in respect for authority. So, once again, unexamined expectations led to false conclusions that further undermined already poor home-school relations.

One especially enduring aspect of parent-teacher conferences is educators' belief that the "parents who need to attend the conferences are the ones who never do." This group, of course, is made up of parents whose children are not achieving academically, have behavior problems, or exhibit other types of difficulty in school—such as acting immaturely. Had I not been a teacher, I think I would have avoided the yearly conferences. Parents of children who are having trouble in school would likely benefit from discussing their child's progress with teachers. Instead of assuming that these parents "don't care," we need to actively search out the reasons for their lack of attendance. Recalling Daniel's father's life experiences, as well as Daniel's own propensity for misbehavior, it is easy to understand why this family would avoid conferences and other school activities. It is time to stop finding fault with parents like Mr. Thomas and to concentrate on finding remedies.

LACK OF FAMILIAL CLOUT

As varying family structures become more widely acknowledged, terminology does as well, and not necessarily always in a positive manner. For example, the term *broken family* has become common when referring to single-parent or divorced families. I am certain that prior to my divorce, I used the term *broken family* with casual indifference, oblivious to its hidden implications. However, when my own family joined the ranks of the "broken family" group, the change occurred with so little fanfare that I did not immediately recognize our new status. An acquaintance who inquired how my sons coped with the divorce commented, "It must be so difficult for them, now, coming from a broken family." That remark stayed with me for quite a while, my indifference to the term evaporated, and I became starkly aware that the phrase *broken family* indicated a nonfunctioning unit, a "lesser than" situation.

In the same manner, *dysfunctional family* is often the catchall term for families experiencing difficulties that affect their children's ability to perform effectively at school. *Dysfunction*, the "failure to function normally" (Encarta Dictionary in Microsoft Word), encompasses the *chronic* struggles that interfere with usual routines, interactions, and ways that the family operates (Boss, 2002). Families, described by characteristics such as perfectionism, workaholism, compulsive overeating, intimacy problems, depression, and problems in expressing feeling, experience persistent problems that involve a high degree of seriousness. Other descriptions include parents who are controlling, deficient, alcoholic, or abusive. Alternatively, families who experience *temporary* troubles return to their prior level of functioning more quickly.

As a principal, I felt that students and their families should be protected from such labeling and the indignation that they should accept their "rightful" position as a broken or dysfunctional unit. In school settings, these terms were often used as a means of blaming parents and making excuses for students' academic and behavioral problems, and alleviated the need for further intervention on behalf of the child—indicating that nothing could be done for broken or dysfunctional family units. From my experiences as a principal, I witnessed teachers contacting divorced parents less often and having fewer meetings with them because of the perception that the parents chose to be less involved. Families who were termed *dysfunctional* tended to receive less attention and support because they were viewed as incapable or disinterested. As a result of these preconceived notions, families experienced alienation and their children risked slipping through the cracks (Rishel, 2004; Rishel & Miller, 2004).

I recall a third-grade teacher who was having difficulty with a student named Emily, whose parents had recently divorced. Despite her average academic ability, Emily worked below grade level, regularly skipped homework assignments, and often incurred discipline in the classroom. The teacher, who seemed genuinely concerned about Emily, framed Emily's problems around her home situation ("but she is from a broken family, so. . ."). By doing so, he absolved himself of responsibility for resolving her problems, when, in reality, Emily's "broken family" worked more cohesively than many intact families. Although divorced, her parents were involved and provided consistent, visible support.

Emily's teacher, in using the phrase *broken family*, was referencing the notion that children of divorced parents often behave poorly, have academic difficulties, and have trouble fitting in with peers. The problem is that these characteristics are not limited *only* to these children. Emily may have had the same difficulties and characteristics if her parents had remained married. Although educators must take into consideration the needs and dynamics of children who are from divorced families, it is dangerous to enable this characteristic (divorce) to be the sole or main explanation behind a student's actions. To help Emily's teacher focus more effectively, I shared that by shaping his interactions based on her "assigned" identity limited him in understanding her behavior and resolving her problems. (I also added that, in my opinion, Emily was from a divorced family, not a broken one.)

A similar situation occurred when the staff (erroneously) labeled and blamed the parents of two students as a result of their "dysfunctional family," whose problems were reported to be that the father worked too much, the mother ignored the children, the children were unsupervised, and the students did not hand in homework regularly. Concerns mounted when Bart, the oldest of the boys and a fourth-grader, stood on his chair at lunch and screamed, "I hate this school!" As one teacher announced, it was "Just another one of those dysfunctional families for us to deal with!" The story unfolded quite differently when I met with Bart's parents. I learned that upon their recent move to the community, their regular routines and ways of functioning were dramatically changed due to the father's employment, which now included working the midnight shift instead of days. This resulted in less time and a lack of quality time as a family. The boys' difficulty fitting into a new school was exacerbated by the fact that they enrolled in the middle of an academic year, which presents its own distinct set of problems for most children.

Alluding to the accusation that the mother "ignored" the children, it emerged that her role had shifted to being the morning caretaker of the children, thereby leaving time after school for them to interact with their father. Far from ignoring her children, she was attempting to adjust to a new situation, where evenings were stressful and rushed because of homework. When they learned that homework was not being turned in, the parents realized that the children had substituted family time for homework. Under great stress, they were simply attempting to adjust to the move and to the uncomfortable daily challenges.

In resolving the issue, I began questioning the damage that occurs when misinformation and the labeling of others interferes with reality and responsibility. Questioning how terms are easily misconstrued, I saw these incidences as indicative of the further alienation of families within the school culture. Was it just a perspective—that what appears to be "dysfunctional" or "broken" by some is indeed quite the opposite? Or was it that as a principal, I had to maintain an open mind and seek the truth, whereas when I was a teacher, I readily applied false terminology? Did I suddenly have the unique vantage point of viewing families through a different lens and being privy to the inside stories? Or was this knowledge accessible to the teachers as well? Recognizing that the responsibility is for all school personnel to be equally aware, the topic for the next faculty meeting was the alienating use of the terms *dysfunctional* and *broken* to describe the families of our school community.

CONCLUSION

My personal and professional life situations—and the insights I gleaned from them—have provided the experiential knowledge that guides my thinking, decision making, teaching, and writing about educational issues. As the examples presented in this chapter show, the significant difference between misperceptions, misinformation, and a narrowly defined understanding can have crushingly negative effects on some families, shaping both the overt and hidden ways in which they experience schooling. Although the examples represent only a tiny fraction of all the stories that could be told, they reveal how important it is for educators to ask the "why" questions, to hunt for the answers, and to use them as the basis for decisions. The stories in this chapter also show how infrequently we do any of these things. In failing to question, we surrender to the status quo, excusing ourselves from further effort on the grounds that "this is just the way it is." Thus, we passively participate in hegemonic practices and reinforce a singular ideology and a discourse that provides the consistency and tradition of comfort. The wheel continues to turn and we turn with it. Yet, on any given rotation, we could contribute to changing the direction of the wheel, or at least, we could slow it down enough to provide time to ask—and answer—the "why" questions. The challenge is to move our focus beyond the outside layer, digging deeper and looking beneath, where the hidden, but often most important, clues lie.

QUESTIONS FOR REFLECTION

1. Reflect on the issue of ideology and its impact on the school environment. How did ideology shape your school experience? In what ways did it serve you well? In what ways did it negatively impact your experience?
2. Explain how dominant ideology affects curriculum and curricular decisions. Give examples of how lack of sociocultural, familial, and educational-experiential clout are affected by these decisions.
3. Thinking back over the ways that families are sometimes excluded and alienated from the school environment, can you think of examples of when this occurred in your own experiences in school? What families were alienated? Why? At that time, what were your feelings about this?
4. Describe how family financial clout serves as a hegemonic device in the culture of schooling.
5. Explain the cycle that resulted in the exchange between Daniel's father and the principal. What type of clout was Daniel's father lacking? What type was Daniel lacking?
6. How does the "lack of familial clout" affect a student's abilities to fit into the school environment? What roadblocks do the student and the family face?

NOTE

1. The shooting at Columbine spurred a rash of school-inovked policies based on the concept of zero tolerance. Substantial information is available from the Center for Mental Health in Schools at UCLA: http://smhp.psych.ucla.edu/qf/zerotol.htm.

REFERENCES

Apple, M. W. (1993). *Official knowledge: Democratic education in a conservative age.* New York: Routledge.

Apple, M. W. (1995). Cultural capital and official knowledge. In M. Berube & C. Nelson (Eds.), *Higher education under fire* (pp. 91–106). New York: Routledge.

Aronowitz, S., & Giroux, H. (1993). *Education still under siege* (2nd ed.). Westport, CT: Bergin & Garvey.

Auerbach, S. (2002). Why do they give the good classes to some and not to others? Latino parent narratives of struggle in a college access program. *Teachers College Record, 104*(7), 1369–1392.

Ayers, W. (2001). *To teach: The journey of a teacher* (2nd ed.). New York: Teachers College Press.

Beane, J.A. (1990). *Affect in the curriculum: Toward democracy, dignity, and diversity.* New York: Teachers College Press.

Boss, P. (Ed.) (2002). *Family stress: Classic and contemporary readings.* Thousand Oaks, CA: Sage.

Building Blocks for Youth. (2006). *Zero tolerance fact sheet.* Youth Law Center, Washington, DC. Retrieved September 10, 2006 from http://www.buildingblocksforyouth.org/issues/zerotolerance/facts.html.

Connelly, M. F., & Clandinin, D. J. (1988). *Teachers as curriculum planners: Narratives of experience.* New York: Teachers College Press.

Darling-Hammond, L. (1998, August). Alternatives to grade retention. *The School Administrator, 55*(7), 18–21. Retrieved July 22, 2005, from: http://www.aasa.org/publications/sa/1998_08/Darling-Hammond.htm.

Ferrandino, V., & Tirozzi, G. (2000, January 26). Zero tolerance: A win-lose policy: Principals' perspective. *National association of elementary school principals.* Retrieved September 10, 2006 from http://www.naesp.org/ContentLoad.do?contentId=908.

Henderson, J., & Kesson, K. (2003). *Curriculum wisdom: Educational decisions in democratic societies.* New York: Prentice Hall.

Jackson, P. W. (1990). Life in classrooms. New York: Teachers College Press.

Jackson, P. W., Boostrom, R. E., & Hansen, D. T. (1993). *The moral life of schools.* San Francisco: Jossey-Bass.

Jimerson, J., Pletcher, S. M., & Kerr, M. (2005, February). Counseling 101: Alternatives to grade retention. National Association of School Psychologists. Retrieved October 15, 2006 from http://www.nasponline.org/resources/principals/Retention%20WEB.pdf.

Nagaoka, J., & Roderick, M. (2004). Ending social promotion: The effects of retention. *Consortium on Chicago School Research,* University of Chicago. Retrieved October 15, 2006, from http://ccsr.uchicago.edu/publications/p70.pdf.

Rishel, T. (2004). Maneuvering the emotional and social demands of the classroom. In P. C. Miller (Ed.), *Narratives from the classroom: An introduction to teaching* (pp. 164–182). Thousand Oaks, CA: Sage.

Rishel, T., & Miller, P. C. (2004). Positive relationships for effective teaching. In P. C. Miller (Ed.), *Narratives from the classroom: An introduction to teaching* (pp. 127–145). Thousand Oaks, CA: Sage.

Schwartz, D. (1997). *Culture & power: The sociology of Pierre Bourdieu.* Chicago: The University of Chicago Press.

Chapter 4

A Welcoming Tone in the Classroom: Developing the Potential of Diverse Students and Their Families

Lisa Rieger

Imagine. . . the first day of school in a first-grade classroom. It is a year full of wondrous expectations for students, parents, and teachers. Often called a magical year, first-grade is the time when young children are expected to learn, practice, and independently use specific strategies that will help them become effective communicators, creative problem solvers, and flexible thinkers. As I enthusiastically welcome the many students, parents, and siblings who arrive at my door, I am conscious of the parents' sense of hurriedness to get out of my way. I keenly take note of my students' various reactions to this and am not convinced that they agree it is such a prudent idea. Unfortunately, many parents assume that this may be their brief and only opportunity to catch my attention, to relay pertinent information, and personally to chat with me until the first parent-teacher conferences in mid-November. *That is a mind-set worth changing.*

As excited as I am to begin shaping our classroom community of motivated, positive, and determined young children, I believe there is a more pervasive tone worth setting with my students and their families. In many ways, this tone is atypical of the culture of school, where teachers often avoid getting "trapped" by needy or aggressive parents. Often feeling too busy, we begin listening to a parent concern only to find ourselves unable to really do so. The competing internal tick of the school clock prevents us. We dismiss many conversations with a polite request to call and arrange a convenient meeting time or we redirect parents to the school nurse, counselor, or principal. At times, our own discomfort with difference and our overwhelming feelings raise our shoulders to our ears and keep our hands wrapped tightly around the classroom doorknobs. We radiate an anxiety that propels us to close our doors quickly so we can be free of the chaos surrounding our students' lives. We are overeager to begin conforming children to our rules and expectations of school. However, the results can be disastrous for teachers, parents, and students—alienation, unnecessary power struggles, and a general mode of complaining and unhappiness can soon creep in and take over. The truth is *teachers really do need parents* to help support their children as they transition into early childhood classrooms (Balaban, 2006).

BEING RESPONSIVE TO FAMILIES

With body language and eye contact, I try to communicate my desire for a different kind of classroom. There will be no "shooshing" parents or family away, especially today. It is important for me to learn their names, shake their hands, smile, and look directly into their eyes, just as I will do with their children. I am reminded that there will be times when I will want and need to ask parents, "How are you?" Many parents will eagerly begin to share some of their lives with me if they sense I am genuinely interested. These kinds of exchanges are enriching and insightful. They can and will happen if parents sense that the classroom climate is safe and free of personal judgment. Consider the following story:

> Cameron's father was standing in my room one morning helping him unload his backpack. I sensed that he was rather beside himself and knew he was not usually on "drop-off duty." As Cameron happily made his way down to breakfast, I sat down on the tabletop and casually asked the father, "How are things today?" Trying to ignore his quickly tearing eyes, the father told me that his ex-wife had been arrested last evening for drug possession. I knew Cameron was well-loved by both of his parents and immediately expressed my empathy. Trying to regain composure, the father said he wasn't sure how the situation would affect Cameron, but was worried that he might appear out of sorts for a while, especially since he wouldn't be with mom at night, as usual. I assured him that we would keep a close eye on his son and allow him to talk about what happened if he wanted to. I told him that his son's classmates loved him and would be supportive in their own ways, too. Finally, I promised him that I would let him know if Cameron showed any signs of needing additional support and explained some school services that might be of help to Cameron and his family.
>
> The father appeared comforted by my receptiveness. He broke down further and admitted that he blamed himself for much of the disruption in his son's life. I learned that he had been arrested for assault, but had made

a consistent and positive effort to regain control of his anger. He loved his
son and was strongly committed to working things out with his ex-wife.
He was taking concrete steps in that direction. He desired, more than anything, for them to function as a family again. I sincerely expressed my respect
and support of his efforts, which were in his son's best interest. We agreed
to keep in touch more frequently regarding his son's progress. As he left, I
couldn't help but wonder if I would ever have known the internal struggles
of this father or his family had I not asked this morning. Initially, my parent
rapport had developed more with Cameron's mom, who usually brought him
into school and sat with him during breakfast. I hope my interaction clearly
communicated to Cameron's father that it was not my place to judge the
actions of either parent or to think of Cameron as any less capable because
of them. The father, although eager to talk, was clearly not certain if it was
appropriate to approach me with sensitive/private family information. I was
grateful he did! Both parents showed a vested interest in their son's education.
      Cameron, who was usually motivated and enthusiastic about school,
making progress, and eager to please, was curled up on the classroom floor
sound asleep that afternoon, despite the usual buzzing of lively first-graders. A
kind friend gently covered him with his sweatshirt.

Cameron never mentioned the incident, but I was thankful I could correctly attribute his exhaustion and listlessness to changes in family dynamics rather than other prior notions I held. Cameron's mom and I had previously discussed with him the importance of bedtime. Cameron was one to
sneak out to the couch and catch some late-night TV when he couldn't fall
asleep. If I hadn't created the opportunity to talk with his father, I may have
assumed that Cameron's anxiety about going to bed simply related to some
inconsistent routines and expectations at home. Evidently, the situation was
much more complex.
    As the story of Cameron demonstrates, establishing a personal rapport
with *all* parents is a must. It is well worth the extra effort to create these
relationships, especially with parents who shy away from school due to barriers of language, religion, culture, and socioeconomic class. Barriers may
also be rooted in their children's previous school years, their own school
experiences, or the current stresses that daily life brings. More often than
not, it is from these parents that I am going to request additional support
as their children learn to navigate the world of school (Epstein et al., 2002).
Parents need to feel they can walk into a classroom, look around, and even
stay a while. Often, I invite them to sit down near their children. My priorities each morning must consider theirs as well. Ensuring that neither my
students nor their families leave one another without the necessary words,
hugs and kisses, or mature "quick glance and cool wave" good-bye is vital

to our learning. To combat my internal school clock, I am not in the habit of waiting for parents to leave before I begin. In fact, I secretly hope that my approach encourages some to stay. Simply, I welcome everyone to begin our day with us. There is always much to show my students and their families about our learning and routines. Why wait until curriculum night or until a problem arises? If parents can spare some extra precious moments, the moments are mine to welcome.

Setting the tone I describe is a challenge in today's classrooms. It demands purpose, consistency, and the continuous efforts of everyone who comprises the classroom community, including the multitude of specialists, volunteers, mentors, and student teachers. As the first weeks of school ensue, the attitude that everyone is valued and has a voice in the classroom community nurtures the strong relationships I desire with my students. Daily, I model the kind of supportive, ever respectful, and compassionate companionships that I want my students to develop with one another. Seeding such relationships enables me to set high and rigorous expectations for quality learning. When my students have a vested interest in maintaining the fertile ground for learning and growing, they hold me and one another accountable. The many hands make for a rich harvest! Having the gift of Samuel in my class reaffirms that first-graders know much more than we might expect about creating a welcoming classroom environment.

> Samuel is a Jehovah's Witness. In my experience, these children do not celebrate holidays or birthdays and cannot participate in any kind of activity associated with them. Samuel's parents are aware of how celebrations have been commercialized and how they seep into the school culture and curriculum. They believe Samuel knows and participates within the boundaries of his faith, but sometimes it is understandably difficult for him to be excluded from parties or activities that are related to various celebrations. In the past, he has been removed from class or school when such activities occur. His parents have found this to be the best way for Samuel and them to handle situations with which they feel uncomfortable. Samuel's parents check in often and want to be well-informed of our classroom activities. They appreciate discussing any concerns I have and they help prepare Samuel when "necessary arrangements" must be made.

Some teachers' first reactions may be to moan and groan over having to accommodate a child whose family has specific religious observances. Worse yet, these teachers will continue to adorn their walls with holiday decorations and will continue to celebrate most of the commercialized Christian holidays with their students. Children like Samuel will be removed accordingly, and his classmates will think it strange if no explanation is given.

If one is given, students will learn to accept that Samuel is "different" and learn that it is all right to exclude him during the activities and celebrations that their teacher has them looking forward to. I offer a different mindset. I am genuinely grateful and somewhat relieved to have students like Samuel in my classroom. My challenge is *never* to have students like him removed from our classroom community. If Samuel is required to attend, fully participate, and respectfully follow the expectations of school, then it is my responsibility to make sure he can do so. Having students like Samuel can help advocate that classroom activities and school-wide celebrations remain inclusive of everyone. As the year unfolded, my students and I developed many universal ways of "celebrating" that became ingrained in my practice whether or not there were families present that had specific cultural or religious observances.

Working with Samuel and his parents, I showed them that my curriculum lent itself to more encompassing themes that would not offend their religious beliefs. Birthdays became optional for everyone and occurred during snack time. This way, Samuel and everyone else had the alternative choices of a school snack or a snack brought from home. I gave the children the responsibility of making sure everyone was satisfied before anyone could eat, and they readily took this responsibility to heart. Samuel participated enthusiastically. He eagerly showed his desire to share and care for his classmates by always bringing two or three extra snacks from home. Birthday or not, there was rarely a day when the rumbling tummy of a friend would deny his offering. During the month of December, we decorated a nontraditional tree with beautiful words. This was inspired by the reading of *Frederick* (Lionni, 1985). I use this story to inspire children to acknowledge the work and gifts of everyone in a family. We learn that sometimes gifts may be hidden or misunderstood, but that does not diminish their importance. Frederick reminds them how powerful words can be in helping to imagine or remember what brings us joy. Children who cannot get beyond the visions of "sugar plums" in their heads are free to put a word like *Santa* on the tree. However, Samuel and the majority of his peers preferred words such as *puppy, sunshine,* or *pepperoni pizza.* The students experiment with secretly making and exchanging a homemade surprise for a fellow student whose name they had secretly drawn. With the strict stipulation of no store-bought, holiday, or parent-assisted projects, the exchange between students is priceless! Samuel used stuffed fabric, a sock, and some paint to make a homemade baby doll, a delightfully well-thought-out gift for his unsuspecting friend. She tenderly cradled it the entire afternoon! Without the context of economic status or commercialism attached, the children's genuine excitement, mixed with some discomfort and awkward moments, is of great pedagogical value. Not only do children learn the excitement of giving, but the art of graciously receiving something that is the handiwork of a peer. All children can discuss and experience the intrinsic good feelings associated with giving. Even though they are young, I have not met a first-grader who is unable to rise above the preconceived notion of a "present" and place the true emphasis of this activity where it belongs—in the heart of human expression.

My memories of Samuel and his classmates poignantly illustrate that children have much to teach us about creating environments inclusive of all families. His classmates were open to learning about what he could or could not participate in and they readily accommodated him. Fueled by their sincerity, Samuel and his parents made an effort to join the classroom culture. I was pleased when Samuel's parents okayed his request to treat the entire class to a snack "just because." This reaffirmed that Samuel perceived himself as an equal and vital contributor to our classroom. There is a powerful lesson in Samuel's story for us all. If today's classrooms are to be truly welcoming places for every family, they cannot reflect the teachers' biases and beliefs or those of the majority—they must reflect all the children that comprise them (Derman-Sparks, 1989).

RECOGNIZING FAMILY DIVERSITY

The first few weeks of school reveal the diversity and complexity of today's classroom in a small northeastern city school district. A quarter of my class consists of students whose families are from foreign countries. They come from places such as Russia, Ukraine, Iraq, Kurdistan, Vietnam, Thailand, China, Puerto Rico, Somalia, Cuba, and Bosnia. These families primarily speak their native languages at home and expose their children to the customs, traditions, and celebrations of various religions and cultures. At the same time, many are transitioning into various facets of American culture. Over half of my students are not living in the traditional family structure of one house with two parents whom they refer to as Mom and Dad. There are single-parent families, stepparent families, gay/lesbian-parent families, adoptive-parent families, foster-parent families, biracial families, and extended-family families (children living with a relative). Some children have more than one home and more than one family. This is confusing at first, but well worth taking the time as an educator to understand. A quarter of my class qualifies or will qualify for special education services. However, within the existing diversity and differences in family structures in today's classrooms, I believe it is vital to keep in mind that *all children's families deal with the individual challenges of their children.* Some of these challenges will affect children throughout their school careers—autism, learning disabilities,

deafness, ADHD, asthma, allergies, physical disabilities, and behavioral/
emotional challenges walk through our doors. So do the "unlabeled"
challenges of painful shyness, inability to take risks, low self-esteem, difficulty transitioning, poor peer relations, competitiveness, control, and, my
personal favorite, "in need of an attitude adjustment!" In our classrooms,
all children have special needs, and we must attend to them all.

In a classroom comprised of different languages, different cultures and
beliefs, different customs and traditions, different socioeconomics, and
different family structures, where does one begin to weave the common
threads that will hold us all together? I do believe there is a lasting fabric
that withstands the weathering of intolerance. The cloth takes form in
knowing that *all children's families are or will be in the midst of changing
family dynamics at some point throughout the school year*: arrival of a new
sibling; adoption; separation; divorce; marriage; incarceration of a parent or
relative; a new house; an older sibling going off to college; parents gaining,
losing, or changing employment; a new pet; a vacation; visits with relatives;
and sickness or loss of loved ones. My students and their families have
taught me wisely. They have ingrained in me a philosophy that no matter
where I teach or what my class makeup, I must withhold personal bias so I
can genuinely welcome all children and their families as they are. It is their
stories about their changing lives and experiences that will hold us together
and drive the curriculum. (Bullard, Carnes, Hofer, Polk, & Sheets, 1997).
I must listen and learn from them. I must allow many opportunities for
them to express who they are. We must create the learning agenda together.
As I do, the classroom becomes the blanket—the warm and supportive
environment children will need when changes in family dynamics do occur.

MAKING CONNECTIONS THROUGH
A CLASSROOM LEARNING LENS

Time. Not enough of it remains a constant pressure for teachers and students in today's educational system. As educators, we must ask ourselves,
is it possible or even good practice to cover required curriculum for the
sake of covering it? I have heard the complaint that the well-intentioned
district-wide curriculum maps take the fun out of school. Many teachers
feel it is impossible to cover everything within the allotted time frames, and
if they do, it certainly won't be as in-depth or meaningful as they'd like.
Worse yet, I have also heard the complaint that there is no longer room for
the "fun" projects or special activities that provide children with enriching
opportunities to get to know and understand one another in creative ways.

This pressure of time infuses a disturbing, disconnected, and chaotic atmosphere into school culture. Many of our classrooms and students are out of control because we are dancing from one unrelated activity to the next, unable to take note of students' true understanding. On top of the pressures of curriculum, most outsiders don't realize how little time teachers actually spend with some of their students on a consistent basis. We must deal with the revolving door of disruptions: school-wide announcements; specialists pushing-in and pulling-out students for physical therapy, occupational therapy, speech, ESL, and extra help; mentors; appointments at school-based health clinics; and individual or group counseling sessions (Kralovec, 2003). If we are not careful to minimize the disruptions, we lose our focus. Our sharp demands for quiet, attention, and respect so we can get through the lessons must wave a warning flag in front of our students. Our own distraction due to the disruptive flow clearly signals to them that their learning needs and ideas cannot sustain priority.

How can we as educators truly foster quality learning environments for young children, knowing that the pressure of time remains a constant and mandated testing is becoming the way to hold schools accountable for mastery of the curriculum? If you believe it is possible, it requires extra time, extra planning, and extra work. In order to fit it all in, teachers need to think about how to integrate and redesign the curriculum, be ever reflective practitioners, and collaborate more than ever. Perhaps the most powerful idea I have found is the use of what I call *my learning lens*. This is the lens through which my students and I design and develop my classroom activities and channel the majority of my instruction for the entire school year. The learning lens has to be broad and encompassing enough for my students and me to connect to it continually as we move from idea to idea, subject to subject, and experience to experience. The learning lens is philosophical and pedagogical—*it changes as you change as an educator*. It changes as you gain insight and expertise into the age and development of your students combined with the curriculum in which you must engage them. I bring it to your attention because I think every reflective educator has a learning lens, even if you have never named it for yourself or your students. Your learning lens is your power because it is your hook. It is worth some serious contemplation and attention.

Before I present some very specific ideas regarding the topic of families, I think it wise to reveal my own lens. It has changed several times over the course of my career, and I am sure it will change again. Clearly, I share it not to promote it as *the way* of thinking about curriculum, young children, and their education. A learning lens is not a theme—it is a very conceptual approach to learning that must continually grab hold of students at their intellectual, social, emotional, and spiritual levels. I share it so you may gain some insight into the ideas presented and be persuaded to think about your own lens. At present, I term my learning lens *transformations*. I believe this lens is a powerful hook for me and the first-graders. The lens of transformations has richly layered and complex personal, environmental, academic, family, community, and world connections. I have found it particularly inspiring when thinking about how to develop curriculum projects that will be meaningful and motivating to young children. It supports Carlsson-Paige's (2001) claim that schools must nurture the wholeness of the human experience and that, although challenging, it is vital that today's curriculum connect to children's perceptions of the world. I want my students to take note of the transformations in themselves, in their families, and in their worlds. I want them to grapple with how and why such transformations occur. I want to create opportunities for them to experience transformation in a positive way. Most important, I want them to believe in the possibility of personal transformations enough not to live in fear of making them. First grade, in my mind, is an incredibly transformative year. I cannot help but recognize that everyday I ask that my students be willing to take personal learning risks and muster the determination that such risks require. The transformations learning lens is a tribute to them.

You may be thinking that my lens is far too abstract to discuss with 6-year-olds! What I have presented above is quite philosophical and absolutely meaningless unless it can be translated into practice. Once first-graders understand the meaning of the word *transformations,* they can make many relevant and concrete connections to their lives and school experiences. We begin very literally. As students tell stories or make personal connections to a transformative idea, their passions bring opportunities for deeper levels of understanding. Below are a few examples of first-graders' perceptions related to the idea of transformations:

> infant—toddler—child—teenager—adult—senior
> seed—sprout—seedling—flower
> egg—larva—growing caterpillar—chrysalis—butterfly
> winter—spring—summer—autumn
> morning—noon—evening—night
> letters—words—sentences—stories
> country—town—city
> ice—water—vapor
> 1+1=2 2+1=3 3+1=4
> whole chocolate chip cookie—one bite taken—more bites taken—crumbs

Transformations are part of the human experience, and they can be explored in all areas of the curriculum. As the year unfolds, students see transformations happen. Growing pumpkins, hatching ducklings, losing teeth, gaining inches, getting glasses, learning to read and write in sentences, and understanding number patterns—all contain transformative elements. It is invaluable to have students discuss and bring in samples of the transformations they observe in their natural and built environments. Students live transformations as they learn content and about one another. The learning lens is their open platform to share the changes they perceive in their own lives and in our ever-changing world. It is the focus that ignites and drives our learning throughout the school year.

BRINGING THE FAMILY INTO THE CLASSROOM

I am fortunate to work in a school district with diversity. I have been able to utilize my students, their families, and the diversity that exists within the school community as a basis for exploring changing family dynamics, traditions, and cultures. No matter what the makeup of a class, it is important always to start with the students in it. Yes, there are wonderful resources available to us today—multicultural children's literature, videos, and books filled with excellent activities and explanations for virtually any culture of interest. Yet, if we rely solely on these, difference can easily be interpreted as something "out there," far removed from our world versus "right here" among us.

Within the first few months of school, I usually send home a simple family interview. I ask parents for the following information: (1) the names and ages of everyone in the family; (2) the family's ethnic heritage and/or the places they are from; (3) an explanation of holidays celebrated, traditions/ beliefs practiced, or special times the family spends together; and (4) an explanation of the changes or transformations that have taken place in the family and how this has affected the family (e.g., births, new schedules, moving). After reading aloud *Tar Beach* (Ringgold, 1991), the first-graders add some wishes for their family to the interview information. Once I receive all the interviews, I invite any interested families in to visit and share the information with the class. I remind parents that family has been defined as the people living in the children's homes who love and care for them. *All families*, including adoptive-parent families, foster-parent families, and gay/lesbian-parent families will be welcomed and respected. Children and their families are also free to talk about family members who may not be with them right now, due to difficult circumstances such as incarceration, divorce, or death, as they feel comfortable. Families are welcome to bring pictures, albums, or special objects with them. All students have a special day to share. Whoever is sharing sits next to me or their family members in our sharing circle. I do not have to read much of the information before it is delightfully brought to life by the voices of the children. The mention of an expecting mom, a new washing machine, a yearly camping trip, the death of grandpa, or a favorite meal brings a multitude of questions and related experiences from eager peers. Children are curious about one another and seek the common threads among their peers.

To visualize and complement each family interview, we construct a color-coded concentric circle family map. In the center is the student's name and age. This is surrounded by a circle of family members' names and ages. Around these names is a circle with key words or phrases that tell about the family's celebrations, traditions, and special times. The final circle contains key words and phrases dealing with the family's transformations. The child's wishes for his or her family are added in kite-tail fashion. The family maps are displayed in different places all around the classroom for the remainder of the year. It is interesting and exciting to watch children read, compare, and change information as a birthday arrives or a new wish is sought. The maps are visual representations and a constant reminder of the stories of the children's lives. I have watched first-graders eagerly take visitors by the hand over to the maps to tell them their stories and, as you might imagine, it is not long before the newcomer finds him- or herself being "interviewed" in hopes of a valuable exchange.

Another way to learn more about students and their families is to send home a family artifact request. The artifact can be any object that tells a special story. It can be an object that has been passed down through generations or that serves as a reminder of a memorable time. I urge parents and children to think as broadly as possible and assure them that all items and stories will be treated with respect and as an avenue for the children to learn more about one another's lives. The objects will be treated as "treasures," not toys and, with parents' permission, are often displayed in museum style at our end-of-the-year celebration. I am always impressed with the objects brought in and the stories that accompany them. Here are just a few examples of how seemingly ordinary items take on an irreversible reverence once their value is understood:

> Kylishka is a beautiful, quiet-natured girl. She struggles in school, but is never one to complain, works twice as hard as many of her peers, and consistently displays a persistent and positive attitude. Her presence is one of pure sweetness, and she is eagerly sought out by her peers when they need help, a kind word, or a loyal friend. Kylishka carefully began to unpack what looked like a worn blue denim family picture album wrapped in a plastic grocery bag. This morning I am caught by her eyes—large, warm, and brown—looking a

bit unsure but with urgent sincerity into mine. She is not about to relinquish her grasp on this artifact and pile it, for now, on the designated display table without grabbing my arm and softly saying, "My mom said we must take special care of this and she wants it back as soon as we're done." Aware that I do not yet know the "story" of the album, I smile and tell Kylishka that if she'd prefer, we can keep it in the bag on my desk until she shares with us. Her unforgettable smile reveals her satisfaction, and she determinedly makes her way to my desk, takes a moment to secure just the right spot, and gently places the album on it. Later that afternoon, unable to contain my own curiosity any longer, I ask Kylishka to share her album with us. In it are pictures of her family with a baby brother who had died within his first year of life. Kylishka assures me and her classmates that even though the family misses him, her brother is up in heaven watching over them all the time. She is certain that he helps her sometimes when she asks him to. Kylishka was still quite young when her brother was born and she admits that she remembers him only a little bit. The album is used by her mom and dad to share the happiness he had brought to their lives with Kylishka and her siblings. Her mom's write-up is full of the joyful memories of this baby boy, which have been passed on to Kylishka, who could tell us many details of his brief babyhood.

The class and I were awestruck by Kylishka's presence, clarity, and bravery. I did not have to say a word about the sanctity of this album once it was placed on the display table. The first-graders always asked Kylishka if she would hold the album and look at the pictures with them so they could hear the stories again and again.

Hakeem was struggling to keep his hands steady as two giant crumpled balls of tissue paper emerged from his backpack. Cradling them around one arm, he sat and unloaded the rest of his things with his free hand, impatiently calling to me for help. Eager to free himself of their fragile care, he brusquely blurted out, "You can take these." I speedily whisked them up and away from any possible morning mishap. Hakeem blew a forceful breath of relief and sheepishly smiled at me, grateful to be relieved of his burden. "Hakeem," I said, "I can't believe they survived the bus ride!" He looked and me and shrugged, "Me either. What was my mom thinking?" At that, we both cracked up! As I scrounged through the "bus-proof" package, I discovered two painted ceramic birds. To my dismay, both were quite chipped and nicked. Hakeem noted my obvious concern and said, "Don't worry, Ms. Rieger, those were there." Later that week, Hakeem shared the story of the birds. They had been shipped to his family from Kurdistan. We learned that his uncle and cousins were still there. Hakeem was close with his cousins and looked up to his uncle. He shared many fond memories of playing together. Hakeem was eager for them to come to America. In the meantime, they communicated through letters and packages. The birds were kept in the living room on the entertainment center. The chips and nicks came from Hakeem's 2-year-old brother who occasionally got his hands on them!

I was struck by Hakeem's overwhelming sense of responsibility for these well-worn items. He handled these objects much like a father would a newborn. Their significance lies not so much in their appearance but in the story of heartfelt separation that they represented. Hakeem initially approached learning tasks with an irrational sense of hurriedness, but impressed himself and his peers with his attention to detail and color while painstakingly creating an artistic rendering of the two small statues.

Baby blankets, souvenirs from family vacations, trophies and certificates, pictures of loved ones, trinkets from adoring relatives, a worn baseball glove, a wooden spoon, a rubber ducky—the stories go on and on. I often culminate the family artifact experience by photographing the items with their owners. Before they leave us, the children create their own artistic representation of the object and tell its story in their own words. The photos, pictures, and stories are compiled in a class book. This book is often revisited and accompanies us on a field trip to our local museum. There, the children examine artifacts brought by immigrants and various ethnic cultures that comprise the local community. They are excited and enthusiastic to discover that many of these objects are as ordinary as and similar to their own! The first-graders are now eager and well-prepared to examine these objects and ask questions that uncover the stories of others. They begin to internalize that a valuable way to learn about people is to listen to their stories and examine their treasures.

There are countless ways to provide young children with opportunities to voice their stories. The two activities described above take considerable time. Although all students are eager to share, having one or two students present each day provides each student with unlimited time to tell stories, answer questions, and discuss connections and perceptions that are meaningful to the class. Once assured that everyone's turn will come, students relax and can truly listen to and interact with the individual who is sharing. This kind of listening is demanding, but is also invaluable and enriching. Eliminating the pressure of time and consistently practicing active listening enables everyone to obtain a wealth of information. I know that this information is powerful and more valuable than any curriculum I will ever teach. My task is to integrate the children's ideas and perceptions with the skills and concepts I know they must acquire. My students' stories and discussions from these kinds of activities often fuel the journaling, writing workshop topics, and creative projects throughout the year. The more their lives and their perceptions of the world are welcomed into the classroom, the more of a genuine investment they have in their learning and in working with each other (Wells & Chang-Wells, 1992). Creating this high level of investment makes school a very exciting place to be!

CELEBRATING CHILDREN AND THEIR FAMILIES

Imagine again. . . it is May. One cannot help but sense the excited anticipation this morning as students make their way to the classroom. On the way down the hall, they are greeted by a row of brightly colored chairs set upon some dropcloths pushed against the wall. Above each chair hang layers of elaborate plans—first-graders' blueprints of the color patterns and designs they've created for their chairs. Below each chair is a work kit containing brushes, stencils, stamps, pictures, tiles, flat marbles, and a variety of decorative tools and materials. "When is Yvonne coming?" "Are we going to finish the purple today?" "Did you find wheels for our bus?" Within 10 minutes of unavoidable chaos, my class is sitting in front of me colorfully transformed! They have hustled into their paint outfits, and it is nearly impossible to contain my laughter as I stand before them. I am thinking that any visitor could easily match each child to his or her corresponding chair upon examination of the color swatches on their paint clothes! Yvonne, a local artist and my loyal partner in this weekly artistic venture, arrives shortly after our morning announcements, followed by a committed parent volunteer, the reading teacher, and three fifth-graders. For the remainder of the morning, the first-graders are actively engaged in painting and decorating their chairs. The hallway and classroom hum like a bustling workshop. The adults and older students are busy docents for the young artists—pouring paint, wiping stencils and stamps, cleaning brushes, catching drips, and touching up.

The chair project is the result of an arts grant. I wanted to meaningfully provide my students with the opportunity to (1) learn an art form from a local practicing artist, (2) creatively and successfully express themselves, (3) actively transform something ordinary into something beautiful, and (4) give back to their families and their community in a caring and positive way. The project supports the ideas that young children should be engaged in self-directed, meaningful investigations (Helm & Katz, 2000) and that actively experiencing the arts provides a powerful form of interaction between children and their world (The Task Force on Children's Learning and the Arts, 1998).

In phase one of the project, students work in pairs to learn the art of decorative furnishing. They sand, prime, design, paint, and decorate a chair for a place of their choosing within their school or community. The chairs reflect the story of the place for which they are designated, and the first-graders spend considerable time discussing and voting on deserving places.

During the second phase, each student designs a chair for his or her own home. Again, students designate a space of their choosing, such as their bedroom, the living room, the porch, or the kitchen. To my amazement, a few students generously choose to gift their personal chair to a brother or sister who doesn't live with them, a kind neighbor, or a best friend.

The project begins in January and extends until the end of the school year. The excitement it generates school- and community-wide is contagious as students, faculty, and families continually peek in to check on the progress of the chairs. All chairs are gifted at our end-of-the-year celebration. When students are not painting, they are busy writing stories, poems, and songs to accompany each of the chairs. Photos are taken at each phase of the project so that students can create personal scrapbooks of the process. Students eagerly make a guest list, design and send invitations, and plan their exhibit opening with great anticipation. They sing and dance with their chairs, thank everyone who helped with beautiful bouquets of flowers, and personally gift their chairs to community members, school personnel, and their families. We celebrate with lots of hugs, lots of pictures with families and friends, and lots of cake!

Early on in my teaching career I learned the value of creating opportunities for students to showcase their work. Establishing community and arts partnerships has been one of the most successful ways for me to create this kind of opportunity. I strongly believe that all students need to celebrate themselves and their accomplishments. Every year, not just the traditional years reserved for graduations, is a great milestone for children. Creating interesting and compelling reasons for celebration highly motivates students and often catches family and community interest as well. Providing children with a platform such as the chair project, which culminates in a public celebration is an incredibly powerful and unforgettable experience for children and their families. The exhibit openings generate 100% attendance by my students and their families. This kind of turnout for any event in our school is nothing short of miraculous!

Celebrating does not always need to take the form of magnanimous endeavors. It is important to let families know that they are always welcome to attend school-wide celebrations, field trips, and special classroom activities. In my parent-teacher conference request letter, I insist that parents bring their children with them. It is important that parents peer through journals, listen to their children read, and examine their children's current inspirations and projects. The first-graders, with a little prodding, can usually run most of their conference on their own. There are no surprises, as most children and parents are already aware of the behaviors and skills that are in need of improvement. It is my intention, no matter how much a child is struggling in school, to make these interactions well-meaning and positive.

Creating nonthreatening family involvement activities is another way for children and families to celebrate learning. What could be more fun than bringing your family to school at night decked out in your pajamas? Listening to funny stories by flashlight snuggled among blankets and stuffed animals, munching on cookies and milk, with no secret agendas other than relaxation and enjoyment. Teachers, families, and children need celebrations like these to rejuvenate and be more personable with one another. To me, there is nothing more delightful than watching families and children enjoy themselves in the classroom.

Welcoming children and their families into our classrooms requires educators to critically examine the culture and climate in today's schools. I would not be an educator in the public school system if I did not believe that there are excellent people, initiatives, programs, and resources in place to serve the needs of today's children. However, we cannot ignore the prevailing attitudes, structures, and practices that are in place along with our own personal biases, which can potentially dishearten and dissuade students and their families from seeing themselves as viable contributors. We must welcome our students and families as they are, learn as much as we can from one another, work together, and always create opportunities to celebrate our accomplishments.

QUESTIONS FOR REFLECTION

1. How can you prepare and sustain a welcoming classroom for all students and their families?
2. Where are the excellent opportunities in the curriculum to integrate learning about students and their families?
3. How will you ensure that all students are given equal "voice" in sharing themselves, their families, and their lives with each other?
4. Take some time to reflect upon your present teaching philosophy, your beliefs about how children learn best, and what you most want your students to take away from their educational experiences with you. Combined with the curriculum that you are required to teach, what possible learning lenses do you have in place to integrate content and inspire your students?

REFERENCES

Balaban, N. (2006). *Everyday goodbyes: Starting school and early care: A guide to the separation process.* New York: Teachers College Press.

Bullard, S., Carnes, J., Hofer, M., Polk, N., & Sheets, R.H. (1997). *Starting small: Teaching tolerance in preschool and the early grades.* Montgomery, AL: Southern Poverty Law Center.

Carlsson-Paige, N. (2001). Nurturing meaningful connections with young children. In L. Lantieri (Ed.), *Schools with spirit: Nurturing the inner lives of children and teachers* (pp. 21–38). Boston MA: Beacon Press.

Derman-Sparks, L. (1989). *Anti-bias curriculum: Tools for empowering young children.* Washington, DC: NAEYC.

Epstein, J. L., Sanders, M. G., Simon, B. S., Salinas, K. C., Jansorn, N. R. & Van Voorhis, F. L. (2002). *School, family, and community partnerships: Your handbook for action* (2nd ed.). Thousand Oaks, CA: Corwin.

Helm, J. H., & Katz L. (2000) *Young investigators: The project approach in the early years.* New York: Teachers College Press.

Kralovec, E. (2003). *Schools that do too much.* Boston: Beacon Press.

Lionni, L. (1985). *Frederick's fables.* New York: Alfred A. Knopf.

Ringgold, F. (1991). *Tar beach.* New York: Crown.

The Task Force on Children's Learning and the Arts: Birth to Eight. (1998). *Young children and the arts: Making creative connections.* Washington, DC: Arts Education Partnership.

Wells, G., & Chang-Wells, G. L. (1992). *Constructing knowledge together: Classrooms as centers of inquiry and literacy.* Portsmouth, NH: Heinemann.

Chapter 5

Wards of Wisdom: Foster Youth on a Path Toward Postsecondary Education

Ilyana Marks

Young adults who emancipate from foster care are underrepresented in postsecondary education and overrepresented in state welfare and social services (Jim Casey Youth Opportunities Initiative, 2006). Initially designated wards of the court, youth placed in foster care encounter a series of family and academic transitions. Consequently, academic achievement for this unique population is frequently thwarted by an education gap. This chapter looks at how professional school counselors (PSCs) and educators can collaborate to close the education gap by supporting foster youth on a path toward postsecondary education. Writing as a PSC, I offer a strengths-based approach to equip foster youth with the assets and resilience necessary for school success. A review of federal and state child welfare legislation orients readers with the context of relevant policy and available services. Purposeful, proactive, and systemic supports initiated by educators are necessary to close the education gap. Equity, access, and transformation emerge as themes that can help foster youth triumph on the path toward postsecondary education.

THE EDUCATION GAP: RECOGNIZING THE NEEDS OF FOSTER YOUTH

Annually, more than 800,000 foster youth are served by child welfare, most between the ages of 14 and 17, with an approximately equal percentage between genders (Administration for Children & Families, 2006). During the same years that most high school graduates enroll in college and complete their first degree program, foster youth are more likely to drop out of high school; become single parents; become homeless, incarcerated, or unemployed; or rely on public assistance (Jim Casey Youth Opportunities Initiative, 2006). Unlike the general student body, only a small fraction of foster youth performs at grade level, and close to half are given special education placements due to learning and emotional needs (Zetlin, Weinberg, & Kimm, 2004). Children who become wards of the state experience a lifestyle replete with family upset, chaos of sudden transition, school changes, and multiple home placements. Foster youth are not immune to racial or cultural disparity. Minority youth in foster care account for double the number of White children, with a disproportionately greater percentage of African-American youth compared to those of any other ethnic background (Administration for Children & Families, 2006).

In extreme circumstances, family systems fail. Most family struggles that involve Child Protective Services (CPS) are inextricably linked with poverty. Whereas child abuse and neglect are the leading causes for a youth to become a ward of the state and enter foster care, substance abuse and informal kinship care are also common causes for a child to be removed from the home (Green Book, 2000).

In my own experience, I encounter foster youth whose birth parents suffer from mental health challenges, medical disabilities, and challenges related to immigration and cultural assimilation. Foster youth experience a series of transitions and family upsets before they become wards of the state. Foster care is designed as a temporary remedy with the hope, in many cases, that the family can heal and be reunited. I have worked with several youth who experienced more than nine temporary care placements and home transitions. Subjected to family upset and instability, many foster youth are labeled with behavioral challenges, Emotional Disturbance (ED) or Serious Emotional Disturbance (SED), resulting in special education placements at twice the rate of the general student body and a higher rate of grade retention (Zeitlin, Weinberg, & Kimm, 2004). If they stay in school and are motivated to graduate, foster youth often need to repeat courses for credit, holding them back from a direct route to postsecondary learning.

A child who enters foster care is initially designated a ward of the court and then assigned to a caseworker from the state welfare services. Through a chain of command and protocol based on court orders and judgments, the ward receives placement, care or supervision and age-appropriate or need-based services (Badeau & Gesiriech 2003). A ward of the court may be granted the volunteer support of a Court Appointed Special Advocate (CASA) (National CASA, 2006), a caseworker, and other state welfare representatives, but there is no personalized advocate or court-ordered service for the purpose of education. How do educators fill in the education gap and meet the needs of a youth whose life has been serviced by disconnect? Passing foster youth off to the next placement, social service, education referral, or community resource is not enough to ensure school success.

THE ROLE OF THE PROFESSIONAL SCHOOL COUNSELOR

Educators are vital links for foster youth. In this chapter, the term *educator* encompasses all school staff and education professionals, with a special emphasis on those who work in the primary and secondary schools. National, state, and district standards make the professional school counselor responsible for providing all students with developmental supports and skills for academic and life transitions. The role of the PSC serves as a point of reference from which school change can be initiated for the success of foster youth in postsecondary education.

According to the American School Counseling Association (ASCA, 2005) the PSC's role is based on themes of leadership, advocacy, collaboration, and systemic change. The ASCA offers a national model for school counseling based on proactive and effective supports for individuals and unique populations. This model is a comprehensive guide, not a visual graphic or step-by-step process. The ASCA model can be useful in orienting any education professional with the ideals for school counseling. Referenced collectively by educators at any school site, the ASCA model is designed to enhance services for any unique student population.

PSCs are charged with the duty to support students in the domains of academic, career, and personal/social capacities. In a comprehensive school-counseling program, PSCs draw from each of the ASCA domains to prepare students for future school transitions and a successful adulthood. The ASCA model holds PSCs responsible for using disaggregate data within the student body to build systemic school programs that work to close an achievement gap. Student-needs-assessment surveys, program evaluation, and school administrators can be aligned to initiate school change (ASCA, 2005).

According to ASCA, an achievement gap is closed when education needs are met in a manner of equity and barriers to learning are removed. Effective service delivery for PSCs is constructed with data that are site-specific and implemented systematically through the collaborative support of all school professionals, family members, guardians or caregivers, and community resources. PSCs use school site data to address issues of inequity and marshal the supports for every student to experience academic achievement. Effective action plans include identification of student needs, program development, indirect services based on collaboration and referral, and direct services delivered to students individually or in groups. Accountability practices are designed to monitor student behavior and academic achievement. PSCs can collaborate and consult with educators to modify classroom instruction, align students with school resources and supports, offer group or individual counseling, provide parent or guardian services, and form school teams to infuse counseling opportunities throughout school services and the classroom curriculum (ASCA, 2005).

The ASCA (2005) national model functions as an ideal so PSCs can gauge progress and enhance program design to implement comprehensive services that match the needs of any school setting. Foster youth can be incorporated as a unique group in data analysis and planning for school services. Professional school counselors can focus data collection efforts within their own school site and at the district level to address the needs that are characteristic of foster youth so they do not get lost in the education gap. As a matter of equity and social justice, school systems that seek to recognize and provide support to overcome barriers to learning for foster youth will positively impact the youth's success on a path toward postsecondary education.

CURRICULUM FOR SUCCESS: BUILDING ON STUDENT STRENGTHS

Foster youth experience adversity, however, they are not exempted from federal mandates and standards for academic performance. Despite tremendous loss, some youth prove resilient. To nurture resilience, PSCs utilize a strengths-based perspective to identify a student's assets and promote learning.

Strengths are described as "the capacity to cope with difficulties, to maintain functioning in the face of stress, to bounce back in the face of significant trauma, to use external challenges as a stimulus for growth, and to use social supports as a source of resilience" (McQuade & Ehrenreich, 1997, p. 203). Rather than recognize a student by deficit or pathology, a strengths-based approach will increase the youth's capacity to thrive (Rudolph & Epstein, 2000). Saleeby (1997) lauds a strengths-based approach for "honoring the innate wisdom of the human spirit, the inherent capacity for transformation of even the most humbled and abused" (p. 3). The task of eliciting student strengths involves a process of collaboration. In contrast to a traditional style of discipline, educators who assume a strengths-based perspective can connect with youth in "allegiance with their hopes, visions and values," (p. 14) rather than through methods of penalty or control. "Change can only come when you collaborate with client's aspirations, perceptions, and strengths, and when you firmly believe in them" (p. 49). Professional school counselors and educators who recognize strengths build a positive relationship with youth and empower them.

In the era of No Child Left Behind (NCLB), when documentation serves as an effective measure for tracking student performance, a strengths-based approach can be effective for gauging student abilities (Rudolph & Epstein, 2000). Strengths-based assessments effectively promote a student's "personal, social, and academic development" (p. 207) and prove effective in the school setting. In my own school counseling experience, I have used a strengths-based approach to develop goals for Student Study Teams (SSTs)/ Child Study Teams (CSTs), Individual Education Plans (IEPs), and individual study plans, and to clarify behavioral expectations. In the case of foster youth, concise documentation within a strengths-based framework is critical for students who do not have the advocacy of family members or a constant guardian.

Asset building is a strategy that speaks to strengths-based practice and can support students at various developmental stages. The Search Institute, a nonprofit organization devoted to healthy child development, promotes asset building as a method for recognizing students for what Scales and Roehlkepartain (2003) describe as the "positive factors" that have been proven to raise grades and test scores. Assets are characterized as either internal or external attributes. External assets include the factors that provide a student with sources of support and empowerment, boundaries and expectations, and constructive use of time. Internal assets are the factors that represent a student's commitment to learning, positive values, social competencies, and positive identity. Not all assets are necessary for school success; however, studies show a direct correlation to higher grade point average (GPA) when more of the external and internal factors are present. The impact on GPA is made possible by a systematic school effort to recognize the assets in individual students and to incorporate asset-building practices in student service, school programs, and classroom curriculum. Educators can institute asset building throughout a school without adding to their workload. The focus on asset building enhances teaching efforts by "promoting the conditions for learning" and proves effective for "all groups of students" (p. 9). Asset building is key in the support of students such as foster youth who may encounter developmental upsets, since this strategy "focuses on human development as a core process in promoting student achievement" (p. 9). Asset building can characterize a school community as one that is caring and supportive, a climate that contributes to the success of every student.

A school that honors student strengths and identifies assets nurtures resilience. Resilience is a character trait that is described by Doll and Lyon

(1998) as one's ability for "successfully coping with or overcoming risk and adversity or the development of competence in the face of severe stress or hardship" (p. 348). Efforts to build resilience result in protective factors that can contribute to the prevention of child abuse (Tomison & Wise, 1999). A variety of resilience-based programs are instituted at the state, district, school, and classroom levels.

The study of resilience extends to ethnically specific strategies that can promote a culturally sensitive approach to student service. Connell, Spencer, and Aber (1994) report practices that bear evidence for educational resilience in African-American populations, which represent the largest minority of youth placed in foster care. Educators serve as liaisons to support youth in their exploration of culture and race, and PSCs are specially trained to address such identity development. Schools introduce students to diverse leaders and history, but this education may not facilitate the development of an individual's ethnic or cultural identity. Foster youth may encounter barriers with regard to social, ethnic, cultural, gender, and family roles that impede academic achievement. Each culture embraces life with a unique set of attitudes and traditions, and ethnicity emerges in the diverse ways that families cope, respond to problems, seek help, express themselves, and interact individually or in groups (McGoldrick, Giordano, & Pearce, 1996). The plight of refugees or the cultural stigma of mental health challenges in certain cultures can heighten family torment for many foster youth. PSCs are poised to offer individualized support so that students can recognize the context of race, culture, and family history that impacts their identity development and school experiences.

Educators who help foster youth to utilize strengths in order to succeed in school and work through challenges choose not to regard students as a product of dysfunction and can thereby empower them (DeJong & Kim Berg, 2002). When they are empowered, foster youth can identify healthy coping skills to persevere during times of transition or loss. Schools that incorporate opportunities to identify strengths and assets can nurture resilience among all students. The school that identifies strengths establishes a healthy community that a youth in foster care may not have previously encountered.

LIAISONS FOR DEMOCRACY:
ASSESSING LEGISLATIVE SUPPORT

Susceptible to the education gap, foster youth may not have access to the same learning opportunities as most students and stand to benefit from educators who promote school practices guided by democracy and social justice. Schools committed to the ideals of democracy and social justice speak to the morals and virtues that involve an individual's well-being within the context of a greater community. Advocate for child welfare and educator John Dewey (1916/2004) charged schools with the responsibility "to see to it that each individual gets an opportunity to escape from the limitations of the social group in which he was born, and to come into living contact with a broader environment" (p. 20). An initial step toward democracy and social justice in service delivery within the context of a school is to understand the limitations of federal or state initiatives for child welfare. The federal No Child Left Behind Act incorporated the McKinney-Vento Homelessness Assistance Act to outline support for youth in transition and to ensure a Free and Appropriate Public Education (FAPE). The John H. Chafee Foster Care Independence Program has worked to enhance access and accountability for foster youth in postsecondary education. State services for foster youth complement the federal system for child welfare and school accountability, but local resources will vary depending on the accessibility and availability.

The McKinney-Vento Act introduced a system of accountability for the identification, enrollment, attendance, transportation, special needs, homelessness, and circumstances of poverty (see also Chapter 9, this volume) that become barriers to learning for youth in transitional circumstances (Webb & Rutkin, 2003). Under the McKinney-Vento Act, states and schools are held accountable for service delivery to homeless or transitional youth at the district level. Every school district is required to designate a liaison to identify youth who are eligible for McKinney-Vento services. These services are extended to family members who assume responsibility for youth under informal kinship care. The McKinney-Vento district liaison collaborates with schools and community agencies to ensure that eligible youth are given the services they need so their education rights are provided for. Accountability for enrollment under the McKinney-Vento Act starts as early as preschool and can extend to Head Start or Even Start programs if they are administered by state and local education agencies. Enrollment is required to be immediate, may be specific to a student's school of origin, and cannot be delayed due to the absence of required documents such as birth certificates, previous school records, immunization records, or other medical documents. Enrollment includes a student's opportunity to participate fully in all school activities, including sports and extracurricular activities, so they are not turned away due to attendance records or fees. For students whose attendance suffered due to transition, the McKinney-Vento Act requires due credit for partial completion of coursework and for students to be placed in the appropriate grade level and learning environment. Grades cannot be lowered due to barriers related to homelessness or transition. Transportation challenges should not thwart attendance, and the McKinney-Vento district liaison is prepared to coordinate alternatives (National Association for the Education of Homeless Children and Youth [NAEHCY] & National Law Center on Homelessness & Poverty [NLCHP], 2004).

The McKinney-Vento Act institutes inclusive practices for youth who have special needs. Schools must accommodate students who qualify for support under the Individuals with Disabilities Education Act (IDEA) and modifications determined by Section 504 of the Rehabilitation Act of 1973 and of the Americans with Disabilities Act (ADA). According to NAEHCY and NLCHP (2004), students who receive McKinney-Vento support are ensured that appropriate services will be continued immediately upon enrollment. In the case that school records for Individualized Education Plans (IEPs) are not maintained, the district liaison establishes interim services or initiates a new IEP meeting. Maintaining IEPs is important in particular for foster youth who may not have a single caregiver who follows their education progress. Students eligible for services under the McKinney-Vento Act are also eligible for Title I, Part A of the Elementary and Secondary Education Act, which addresses barriers to learning due to poverty. Title I, Part A funds are used to provide services that help students "to succeed in school and meet academic achievement standards" (p. 26). The funds can provide relief for a variety of student needs by way of mentorship, academic supports, and fees for college entrance exams or other activities.

For issues relating to access or accountability under the McKinney-Vento Act, such as compliance or mediation support, educators or caregivers can turn to the district liaison or the U.S. Department of Education (USDE). The USDE offers a clearinghouse specifically designed for the McKinney-Vento Act, and states are required to establish procedures for dispute resolution. Additional research, guidance, and planning materials are provided by NAEHCY and NLCHP (2004).

Even after foster youth leave school or turn 18 and emancipate to a life of independence, there are still federal supports. In December 1999, the John H. Chafee Foster Care Independence Program replaced the Independent Living Initiative under Title IV-E of the Social Security Act. The Chafee Independence Program enhanced assistance to young adults between the ages of 18 to 21 who are transitioning out of foster care. Funding is designated for independent living activities, housing, cost of food, Medicaid, and accountability practices. Designations are broadly defined so that service delivery is left to the jurisdiction of the state, and program implementation will differ according to local resources (National Foster Care Awareness Project, 2000). The Chafee Independence Program supports both dependent and emancipated foster youth on a path toward postsecondary education by way of state, not-for-profit, or private funding. Such funding can be used toward database maintenance to identify eligible young adults, provide tuition for vocational or job training and college, and offer funding for entrance exam preparation, application and exam fees, housing, preventive health services inclusive of substance abuse, and mentorship (National Foster Care Awareness Project, 2000).

Although McKinney-Vento services are mandated and necessary for removing the barriers that contribute to the education gap, these provisions do not provide the personalized opportunities that facilitate school success. Proactive supports and longitudinal planning are reliant upon an educator's own conviction to collaborate for change. Ill-defined or poorly implemented federal legislation can emerge as a labyrinth. Finding the resources and services available for emancipated youth can be likened to a scavenger hunt. Depending on local resources, there may or may not be a full array of Chaffee supports available. School liaisons can implement child welfare services for state and federal legislation effectively, but this effort may not achieve ideals for social change. Dewey's (1916/2004) democratic ideals for education encapsulated the hope that "as a society becomes more enlightened, it realizes that it is responsible not to transmit and conserve the whole of its existing achievements, but only such as make for a better future society" (p. 20). Districts employ liaisons for child welfare, but have yet to employ liaisons for democracy; therefore, it is up to each educator who encounters foster youth to provide them with a learning climate for social change.

SCHOOL SYSTEMS AND PARTNERSHIPS FOR CHANGE

Systemic service delivery in the school setting is effective for building connections with foster youth who get lost in the education gap. Educators who collaborate to provide a systems approach consider the context of a student's living situation, transitions, and the potential resources available at the school site that will maximize the student's learning experience. White and Mullis (1998) suggest that the interaction of system components inclusive of a team approach and participation of the student can result in timely service, efficient consultation, and effective counseling methodology and theory. They also report that results become evident in student behavior and the frequency of positive learning experiences. A systematic approach offers comprehensive student service that will address the complex and developmental needs of students at multiple grade levels. Many of the challenges that foster youth encounter in their daily life occur outside of the classroom. School systems that incorporate partnerships for change by teaming with child welfare agencies, nonprofit organizations, and local youth programs can extend the education experience outside of school time.

Mentor-program relationships offer youth the opportunity to expand visions for postsecondary education to new horizons. Organizations that train and match youth with mentors can be found in every state, including of Big Brothers Big Sisters, The Boys & Girls Clubs of America, and other community-based programs. Mentoring can influence a youth's behavior, academic attitudes and performance, family and peer relationships, self-concept, and cultural understanding (Tierney, Grossman, & Resch, 1995), as well as psychological well-being and physical health (DuBois & Silverthorn, 2005). In my experience, the foster youth I have worked with most frequently aspired to become a teacher, social worker, lawyer, or police officer. These are the professionals they know from life experience. Foster youth may spend more time with life's heroes than children in traditional families, but through mentorship, they are introduced to or encouraged to discover new possibilities. Mentorship can empower foster youth to take charge and bridge the education gap independently. In the company of mentors, foster youth can be validated as they work through personal challenges and develop their own voice as they engage in conversations at a coffee shop or over the telephone, share poetry, correspond through email, attend outings, participate in games or sports, and attend program meetings.

The Jim Casey Youth Opportunities Initiative (2006) provides up-to-date research studies, guides, and strategies for best practice and partnerships that help foster youth attain success in postsecondary education. The wealth of the Casey resources indicates that there are several ways to construct a path toward postsecondary education for foster youth. Educators can reference the Casey program resources to inform school site service delivery and identify key partnerships in the local community.

There are stepping-stones beyond the traditional path to postsecondary education that may bring hope to a student who has become disoriented by the education gap. Earning straight D's in the junior year of high school does not mean a student cannot attend a prestigious university someday. Stepping-stones surface when the academic path is broken down to a personalized path. For students lost in an education gap, knowing there are a variety of options to advance in education can keep them engaged. Community partnerships will enhance the efforts of school systems and individual educators to close the education gap for foster youth.

TRANSITION, TRANSFORMATION, AND TRIUMPH:
GUIDANCE FOR FOSTER YOUTH

Supported transitions present opportunities for transformation and triumph. Numerous school and nonprofit programs are designed for at-risk youth; however, few recognize the needs of foster youth as a unique population.

In March 2002, Jane Goodall appeared at a National Hockey League rink in southern California to accept commendation for forming a chapter of her Roots & Shoots program at a local university. Goodall greeted the audience with an ape call that reached to the far ends of the arena. She discussed Roots & Shoots, a global program devoted to science exploration for students at elementary, secondary, and postsecondary levels. Soon after this visit, Goodall extended the Roots & Shoots program and the power of her voice to foster youth by way of a guide entitled *Foster Care Handbook: Roots & Shoots for Youth in Transition* (2005). Goodall's guide uses a transitional model to help youth work through personal loss by way of exploring their own learning abilities to embrace new beginnings and find opportunities for civic engagement. The format is designed to help foster youth address their own behavior and develop skills for intervention strategies, goal setting, and reflection. Goodall's guide complements the services offered by PSCs and can easily be integrated to an academic or after-school program. The spirit of Goodall's guide provides a positive approach to youth development and community building on a global scale. The critical element of this guide is based on active participation of foster youth and effectively draws upon their power of voice, an element that is often lost or ignored as they transition through multiple placements or impersonalized systems of care.

Equal Justice Works Fellow for the National Center for Youth Law (NCYL), Phil Ladew implemented the Foster Youth in Transition Project. In an article entitled "Happy Birthday! You're Homeless", Ladew and his coauthor, Benedetto (2000) remark that the preparation of students for Harvard by way of private school can be less expensive than the cost of educating foster youth who depend on an array of child welfare services. Ladew, a former foster youth himself, experienced firsthand the daunting experience of roadblocks and confusion on the path toward postsecondary education. Proving resilient, Ladew used his awareness to build inroads and inform foster youth en route to emancipation by creating *Fight for Your Rights* (2004). This guide walks foster youth through the red tape, social services, targeted resources, and postsecondary education options that enable emancipated youth to become independent within the system of interdependence.

Educators can incorporate ready-made programs like those published by Goodall and Ladew into the school setting. In this effort, the voice of foster youth should be incorporated into any programming effort as a vital component for planning and service delivery.

POSTSECONDARY EDUCATION EXPLORATION AND CAMPUS CHOICE

Of the fraction of foster youth who graduate from high school, fewer find their way to private colleges or 4-year universities. To contemplate a campus of choice for postsecondary education can evoke feelings of inspiration and challenge for any student: Where to go, how far away, what to study, what does it cost, and how hard will it be? Trade or technical schools may appear as a valid option, but there are pitfalls to taking the shorter route. Community colleges offer specialized training programs similar to those of trade schools, but for a lower cost by way of certification. Students can earn a specialized career certificate and apply the same course work toward an associate degree. The certificate may not sustain a long-term career in a competitive field, but can be a useful stepping-stone toward a more advanced degree.

The admission process at different postsecondary institutions varies. Educators and students should not hesitate to contact admissions officers to ask about supports or funding tailored to those who experienced even the briefest of placements in foster care. There may be a wealth of scholarships, specialized supports, and local, state, and federal funding available to foster youth at a particular campus, but these are often not well-known to youth who are alienated or frustrated by the education gap.

The education experience that is typical for foster youth may not prepare them adequately for competitive college entrance. For foster youth, the campus concept may be foreign terrain. In my experience, all of the wards of the state that I supported on a path to postsecondary education were first-generation college students. Raised without the role models or expectations familiar to traditional students, the college campus is new territory. The term *campus* is centuries old, referring to the camp or field of a military setting or a group organized for training (Oxford University Press, 1989). In essence, the campus is a training or exercise ground for champions. Educators who provide foster youth with life skills to set up camp for their future will empower them to seek out a college campus where they can employ their strengths and emerge triumphant.

Preparing for Campus Life

I participate on a committee that interviews former foster youth for an undergraduate "Guardian Scholarship" that covers costs for tuition, books, food, and year-round housing. Many foster youth do not have a stable home to come back to during summer, winter, and annual term breaks. Year-round housing is not a traditional option; however, Guardian Scholarship committees have been assembled across the nation in the past decade in an effort to retain students who were once wards of the court. As a Guardian scholarship committee member and mentor, I have discovered that many award recipients struggle to fit in once they arrive at the campus setting. Some do not want to be associated with a scholarship label, as they would prefer to leave the mark of child welfare behind. Other Guardian scholars study abroad, mentor younger siblings, and graduate with honors. I know former foster youth who tried to explore the possibility of starting college without a scholarship or network of support. In doing so, they found that campus parking was daunting enough to make them turn around and leave. Some pulled the car over en route to a campus visit as they experienced panic attacks and never arrived.

Campus tours can be a pivotal experience. I chaperoned foster youth on campus tours arranged by the by the local Independent Living Program (ILP). County services and nonprofit organizations offer ILP services to foster youth between the ages of 16 and 21 so they can build skills for emancipation. Topics covered by ILP services include education, careers and relationships, and other life skills. At each of the college tours that I chaperoned, there were typically a number of youth who had just started attending ILP, so this orientation to postsecondary education was their first. Often, the campus tours were not eagerly anticipated; instead, they were regarded by the youth as just another ILP chore. On the day of one such college tour, I arrived at a group home early while the youth were still finishing their house duties. The youth complained more about attending the ILP college tour than the housecleaning. In this group home, many of the youth were labeled Seriously Emotionally Disturbed (SED) and were on antidepressants, demonstrated sexualized behaviors in the school setting, regularly brought home failing grades, ignored homework assignments, had difficulty following directions, or demonstrated resistance and expressed a general disinterest in school. A few of the youth aspired to professional careers, but were not familiar with the pathway to attain such goals. Many of the youth were frequently put on detention by teachers and on suspension for fights, and had meetings with the principal to set up academic or behavior contracts. School did not seem to be a place of learning and positive experience for these youth, but instead an institution that was there to issue penalties and control. Intellectually, these students had checked out.

En route to the campus, the youth continued to complain about the tour and expressed complete disinterest. When we set foot on the college campus, we are greeted by admissions officers and real-life college students who served as tour guides. The tour group was led through dorms and had a chance to sit in classrooms, look at the gym, see the theater, learn about the layout of school buildings, and dine in the cafeteria. At the end of this tour, I noticed a gradual shift in their characters. At the end of the visit, we returned to the bus with stickers, pennants, and college applications. During the ride back, the youth vocalized visions for themselves in postsecondary education, on either that campus or another one they visited before. When we returned to the group home, the youth independently sat down to review the application materials. Later, we all sat down together at the kitchen table to discuss topics to write about for their personal statements. As long as I sat with them, they continued to write, to ask questions, and to think about what it would be like and what steps it would take to become a college student.

Putting It in Writing

When combined with campus visits and facilitated writing practice, composing a personal statement for a college application can serve as an activity that may help students visualize a path toward postsecondary education. Putting it all in writing can introduce foster youth to new visions for school engagement and pathways to postsecondary success. Foster youth can fuse school experiences and personal triumphs by practicing writing a personal statement as early as their freshman year in high school to identify their academic strengths and turning points. Grades and SAT scores, among other factors, influence the admission decision, but when the personal statement is an afterthought or unrefined, a student's efforts to communicate become muddled. The strength of character conveyed in one's personal statement is what admissions officers tell me impresses them most.

Navigating for Independence

A campus setting boasts resources and support services devoted to all aspects of student life. Private colleges and universities may provide smaller class sizes to nurture student dialogue and offer a personalized experience, but they may not offer the federally funded support programs found at state institutions. State colleges and universities offer supports for underserved student populations such as minority student services, Educational Opportunity Programs (EOPs), single-parent programs, and even foster youth scholarship programs. Both private and state institutions offer support services for career exploration, writing, students who have learning disabilities, counseling, medical needs and resources for physical fitness, cultural involvement, and faith-based interests, among others. Programs, resources, clubs, and organizations are identified on websites and in handbooks, but students must use their own initiative to seek these out as needed. A major difference in service delivery between the postsecondary campus and the elementary or secondary school setting is that the student is now charged with managing the system independently.

The postsecondary education setting can be characterized by high demand, chaos, and confusion for students who may not know how to identify a healthy network of support. Some campuses boast programs that bridge the transition from high school to postsecondary education, but they occur only once per year and not all students are able to attend. In an effort to streamline services in a proactive and informative manner, I collaborated with local nonprofit organizations, colleges, and universities to identify common campus resources in the form of a guidebook. The guide serves as a "roadmap" to inform students about local postsecondary education resources. Information about campus services are often published in a variety of formats on campus, but for freshmen who are nontraditional students, the identification of resources does not appear as writing on the wall. There is no glory in realizing what could have been done to avoid a failed term paper or emotional meltdown. I encourage new college students to identify all of the student services on campus the first day of matriculation and to visit each of them within that first week. The roadmap includes financial aid resources designed for foster youth, since they qualify for funding differently than traditional students. In this guide, I encourage foster youth to contact school site financial aid counselors or administrators for guidance in filling out the Free Application for Federal Student Aid (FAFSA). The roadmap encourages students to consider safety by identifying the emergency phones en route to class, the dorms, or parking lots, and to visit the department of public safety in the case they ever need to file a report or get a jump start when their car battery dies. Transfer centers at junior or community colleges are featured in this guide, since opportunities for college tours, recruitment events, and guidance activities are offered year-round. To know the hours of the health center can make the difference between a missed day and missed weeks of classes. As students take action to get to know the college campus as a community, they are empowered to engage in learning beyond the classroom and to take life skills for interdependence into adulthood.

IMPLICATIONS AND RECOMMENDATIONS

Implications for educators who collaborate to close the education gap for foster youth will pave the way for opportunities in postsecondary learning. Rather than emancipate to a life of alienation, dependence on social welfare, or continued transitional upset, foster youth who are prepared for postsecondary education can attain a productive and satisfying adulthood. Ensuring that foster youth achieve postsecondary education will enhance the quality of life for those individuals as well as contribute to the local workforce and the greater community.

At present, school site strategies, research, best practice, and program evaluation for support to foster youth on a path toward postsecondary education are limited. PSCs are poised to streamline services by way of collaboration around the ASCA national model. Systemic efforts can be enhanced by community linkages, inter- and intra-district ties, and by policy at the state and federal level. The efforts of PSCs and educators who form school teams for support to foster youth and conduct action research will ultimately contribute to best practice and strategies for replication. Educator initiative serves as a key for design in proactive and systemic student service. Newly credentialed educators who seek to bring about social change can return to postsecondary education for an advanced degree, apply for school site grants, and conduct data collection for comparative analysis or longitudinal research. Teacher preparation and doctoral programs dedicated to social justice enable educators to rigorously pursue research, define best practice, and ultimately enhance service delivery.

As best practice is defined, culturally specific supports and research inclusive of ethnicity and gender affiliation should also be established. Mental health needs in both the high school and postsecondary education settings should be explored in a longitudinal effort. Mental health partnerships beyond the public school setting may be necessary for foster youth whose needs cannot be met by the comprehensive effort of PSCs, school psychologists, district services, and other educators. In my experience as a mentor and in working with panels of former foster youth in postsecondary education, these students begin to struggle with family disconnect in new ways once they matriculate. Mental health services that are appealing and proactive will help current and emancipated foster youth to accept the supports they need to transition through life and postsecondary education so their energy can be maximized for student life and the college experience. As PSCs and educators collaborate to design comprehensive programs, they should be inclusive of caregivers, group home staff, and others who have a direct impact on the school experience of foster youth. Foster youth as individuals or teams should be recognized as a valid resource for school-based systems change. States and school districts can take action to ensure change by way of granting educators credential renewal hours and providing professional development and recognition for the effort to streamline services and supports for foster youth on a path toward postsecondary learning. The legislation discussed in this chapter is less than a decade old. New politics and policies can only emerge with new efforts for reform.

The efforts of PSCs are enhanced by the collaborative effort of educators, school services that are proactive and systemic, and coordination of community resources for both foster youth and their caregivers. The benefits for foster youth who are supported on a path toward postsecondary education are limitless and include clarified expectations and new dreams in tandem with their own transformation and triumph. With a common cause for equity, access, and social justice, schools can support foster youth to emancipate as empowered individuals, ready for success. Wisdom on the topic of postsecondary education for foster youth is created when educators target the education gap and marshal supports for change. Wisdom is gleaned when foster youth are successful in postsecondary education.

QUESTIONS FOR REFLECTION

1. Young adults who emancipate from foster care are underrepresented in postsecondary education and overrepresented in state welfare and social services. How do these statistics affect your role as an educator? As a citizen?
2. How can issues of race, class, gender, culture, and ethnicity be addressed for foster youth? Why would such issues of diversity be important to address for foster youth en route to postsecondary education? What are some strategies to support foster youth in their identity development in the classroom or general school setting? Discuss your role or own experience in working with foster youth who may have struggled with a family background that may not fit with the Western standards in the typical American classroom.
3. Do you have any predisposition to servicing or educating foster youth? How do you see your role? For educators who are not familiar with the struggles that are particular to this population, how can you initiate collaboration?
4. How visible should support services be for foster youth in the school setting? Create an action plan to introduce a strengths-based curriculum that features asset building and nurtures resilience for foster youth in your school setting. Who do you have to convince for school-wide buy-in? Would you start small or work from the top down?

REFERENCES

Administration for Children & Families. (2004). *Trends in foster care and adoption*. Washington, DC: The Children's Bureau.

Administration for Children & Families. (2006). *The AFCARS report*. Washington, DC: The Children's Bureau.

American School Counselor Association. (ASCA). (2005). *The ASCA national model: A framework for school counseling programs*. Alexandria, VA: Author.

Badeau, S., & Gesiriech, S. (2003). *A child's journey through the child welfare system*. Washington, DC: The Pew Commission on Children in Foster Care. Retrieved April 20, 2006, from http://pewfostercare.org/docs/index.php?DocID=24.

Connell, J. P., Spencer, M. B. & Aber, J. L. (1994). Educational risk and resilience in African-American youth: Context, self, action and outcomes in schools. *Child Development, 65*(2), 493–506.

DeJong, P., & Kim Berg, I. (2002). *Interviewing for solutions* (2nd ed.). Pacific Grove, CA: Brooks/Cole.

Dewey, J. (2004). *Democracy and education*. Mineola, NY: Dover Publications. (Original work published 1916)

Doll, B., & Lyon, M. A. (1998). Risk and resilience: Implications for the delivery of educational and mental health services in schools. *School Psychology Review, 27*(3), 348–363.

DuBois, D. L., & Silverthorn, N. (2005). Natural mentoring relationships and adolescent health: Evidence from a national study. *American Journal of Public Health, 95*(3), 518–524.

Goodall, J. (2005). *The foster care handbook: Roots & shoots guide for youth in transition*. Silver Spring, MD: The Jane Goodall Institute.

Green Book. (2000). *Section 11—Child protection, foster care, and adoption assistance*. (Ways and Means Committee Print WMCP: 106-14). Washington, DC: Administration for Children and Families.

Jim Casey Youth Opportunities Initiative. (2007). *"Resources."* Retrieved March 12, 2007, from http://www.jimcaseyyouth.org/resources.htm.

Jim Casey Youth Opportunities Initiative. (2006). *"Resources."* Retrieved July 14, 2005, from http://www.jimcaseyyouth.org/aboutus.htm.

Ladew, P. (2004). *Fight for your rights: A guidebook for California foster youth, and those who care about them*. Sacramento, CA: National Center for Youth Law.

Ladew, P., & Benedetto, M. (April–June, 2000). Happy birthday! You're Homeless. *Youth Law News*, 1–7.

McGoldrick, M., Giordano, J., & Pearce, J.W. (1996). *Ethnicity and family therapy* (2nd ed.). New York: Guilford.

McQuade, S., & Ehrenreich, J. H. (1997). Assessing client strengths. *Families in Society: The Journal of Contemporary Human Services, 78*(2), 201–212.

National Association for the Education of Homeless Children and Youth (NAEHCY) & National Law Center on Homelessness & Poverty (NLCHP) (2004). *The 100 most frequently asked questions on the education rights of children and youth in homeless situations*. Washington, DC: Author.

National CASA (2006). *"Overview."* Retrieved March 12, 2007, from http://www.nationalcasa.org/about_us/index.html.

National Clearinghouse on Child Abuse and Neglect Information. (2003). *Foster care national statistics*. Washington, DC: The Children's Bureau.

National Foster Care Awareness Project (NFCAP): Allen, M., Nixon, R., Pizzigati, P., Meitner, L., & Epstein, H. (2000). *Frequently asked questions about the foster care independence act of 1999 and the John H. Chaffee foster care independence program*. Washington, DC: Connect for Kids.

Oxford University Press (1989). *Oxford English Dictionary* (2nd ed). Oxford: Author.

Peace4Kids.org. (2005). Retrieved July 1, 2005, from www.peaceforkids.org/programs_life.html.

Rak, C. F., & Patterson, L. E. (1996). Promoting resilience in at-risk children. *Journal of Counseling and Development, 74*(4), 368–373.

Rudolph, S. M., & Epstein, M. H. (2000). Empowering children and families through strength-based assessment. *Reclaiming Children and Youth, 8*(4), 207–211.

Saleeby, D. (1997). *The strengths perspective in social work practice* (2nd ed.). New York: Longman.

Scales, P. C., & Roehlkepartain, E. C. (2003). Boosting student achievement. *Insights and Evidence, 1*(1), 1–10.

Tierney, J. P., Grossman, J. B., &, Resch, N. L. (1995). *Making a difference: An impact study of big brothers big sisters*. Philadelphia: Public/Private Ventures.

Tomison, A. M., & Wise, S. (1999, Autumn). Community-based approaches in preventing child maltreatment. *Child Abuse Prevention, 11*, 2–19.

Webb, J., & Rutkin, G. (2003). Press releases: Education department issues guidance for homeless students under no child left behind act. Retrieved July 21, 2005, from *http://www.ed.gov/news/pressreleases/2003/04/04082003.html.nn*

White, J., & Mullis, F. (1998). A systems approach to school counselor consultation. *Education, 119*(2), 242–253

Zeitlin, A., Weinberg, L., & Kimm, C. (2004). Improving education outcomes for children in foster care: Intervention by an education liaison. *Journal of Education for Students Placed at Risk, 9*(4), 421–429

REPRESENTATIONS OF FAMILY IN SCHOOL CULTURE AND CURRICULUM

The chapters in Part II of the book are research-based and analytical contributions that examine representations of family in American school culture and curriculum. Drawing on sociocultural, critical, sociological, and interpretive theories, these chapters further explore the representations of family that have been introduced in Part I.

In Chapter 6, Monica Miller Marsh draws our attention to the fact that as we enter the 21st century, families consist of a multitude of arrangements. She explores how arrangements have indeed shifted over time in response to economic, demographic, social, and philosophical transformations, and demonstrates that "nontraditional" types of family arrangements have always been a visible part of the fabric of our nation. In particular, she examines three distinct family types that coexisted alongside one another in colonial Pennsylvania.

Chapter 7 surveys the challenges and opportunities that gay and lesbian families bring to school communities by reexamining teachers' work, parent community networks, and accommodations or shifts in curriculum experiences for all children. Janice Kroeger contends that although families expect their children to be served well in schools, gay and lesbian families pose myriad challenges to some educators. In the best interests of their students, teachers often have to reexamine their classroom practices to provide suitable and equitable experiences for the children of gay and lesbian families

In Chapter 8, Leslie Colabucci and Matt Conley focus on picture books and nonfiction books to explore the multiple ways family is portrayed in children's literature. Using textual analysis and critical review,

Colabucci and Conley provide an overview of how family is represented, not represented, and misrepresented in recent, highly acclaimed, and landmark books.

Chapter 9 focuses on homeless families, with young children being the fastest-growing sector of the homeless population. A growing concern in the nation, homelessness is becoming a key educational and societal issue that is addressed neither in practice nor in research. Tracy Thoennes elucidates the experiences and representations of homeless families in school and culture, pointing out the impact of social policy upon homeless families and what teachers, administrators, and school personnel can do to support homeless students and their families.

Finally, in Chapter 10, Tammy Turner-Vorbeck looks beyond the traditional forms of curriculum and focuses instead upon an examination of the more elusive, yet highly impactful hidden and null curricula on family in schools. Supporting the theoretical with the experiential, her writing provides the reader with an understanding of the complex relationship between the primary forms of curriculum at work in schools in order to fully illuminate the real-life consequences that various curricular messages about the concept of family create for students. Overall, this chapter, along with the others in this book, reveals that when curricular representations of family are restricted to typical family structure, other forms of family are omitted and thus devalued.

Chapter 6

Evolving Images:
Crafting Family Lives in
Colonial Pennsylvania

Monica Miller Marsh

Family is a culture's way of coordinating personal reproduction with social reproduction—as the socially sanctioned place where male and female reproductive activities condition and are conditioned by the other activities into which human beings enter as they perpetuate a particular kind of society, or try to construct a new one. (Coontz, 1988, p. 1)

Four years ago, my husband and I found ourselves constructing our notions of family when we returned from a 6-week stay in Poland with three children. We knew our lives would be changed forever, and we welcomed that change. What we didn't expect was how hard we would have to advocate for our children in schools that did not sanction them as capable, knowledgeable, and accepted. My oldest son was 5½ years old at the time, and we never won the battle of having him accepted into the local public school kindergarten. The school argued that his IQ score of 55 meant that he would not be able to function in a mainstream classroom setting. We argued that he had taken a test in English without a Polish translator shortly after he arrived in this country and that he did not have a valid IQ score. The school had rules, and with his scores he would need to be bused 45 minutes away to a classroom with children who were considered to be extremely low-functioning. Rather, we perceived him as needing a school with a language-rich environment. Fortunately, we were able to enroll him in a local parochial school where he was included in the regular kindergarten classroom and did just fine. I am happy to report that although he still does struggle with the English language, he is currently in a third-/fourth-grade multiage classroom and enjoys reading, playing piano, and being a member of the community basketball team.

Although overt issues of equity are ones that my husband and I are able to battle for our children, there are also those issues that are part of the hidden or null curriculum (see Chapters 5 and 10, this volume) that constantly remind my children that they do not come from a family that is legitimized in school. When I think about my youngest child, a story comes quickly to mind. One of her very first assignments in preschool was to send in her baby picture and to ask us about how she got her name. Of course, there are no baby pictures, and none of us knows how she got her beautiful first name. Although we are able to adapt assignments—in this case, we talked about her middle name, which we did choose for her, and took in the first picture of her that was sent from the adoption agency— these assignments always turn out to focus on the many losses my children have suffered—the loss of a birth family, their culture, their memories, and a significant part of their childhood.

One of the most painful assignments for our entire family was given last year when my husband was spending the morning in my middle son's second-grade classroom for the annual father/child visitation. My middle son was going through a hard time and exhibiting some signs that perhaps he wasn't as attached to us as we had first thought. As parents, we were trying to do everything we could to help strengthen our bonds with him to create the foundation of security he would need to thrive, not just survive. We believed that the father/child visitation would be the perfect opportunity for our son and his father to spend some special time together. When our son got home that afternoon, he was in a dark mood. During the visitation, father and son had to work on a math assignment that asked them to use the child's weight at birth to calculate mathematics problems. Our son had reported that all of the children were talking about when they were babies and that he and Daddy had to "make it up." I wonder how many children are being forced to "make it up" as schools continue to endorse one hegemonic family form (see Chapter 1, this volume).

There is no one way to be a family, and there is plenty of historical evidence to support the claim that there is no ideal family. As a family historian, Stephanie Coontz (1997) maintains that there have always been a "tremendous variety of family types that have worked—and not worked— in American history" (p. 2). These successes and failures have as much to do with the social context in which families are living as with the groups of individuals who are trying to craft a life together. Families are ideologies that emerge within very specific cultural contexts. Ideologies are systems of beliefs, values, and ideas that are predicated upon a specific set of social, economic, and political principles/philosophies (Shapiro, 1988). These ideologies of the family structure influence how individual members view the world and position themselves within it. In other words, family forms always were and certainly continue to be shaped by the spiritual, economic, political, and social needs of the groups of individuals involved.

I began to wonder about the families that settled in and around Bethlehem, Pennsylvania, the place that I currently call home. Through conversations with friends and neighbors, I discovered that many different family forms have always existed in this community and have thrived when given a chance. In this chapter, I examine three specific family types that coexisted in and around Bethlehem at the time it was founded in 1741. I examine how the spiritual, economic, political, and social forces surrounding these three diverse groups of individuals led to the fashioning of their very particular family type. The families discussed include those of the Lenni Lenape Indians and two groups of German immigrants—the Moravians and the Lutheran and Reformed Protestants. I discuss the Lutheran and Reformed immigrants as a combined group because once they arrived in Pennsylvania, they frequently united and formed joint congregations (Wood, 1942). Throughout the chapter, I draw upon Bakhtin's (1981) notion of chronotope as I discuss and analyze the family forms of each group.

A chronotope, according to Bakhtin, is a "field of historical, biographical, and social relations" (quoted in Morson & Emerson, 1990, p. 371) that can best be described as the way that time (history and biography) and space (social) become intertwined to create a very specific context in which actions and events take place. It is within this context or "form-shaping ideology" (p. 366) that the historical, religious, social, cultural, and political forces of any given time and place become intertwined. Bakhtin explains that in the chronotope, "time, as it were, thickens, takes on flesh, becomes artistically visible; likewise, space becomes charged and responsive to the movements of time, plot and history" (quoted in Morson & Emerson, 1990, p. 371). In other words, if we are able to understand how a group of individuals structured their lives around the concepts of time and space, we can begin to understand the values and emotions that circumscribed their daily experiences, including their preference of family forms.

Through the use of chronotope, we can make visible the values that have been ascribed to a particular moment in time and space by a specific group of people. These values set the parameters for who a person can become in that historical moment. Chronotopes help us to understand how a particular "image of the person" (p. 371) is made possible within a specific zone of time and space. Since Bakhtin wrote extensively about chronotopes in literature connected to the chivalric romance, let me draw an example from the Middle Ages to illustrate how chronotopes limit or make possible certain images of the person. Imagine, for example, fighting a battle in the

Middle Ages. It would be perfectly appropriate to ride out to the battlefield on a horse wielding a sword and shield while wearing a full set of armor. Yet, these same actions taken on the battlefield today would most likely result in disciplinary action! The meaning that was once tied to the image of being a knight in the Middle Ages doesn't carry the same import in our current era. This is because chronotopes shift and change in response to the social forces that are generated by groups of individuals as they live their lives. The economic and social system from which the feudal lords and the knights who served them emerged are no longer in existence.

It might help to think about the forces of history, economics, politics, and religion as fragments of different narratives or storylines. After all, it is through stories that we narrate who we are with one another. Stories help us to make coherent the values that shape the meaning of our lives (Holquist, 1990). If we think about time as being always fluid, we can envision the forces of economics, religion, politics, and history as storylines that are in constant motion, continuously bumping up against each other to form new and different landscapes on which we live our lives. Within this ever-shifting narrative landscape, different sets of values and meanings emerge as groups of people attempt to make sense of the contexts in which they live. It is within these chronotopes that "the knots of narrative are tied and untied. It can be said without qualification that to them belongs the meaning that shapes narrative" (Bakhtin, 1981, p. 250). Embodied within chronotopes are "the storehouse of images" that individuals draw upon as they attempt to shape their own narratives and the narratives of others. Each chronotope, then, becomes a zone of possibility that carries different images of who an individual, or, in this case, a family can become.

In the rest of this chapter, I narrow my focus to a 20-year time period (1741–1761) to illustrate how three distinct conceptualizations of time and, subsequently, space, embedded within three chronotopes structured individual biographies in ways that made three very different images of family possible. These three chronotopes are based on time as divine, time as corporate, and time as unity. Before proceeding, I want to caution the reader that these chronotopes are my constructions. I am artificially fixing time and space on the page in an attempt to understand better the time/space dimension and how very different notions of the family could emerge and coexist in the same time period. I begin my discussion with the Bethlehem Moravians, not because they were the first to settle the area—of course, the Lenni Lenape were—but rather, because most of the information documenting this time period in southeastern Pennsylvania was recorded by the Moravians. It was customary for each member of the Moravian community to write a memoir. These memoirs are kept in the Moravian Archives in Bethlehem, Pennsylvania, and are available for reading and research.

TIME AS DIVINE

In the early 1700s William Penn's promise of religious tolerance attracted many immigrants from Europe to Pennsylvania. The Moravians were one of these groups. This group's religious philosophy is rooted in 18th-century pietism and the theology of Count Nicholas Ludwig von Zinzendorf. The Moravians initially settled in the newly formed colony of Georgia in 1735, but as this settlement struggled to take hold, some of the group relocated to Pennsylvania, where in 1741 they were instructed by their religious leaders in Europe to begin building the town of Bethlehem. Bethlehem was designated to become the hub of missionary activity that was carried out by the Moravians in North America, South America, and the Caribbean (Engel, 2003).

The Moravians were evangelists who believed it was their calling to spread the word of Christ to all non-Christians around the world. True Christians, they contended, existed in all churches among all groups of people in the world. Everyone could reach salvation, joy, and peace of mind if they opened their hearts to Christ. The Moravians aspired to live lives of "childlike simplicity" in which they worked to cultivate the ability to trust in Christ and believe in him with total acceptance (Smaby, 1988, p. 151). Religious maturity was reached when individuals realized that they were unable to rise above being sinful and that their only recourse was to rely totally on Christ. Once they gave their lives over to Christ, they would be rewarded with forgiveness and eternal life. For the Bethlehem Moravians, the goal of life was to develop a personal relationship with Christ. Their lives were devoted to becoming more intimate with Christ as they anticipated and prepared for the positive experience of death. For Bethlehem Moravians, their time on Earth was inextricably linked to Christ. This divine sense of time was the organizing force behind the Bethlehem Moravians' economy, their way of governing, their communal way of living, and the types of relationships that they were able to form with one another.

Communal Living and Economy

Within this chronotope, time as divine, the Moravians viewed themselves as members of one single household headed by Christ in which they shared all of the work and all of the resources (Engel, 2003; Erbe, 1929; Smaby, 1988). This communal economy or *oeconomie*, which literally translates to mean "household," allowed the Bethlehem Moravians to position and keep Christ at the center of their lives (Engel, 2003). During the 20-year period that the Moravians lived in the communal economy, the number of individuals shifted, yet it is interesting to note that at its height there were around 800 members residing together (Smaby, 1988). Each member of the community was designated a job as either a provider or a missionary. Providers were responsible for carrying out the jobs that sustained and maintained the community. They tended crops, taught and took care of children, nursed the sick, built houses, prepared food, laundered and repaired clothing, or learned a craft or trade. Those community members who were designated missionaries traveled mainly throughout the northeastern United States to preach, baptize, and serve communion. Every member worked for the good of the community and was provided with food, clothing, and shelter in return for his or her efforts. Individuals received no wages, nor did they own any property. However, members could continue to own the assets they brought with them, and there were no restrictions on purchasing things with private funds (Engel, 2003).

Political affairs, within this chronotope, were also, for the most part, left in the hands of Christ. The Bethlehem Moravians relied on Christ to give his opinion about issues through the use of the Lot (Engel, 2003; Erbe, 1929; Smaby, 1988). When an important decision needed to be made, a question was asked, and on slips of paper leaders wrote a series of potential answers that Christ could give. A blank slip of paper was also included, which would allow Christ to reject the question altogether. One slip of paper was drawn—the Lot—and that was believed to be the divine answer. The Lot was used as people sought approval for admission into the congregation, marriage, and other issues.

This intertwining of economics, religion, and political affairs led to a so-cial living arrangement that would support one single household under the direction of Christ. The Moravians had found that individuals experienced similar spiritual needs and spiritual growth around the same stages in life. They believed that community members could best support one another spiritually by living together in groups that were segregated by age, gender, and marital status. These groups were referred to as "choirs." The choir system consisted of a Nursery, Little Boys' and Little Girls' choirs, Older Boys' and Older Girls' choirs, Single Sister's and Single Brother's choirs, a Married People's choir, and a Widow and Widower's choir.

The forming of the choir system illustrates how the notion of time embedded within this specific chronotope defined the use of space as well. Choir members lived together in dormitories in which there were no private spaces. Space was organized so that each member of Moravian Bethlehem was constantly being publicly supported to move closer to Christ. Intimate biological ties among people were nonexistent, since those with whom one lived and to whom one provided spiritual support were age mates and single brothers or sisters.

The choir system spiritually supported individuals throughout each stage of life, beginning when a child was in utero. The Moravians believed that the actions of the mother influenced the child while in the womb

(Smaby, 1988) so it was quite common for pregnant women and women with young infants to travel and continue their missionary work. There is evidence that fathers were an integral part of their children's lives (Smaby, 1999) and that children lived with both of their parents, or with their mothers, until they were done nursing, at which point they entered the Nursery choir. Once children entered the Nursery, they had little contact with their parents. Here, boys and girls resided together, under the direction of a few of the Single Sisters, until they were about 4 years old. This arrangement made sense both economically and spiritually. Parents were freed from their child-rearing responsibilities and could continue to travel or labor for the good of the community. Spiritually, Moravians wished to shape a new kind of person, one who was completely devoted to Christ. This education could happen more readily without the interference or influence of parents, and it took place in earnest when children moved into the Little Girls' and Little Boys' choirs.

The Little Girls' and Little Boys' choirs were segregated by sex, and the children who lived within them were reared by Single Bothers or Single Sisters of the same sex. Religious services played an important role in daily activity, and children were encouraged to begin understanding their own immorality and their reliance on Christ as a consequence (Smaby, 1988). It was not unusual for children at a very young age to write about their wish to go to Christ. At the age of 12 or 13, children moved into the Older Girls' Choir and Older Boys' Choir. Here, they continued their intensive religious education and began an apprenticeship to prepare for their religious and economic contributions to adult Moravian life. The emphasis at this age was on establishing open-heartedness, a willingness to describe personal religious struggles to choir leaders and to let the leaders help in the struggle to attain proper relations with Christ (Smaby, 1988).

At around 19 years of age, individuals moved into the Single Sisters or Single Brothers choir. It was from these two choirs that leaders within the community and candidates for marriage were chosen. Although death was considered to unite individuals with Christ in eternity and it is common to find terms relating the Moravians to Christ, such as "Eternal Husband" for women and "Bridegroom" for men, marriage among men and women was very much supported in Moravian Bethlehem. Most biographies of the time report that marriages were "happy and blessed," and there is only one recorded divorce in the Moravian community during the time of 1741 to 1844 (Smaby, 1988). As reported in the Synod Minutes in 1747, "Marriage is an ordinance of Christ. . . which He Himself instituted and blessed" (Smaby, 1988, p. 163).

Marriage was both a social and an individual decision. The leaders of each choir, who had guided these young adults as children on their spiritual journey, worked together to assemble the names of a group of candidates for marriage. Candidates were chosen who were believed to have a strong and secure relationship with Christ. Their overall disposition, leadership ability, and craft, trade, or mission background were also taken into account. Candidates were then matched together by the choir helpers and their names were submitted to the Lot. If the Lot affirmed the match, then each Brother and Sister was asked individually about the match. Although Christ sanctioned these matches as indicated through the Lot, the individuals involved made the final decision. The Moravians believed that "the certainty of one's heart should be the basis of all [one's] actions, ... what matters most is the joy in one's heart" (Smaby, 1988, p. 160).

The Married People's choir met together for eating, fellowship, and worship. It appears that after marriage, some married couples continued to live in the Single Brothers and Sisters dwellings, while other married couples appeared to have lived together (Smaby, 1988). Married couples, chosen by the central Moravian leadership in Europe, took on the responsibility of running the Bethlehem community. Since women ministered to women and men ministered to men, the leadership responsibilities were equally divided. Leadership positions were made possible for Moravian women that did not exist for other women of European descent living in the United States (Faull, 1997). The sense of the space outside of Bethlehem having boundaries well beyond Pennsylvania when it came to spreading the word of Christ meant that single and married women had travel adventures and experiences like those of their male counterparts. Women were able to focus on these leadership positions because community members cared for the children.

It is interesting to note that the Bethlehem Moravians described their communal arrangement as simply natural, given the circumstances of a small community and frontier life (Engel, 2003). They saw this living arrangement as an economic necessity, not necessarily a religious calling. Consider the following statement written by town leaders in 1747: "Our communal housekeeping is only out of need. It is not a point of religion, much less of blessedness" (Engel, 2003, p. 59). Yet, on two separate occasions, members were asked about dismantling the communal economy and moving into a nuclear family structure. Changing the shape of the family would mean that individual families would now be responsible for supporting themselves. On both occasions, the majority voted for the continuance of the communal economy.

Privatization of Families

By the early 1760s, Bethlehem was a thriving Moravian community. The Moravian church worldwide, however, faced a huge financial crisis, and the governing body of the entire system required that all Moravian communities contribute to paying down the overall debt. The Moravians in Bethlehem were not able to contribute financially to the worldwide church because they were supporting such a large group of members, including the missionaries who were traveling and carrying out their work. In 1762, the worldwide Moravian church legislated that Bethlehem's communal economy be dissolved and that nuclear families concentrate on the economic and social needs of their own members (Smaby, 1988). The move from the communal economy to a private family enterprise highlights how certain structures such as private dwellings and resources to care for and educate children needed to be in place in order for individual family economies to function.

The first task that had to be undertaken as Bethlehem made the transition from a communal economy to private nuclear families was to create physical spaces for all married couples. This was accomplished by constructing single-family dwellings, dividing large buildings into apartments, and expanding apartments that were already attached to inns, craft houses, and mills (Smaby, 1988). Once couples moved into their homes, the second major task was to begin to move children into the homes of their parents. The process of bringing parents and children together was quite gradual and took over a decade to complete. Data from Moravian records report that 2 years after the dissolution of the General Economy, only 24% of the children under the age of 12 lived with their parents, and 8 years later, 49%, or about half, of the children lived with their parents. By the late 1770s it appears that the transition to nuclear families was complete (Smaby, 1988).

The move from the communal economy combined with the death of Count Zinzendorf in 1760, who had promoted female leadership throughout the Moravian church, led to a hierarchy among men and women that mirrored other colonial families living in Pennsylvania at this time. Men fared far better than women as they moved out of the communal economy. Women lost their leadership positions as they were forced to take up the responsibility of individually running a private household and caring for their own children. Single and widowed women struggled to find enough work to care for themselves. Many Bethlehem families struggled to meet their family's needs. This privatization in which families had to become corporate bodies in order to provide for their own nuclear unit was embedded in the dominant chronotope of the era: *Time as corporate.*

TIME AS CORPORATE

Between 1730 and 1760, there was a large population increase in southeastern Pennsylvania, the majority of whom were German immigrants from the Lutheran and Reformed churches (Illick, 1976; Lemon, 1972; Wood, 1942). Becker (1982) explains that the German immigrants belonging to the

Lutheran and Reformed churches were drawn together by their similarities in creeds and practices. They often worshipped jointly or shared a church for services. They became known as "church Dutch," which distinguished them from the many independent Protestant German sects, such as the Moravians and other groups, that were arriving in Pennsylvania around the same time. Lemon (1972) describes this group of German immigrants and the many other settlers arriving from Western Europe at this time, as being "filled with the Protestant (or, perhaps more accurately, the secularized middle-class Protestant) spirit of hard work and success"(p. 6). Lemon cites the following prayer:

> Quickly improve your time while in your power
> And carefully do husband every hour,
> For time will come when you will sore lament
> The unhappy minutes that you have misspent
> Despair of nothing that you would attain
> Unwearied diligence your point will gain. (p. 6)

In this prayer, the term *husband* refers to the economic use and management of not only time but of other resources as well. And, as the prayer further suggests, idleness, laziness, and sin were closely linked to one another (Kollmorgen, 1942). Religion was inextricably tied to hard work, order, frugality, and living simply for this group of German immigrants. Time was to be used productively and profitably.

Within the chronotope of time as corporate, space was configured quite differently from the way it was for the Bethlehem Moravians. This group of settlers moved onto isolated farmsteads, commonly 100 to 300 acres in size. These farms supplied the family members who labored upon them with food and a profit as they sold excess crops both locally and internationally. On a local level, grain, meat, hay, and other products were sold at market. Wheat, flour, corn, flaxseed, meat, lumber, iron, and small amounts of other commodities were sold overseas to the West Indies, London, and southern Europe. As Lemon (1972) reports, "despite fluctuations, exports of wheat, flour and flaxseed from the Philadelphia area rose more than 50% between 1731 and 1760" (p. 223). Within this chronotope, production was based on the use of land that was privately owned.

It is interesting to note that banks were not in existence until 1783; however, wealthy individuals acted as bankers. Drawing upon their strong religious convictions, one of which was piety, this group of German immigrants tended to lend money to family members and friends without charging interest (Kollmorgen, 1942). They planned for their families and themselves much more than they did for their communities, as they placed their "individual freedom and material gain over that of the public interest" (Lemon, 1972, p. xv).

Although maximizing profits and gaining possession of land was important for this group of immigrants, there is scant evidence to suggest that they were involved in community political affairs. This group typically supported the Quakers who held most of the elective offices in the colony of Pennsylvania prior to 1756. It wasn't until 1764 that a Pennsylvania German was elected to the Provincial Assembly of Pennsylvania (Graeff, 1942).

Within this chronotope, the Pennsylvania German farm family was a "closely knit economic unit and was run in true patriarchal fashion" (Kollmorgen, 1942, p. 51). The German farmer was the head of the household, and his wife and children were his property. Women and their grown daughters worked alongside husbands and sons in the fields during the harvest season, and throughout the year their duties consisted of milking cows, processing dairy products, tending chickens, knitting, spinning, and keeping the house running smoothly. Children went to work in the fields at a young age, as work was seen as part of their religious practice. These children were quite familiar with proverbs such as "idleness is the root of all evil" (Kollmorgen, 1942, p. 51). Until the sons or daughters came of age, all of their earnings belonged to their father, and he would use the money at his discretion (Kollmorgen, 1942). This money was typically saved and used to help establish farms on the family property when the children came of age.

This family form could best be described as an extended lineal family. Each generation lived in a separate household, yet the nature of agricultural work and the patterns of inheritance linked individual families together in legal, moral, and customary bonds (Henretta, 1978). The financial welfare of both parents and children were tied to the land and to each other.

Bakhtin (1981) tells us that chronotopes can become interwoven, envelope, or even dominate one another. The chrontope, time as corporate, was the dominant chronotope of the period. It slowly enveloped the chronotope, time as divine, as the Moravians made their move from a communal economy to one based on individual nuclear families, and it completely eclipsed the chronotope in which the Lenni Lenape Indians were embedded, time as unity.

TIME AS UNITY

The name *Lenni Lenape,* translated into English from the Unami dialect, means "the original, common people." The Lenape lived in the area that is currently comprised of eastern Pennsylvania, New Jersey, northern Delaware, and southeastern New York State. The size of the Lenape population has been estimated at between 8,000 and 12,000 during the mid-Woodland period (C.E. 1000–1600), although these estimates are believed to be extremely low (Weslager, 1996; W. Dunn, personal communication, July 20, 2006). These numbers began to fall rapidly after contact with Europeans due to the introduction of diseases that were brought from Europe and conflicts over land. The Lenape were named the Delaware Indians by the English and are most often referred to as such.

It is from the diaries of David Zeisberger, a Moravian missionary, that most of the information we have about the Lenape derives. Wesley Dunn, the president of the Native American Indian Museum in Allentown, Pennsylvania, assured me that "Zeisberger's diaries contain the most accurate and thorough observations of this group of individuals ever recorded" (personal communication, July 20, 2006).

It is interesting to note that one of the things Zeisberger comments upon several times in his diaries is the Lenape concept of time. He writes:

> In reckoning time they do not count the days but the nights…. They divide the year into winter, spring, summer, autumn and these periods are divided according to the moons, though, it must be said, that their reckoning is not very accurate. They cannot agree just when to begin the new year. Most of them begin the year with the spring, that is with March, which they call Chwoame Gischuch, that is the Shad month, because this season this fish goes up the rivers and creeks in great numbers. April they call Hackihewi Gischuch, that is Planting month, though they rarely begin to plant before May or the end of April. (Hubert & Schwarze, 1999, p. 147).

In this entry, Zeisberger struggles with the way the Lenape notions of time are arbitrary and appear to follow natural cycles rather than being precisely measured like European conceptions of time. Zeisberger also commented on the way the Lenape chose to use their time. Consider his words:

> North American Indians. . . are lazy as far as work is concerned. If they are at home and not engaged in the chase they lie all day on their britchen and wander about in disorderly fashion. Whatever time is not devoted to sleep is given to amusements, such as playing ball. . . . Dances take place every night, all young people, men and women attending. (Hubert & Schwarze, 1999, p. 18)

Zeisberger is describing a concept of time that makes no sense to him from his perspectives of time as corporate and time as divine. For the Lenape, the values of sharing and reciprocity (Coontz, 1988) structured their everyday lives and shaped their beliefs about the world. There was no concept of private ownership of land or resources; everything they had belonged to everybody else. Needed items were acquired through a system of exchange. As Dunn contended, "The word *economy* would be inappropriate to use in a discussion of the Lenape since there was no system in which things were produced or traded for any type of profit prior to the arrival of the Europeans" (personal communication, July 20, 2006). This was a classless society in which no one had to work in order to gain access to food, clothing, or shelter because everything belonged to everyone (Coontz, 1988). For example, an individual wouldn't hunt for himself; he hunted for the entire village. If a Lenape male brought home a deer, his wife would take one piece to prepare while the rest of the meat was shared among the entire community. The concepts of hoarding or theft were virtually unknown to this group of people (Coontz, 1988).

Spirituality played a large role in the lives of the Lenape, and spirits were believed to move between the natural and supernatural world to provide guidance in daily living. In addition to the "Great Manito" or "Great Spirit," who was the creator of everything, the Lenape revered many Manitowuk, or lesser spiritual forces that were present in trees, flowers, grass, rivers, rocks, and so forth (Kraft, 1986; Weslager, 1996). According to Zeisberger (Hubert & Schwarze, 1999), the soul was considered to be an invisible being and a spirit. In his words, "Some likened themselves to corn which when thrown out and buried in the soil comes up and grows. Some believe their souls to be in the sun and only their bodies here. Others say that when they die their souls will go to Christ and that they will be at liberty to return to the world and be born again" (p. 131).

One of the central aspects of Lenape spirituality was the guidance that dreams and visions provided, especially in relation to the existence of personal guardian spirits who were considered to be "points of contact between the supernatural world and the sphere of everyday life" (Weslager, 1996, p. 68). Guardian spirits came to individuals, usually in the form of animals or birds, and were relied upon to guide specific individuals when Great Manito was consumed with larger issues. Guardian spirits were a special blessing bestowed upon individuals that usually appeared around the time children were initiated into puberty.

Within this chronotope of time as unity, space was conceptualized as belonging to everyone, as it was a gift from the great Manito. The Lenape believed themselves to be caretakers of the Earth. There was absolutely no concept of private ownership or possession of land. For the Lenape, "land was like air, sunlight, or the waters of a river—a medium necessary to sustain life" (Weslager, 1996, p. 37). "The land was never formally divided" (Hubert & Schwarze, 1999, p. 147), so it was believed to belong to everyone.

The Lenape were careful to give thanks for everything they took from the Earth, and many ceremonies, festivals, and feasts were planned throughout the year to express thanksgiving.

Important decisions were made democratically through talk among all members of the group. Some villages had a *Sakima*, or chief, typically an elder, who represented the group in religious ceremonies and other diplomatic matters. There is much contradiction about who actually chose the sachem. Weslager (1996) reports that the sachems were not chosen by Lenape women, while Kraft (1986) states that the sachem was selected by Lenape female elders. In our conversation, Dunn explained that the women did choose the sakima of the group, and they could also get rid of him if they were not satisfied with the way he was representing the group (personal communication, July 20, 2006). Dunn went on to explain that the Lenape were a matriarchal society in which the women held the power.

The Lenape were also a matrilineal society in which the "rights, obligations, knowledge and patterned social relations" were passed down through the females (Coontz, 1988). A Lenape matrilineage included the mother, her mother, her brothers and sisters, and all of the children on the female side of the family. This meant that the ties to one's unilinear kinship group were much stronger than the ties to one's own nuclear family. For example, a man might have closer ties to his nephews and nieces than to his own sons and daughters, because they belonged to a different descent group from his own (Coontz, 1988). Every Lenape also belonged to one of three *phratrys*, or clans. All three clans were represented in each village. Men and women were not allowed to marry within their own clan. When a woman married, the man would join her phratry. Any children they had belonged to the mother's clan and would be raised by the clan if anything happened to the parents. This kinship system established larger, more geographically concentrated work groups that stayed together over long periods of time (Coontz, 1988). Marrying outside of one's clan also ensured a continual distribution and circulation of goods.

Within this chronotope, where sharing and reciprocity shaped the narratives of the Lenape, the nuclear family was not a self-supporting unit. Individual families that consisted of children and their parents shared living space with their mother's relatives in bands of about 40 to 50 people near streams or on the edge of the forest. They lived in lodge houses or wigwams that were crafted from saplings and tree bark. Lodge houses held up to fifteen families (W. Dunn, personal communication, July 20, 2006), and each family had its own hearth within the lodge house. Benches were built along one side of the wall on which people could sit during the daytime or sleep on at night. On one end of the lodge house was the communal cooking fire. It was here that women worked together to prepare food for the entire group of families. On the opposite end of the lodge house was the communal food pantry.

Men and women had some fairly defined roles within Lenape culture. For the most part, women did the planting and harvesting, although the men would help with these tasks. Women were also responsible for food preparation, gathering firewood, making clothes, weaving baskets, and carrying all supplies on journeys. Men felled trees, cleared the land, built housing, fished, and hunted. Women and girls often accompanied the men during hunting season, and young girls were provided with their own hunting gear (Weslager, 1996). Elders, who were treated with much respect, knitted the fishing nets, scraped and dressed the pelts for clothing, and made clay bowls, wampum beads, and stone implements. One of their most important tasks was remembering and telling the stories of the Lenape so that the culture and history of the people could be passed on through the generations.

Lenape parents were very lenient with their children, and there are many reports that children were not indulged just by their parents but by the entire group. Zeisberger reports that "Ordinarily orphans, even if they have lost but the mother, meet with hard experience and often suffer want. Children who have been given or bequeathed, on the contrary, are almost without exception well cared for" (Hubert & Schwarze, 1999, p. 81). All children were considered gifts from the Great Manito, and the Lenape were fearful that any mistreatment might result in their children being taken away from them.

Young children were rarely separated from their mothers and were carried on their mothers' backs in cradleboards until they were 5 or older. By seven years of age, boys were learning to hunt with the men and girls were learning housekeeping and gardening skills. Both boys and girls learned to cook. At the age of menstruation, girls were considered mature enough to marry. If a girl had not already selected her marriage partner by this age, she could declare that she was marriageable by wearing a special headpiece or modestly covering her face in public. Lenape boys married between the ages of 17 and 19. Both sexes would most likely have had much sexual experience before marriage (Weslager, 1996).

Occasionally, a union would have been arranged by the parents of those intended to be married, but typically young couples made their own choices and decisions about marriage (Weslager, 1996). Divorce was easy to obtain for both men and women. Because the Lenape were a matrilineal society, upon divorce the men would leave and return to their families of origin. Divorce appears to be fairly frequent but usually occurred before children were born (Coontz, 1988).

Within this chronotope, women had a high degree of independence and were greatly respected in their society. They attended council meetings where their thoughts and opinions were heard and deliberated upon. They had the freedom to leave a marriage and to retain custody of their children. It was through Lenape women that the oral history of the lineage was passed down, and women were the keepers of the religious belongings of the entire society.

CONCLUSION

This chapter has illustrated how three very different notions of family emerged from three specific chronotopes that existed in and around colonial Bethlehem, Pennsylvania, during the mid-18th century. Embedded within each chronotope were very different notions of time and space in which particular images of the person were fashioned. These images shaped and were shaped by the individuals who live in groups that we call families. Each of these family types was flourishing during the 20-year time period that I have examined.

The chronotope is a tool that can be used to analyze and reconceptualize notions of family. As this chapter has illustrated, our world is heterochronous. In any given time and place, there are a multiplicity of chronotopes in existence. These chronotopes shift and change in response to the narratives connected to economics, politics, spirituality, and social forces. According to Bakhtin (1981), it is this malleability that holds promise for transformative potential. In other words, if we can develop an understanding of the conditions that have limited or made certain images of the person, and therefore families, possible, then we can consciously work to craft narratives that will create, sustain, and support a variety of family forms.

As teachers, it is our responsibility to accept and legitimize the wide range of family forms that are represented in our classrooms. We can choose to draw upon existing narratives or create new ones that will obscure normative assignments such as those shared in the opening paragraphs of this chapter. Further, we need to design invitational learning situations that are sensitive to the variety of lived experiences of all families. If we do offer these kinds of sensitive teaching–learning opportunities, then no child will ever be left standing embarrassed about an unknown language, an unknown source of a given family name, or an unknown birth history.

QUESTIONS FOR REFLECTION

1. How does this discussion about colonial families expand your notions of family and your notions of teaching and learning?
2. What happens when children don't see themselves in the activities that are presented in their classrooms?
3. Discuss times in your life when you have made insensitive pedagogical choices for your students. Now describe how these could, instead, become invitational learning situations.

REFERENCES

Bakhtin, M. M. (1981). *The dialogic imagination: Four essays by M. M. Bakhtin* (Michael Holquist, Ed.; C. Emerson Trans.). Austin, TX: The University of Texas Press.

Becker, L. (1982). Diversity and its significance in an eighteenth-century Pennsylvania town. In M. Zuckerman (Ed.), *Friends and neighbors: Group life in America's first plural society* (pp. 196–221). Philadelphia: Temple University Press.

Coontz, S. (1988). *The social origins of private life: A history of American families 1600–1900*. New York: Verso.

Coontz, S. (1997). *The way we really are: Coming to terms with America's changing families*. New York: Basic Books.

Engel, K. (2003). *Of heaven and earth: Religion and economic activity among Bethlehem's Moravians, 1741–1800*. Unpublished Dissertation, University of Wisconsin, Madison.

Erbe, H. (1929). *Bethlehem, PA: A communistic Herrnhut colony of the 18th century*. Stuttgart Publications of the German Foreign Institute. Cultural Historical Series/ Volume 24, Stuttgart, Germany.

Faull, K. (1997). *Moravian women's memoirs: Their related lives, 1750–1820*. Syracuse, NY: Syracuse University Press.

Graeff, A. (1942). Pennsylvania, the colonial melting pot. In R. Wood (Ed.), *The Pennsylvania Germans* (pp. 3–26). Princeton, NJ: Princeton University Press.

Henretta, J. (1978). Families and farms: Mentalite in pre-industrial America. *The William and Mary Quarterly, 3*(35), 3–32.

Holquist, M. (1990). *Dialogism: Bakhtin and his world*. New York: Routledge.

Hubert, A., & Schwarze, W. (Eds.). (1999). *David Zeisberger's history of the northern American Indians*. Lewisburg, PA: Wennawoods Publishing.

Illick, J. (1976). *Colonial Pennsylvania: A history*. New York: Scribner's.

Kollmorgen, W. (1942). The Pennsylvania German farmer. In R. Wood (Ed.), *The Pennsylvania Germans* (pp. 27–55). Princeton, NJ: Princeton University Press.

Kraft, H. (1986). *The Lenape: Archaeology, history and ethnography. Newark, NJ: New Jersey Historical Society*.

Lemon, J. (1972). *The best poor man's county: A geographical study of early southeastern Pennsylvania.* Baltimore: The Johns Hopkins University Press.

Morson, G. S., & Emerson, C. (1990). *Mikhail Bakhtin: Creation of a prosaics.* Stanford, CA: Stanford University Press.

Shapiro, M. J. (1988). *The politics of representation: Writing practices in biography, photography, and policy analysis.* **Madison: University of Wisconsin Press.**

Smaby, B. (1988). *The transformation of Moravian Bethlehem: From communal mission to family economy.* Philadelphia: University of Pennsylvania Press.

Weslager, C. (1996). *The Delaware Indians: A history.* New Brunswick, NJ: Rutgers University Press.

Wood, R. (Ed.). (1942). *The Pennsylvania Germans.* Princeton, NJ: Princeton University Press.

Chapter 7

Doing the Difficult: Schools and Lesbian, Gay, Bisexual, Transgendered, and Queer Families

Janice Kroeger

The Lesbian, Gay, Bisexual, Transgender, or Queer (LGBTQ) parents with children in schools demand recognition because of their growing number and because of their uniqueness. Estimates in the last decade have put the number of children with sexual minority parents between 6 and 14 million (Casper & Schultz, 1999, Harvard Law Review, 1990; Ryan & Martin, 2000, citing Patterson, 1992, 1995a); yet, in 2000, the U.S. Census reported nearly 600,000 same-sex couples residing in 99.3% of the counties across the country. Of same-sex couples who responded to the census, one-fifth of the male couples and one-third of the female couples were raising children under the age of 18. Nonetheless, the census overlooks single gay parents, bisexual parents who are partners of someone of the opposite sex, transgendered parents, and lesbian, gay, bisexual, or transgendered people in heterosexual marriages who are raising children. Any of this constellation of possibilities reflects the uniqueness of sexual minority families in classrooms.

Abigail Garner (2004), speaker and daughter of gay parents, is an advocate for LGBTQ families and suggests that the actual numbers of same-sex partners are likely well above reported numbers because individuals do not feel safe declaring that they are in same-sex relationships. Gays are vulnerable if they live in a state where it is legal to get fired for one's sexual orientation, they may be wary of losing their children, or they may be afraid of being targets of hate crimes; simply put, some LGBTQ individuals are vocal about their lives because it is a matter of politics and activism, while others choose less visible expressions because of privacy and protection. Either perspective needs support from people impacting school experiences.

Although Garner points out that numbers are hard to figure, so are family makeup and parental/child decision making. The LGBTQ family encompasses a range of diversity, although much research and media attention focuses on lesbian mothers (Mercier & Harold, 2003; Patterson, 1995a; 1998). While portrayals in media show high-income "out" lesbian and straight mothers procreating by artificial insemination or gay/straight arrangements, children of LGBTQ families are created in different ways, including heterosexual coupling, divorce, co- or stepparenting, and adoption. Media portrayals diminish the complexity of LGBTQ families and make less visible the richness of queer family types. Researchers have only begun to study the variety of LGBTQ families; particularly from children's points of view (Casper & Shultz, 1999; Garner, 2004).

Teachers should note that among LGBTQ families, there may be biological parents who are not actually caregivers or providers, or legal parents, sperm donors, surrogate mothers, and/or birth parents who may or may not perform a range of parenting functions. Likewise, there may be fully functioning parents who have absolutely no legal rights and no biological ties to the child, but perform as if they do. In addition, many LGBTQ families contain more than two parents living in the same household, or more than two parents living in several different households as well as siblings who are from prior relationships but are not biologically related (Garner, 2004; Ryan & Martin, 2000).

DISCOURSE SHIFTS: FROM ACCEPTABILITY AND PRESENCE TO ACCOUNTABILITY AND POWER

Although the simple description of gay and lesbian parents with children in schools is often used, the phrasing simplifies the complexity and needs of sexual minority families. Reviewing recent literature, I found only one common suggestion among past and present authors: Teachers must advocate (Casper & Schultz, 1999; Derman-Sparks, 1989; Garner, 2004; Hulsebosch & Koerner, 1997; Kozik-Rosabal, 2000; Kroeger, 2001; Kroeger, 2006a & b, Marinoble, 1997; Ramsey, 2004).

Advocating for or backing the rights of same-sex couples with children and supporting children of bisexual or transgendered parents is not straightforward, because the individuals within these groups bend categories of thought and behavior. Queer theory has complicated the binary of gay and straight and interrupts heterosexuality as the normal, given, and fixed category of sexual identity as well as procreation (Butler, 1993; Loutzenheiser

& MacIntosh, 2004). Likewise, queering the subjects of family, childhood, and pedagogy opens a host of issues that many educators find inappropriate for the early-childhood classroom but others have embraced (Blaise, 2005; Kroeger, 2006a & b; Ramsey, 2004; Silin, 1995).

As I analyzed literature about LGBTQ families, queer youth, and advocacy, I found at least a twofold change in foci, suggesting cultural shifts in acceptance and responsiveness to LGBTQ parents and their children, as well as the results and priorities of a queer youth movement. For one, the implicit plea for schools to respond to the growing presence of LGBTQ individuals has changed to episodes of accountability and responsiveness on the part of schools. Simple demographic descriptions of the changing terrain of family and queer youth has shifted to portray the power that activist groups have held to change the nature of school culture. By no means do these shifts herald that the work of tolerance and advocacy is over, but they do show that there have been inroads for LGBTQ families at particular times and in certain places.

In the 1980s, the literature tended to focus on the children of lesbian mothers and gay fathers. Studies assessed an array of child and family developmental characteristics. Concerns about developmental difficulties among children of lesbian and gay parents were not sustained (Patterson, 2000). Garner (2004) argues that results of developmental research—that gay parenting would not adversely affect child developmental outcomes—fulfilled a political need that tended to ensure that gay parents would not be denied custody when seeking divorce. Earliest research demonstrated that children of gay parents had no significant developmental differences from children of straights, but it was conjectured that children with gay parents were more interested in nontraditional occupations for their gender and had more flexibility with the idea of same-sex relationships (Stacey & Biblarz, 2001).

The literature produced throughout the 1990s and 2000s tended to focus on the beliefs and practices of teachers, family struggles, or what schools were doing to increase the support to LGBTQ parents and their children (Casper & Schultz, 1999; Hulsebosch & Koerner, 1997; Kroeger, 2001; Marinoble, 1997; Patterson, 1992). Workshop formats, anti-homophobia training, suggested curriculum adaptations, obstacles facing families, and contradictions in the needs of, and the appropriate handling of, heterosexual parents' concerns were common topics.

More recent work has endured a shift to record the impact of the work of LGBTQ individuals and their allies (Kroeger, 2006b; Kumashiro, 2001). Such work examines queer youth, activist parents, the promise of civil unions, changing school policies, curriculum, and the heterosexual and school ally. Such works attest to the growing power and acceptability of LGBTQ parents and the adjustments that schools are making to adapt themselves to be acceptable to and accepting of LGBTQ individuals (Ireland, 2005; Kozik-Rosabal, 2000; Mercier & Harold, 2003; Patterson, 2004).

ONE COMPLEXITY: COMING OUT DECISIONS

Because of family fears of prejudices, uncertainty about language and disclosure is a prominent issue. Teachers need to know, too, that the intersection of race, social class, ethnicity, and gender also influences parent power, so the coming out decisions among LGBTQ families will be based on many things—only one factor being the parent's sense of trust for the teacher. Professional status, education of parents, and geographic location make an impact on coming out decisions as well as visibility and family health (Ryan & Martin, 2000; Garner, 2004; Kroeger, 2001; 2006b). Some same-sex parents are assertive about their status as gays and force schools to respond to their requests. Requests come in the form of cautions, awareness, questions, demands, or insistence that the school address the needs of the family in a particular way. Many LGBTQ parents request that they receive teachers who will accept their families, as in the case of this lesbian mother's description:

> I said, "We're a lesbian couple and what problems are you going to have?" I do it to fish—to see what their reaction is. At the beginning of each school year they have a process for choosing a teacher. We kind of felt that out and looked for a teacher who we. . . anticipated to be a little more liberal and accepting. In the final paragraph of every single letter, (we wrote) "we want (our son) to be in a classroom environment that will foster acceptance. . . for his family which is" [laughing] and then we'd state it (that we are a lesbian parent family). And, you know, we've been pretty successful with teachers. (Mercier & Harold, 2003, p. 40)

Other LGBTQ parents are not just assertive with school people, but push school change through activism to shape curriculum and school policy, and can exert considerable force upon the institution beyond their own child's classroom, as in the case of this activist father's description in my ethnographic study of diversity and home school relationships (Kroeger, 2006b):

> Our request was that the teacher use the term *gay dads* whenever she talked about us, not in response to negative terminology but that she please refer to the term *gay dads*—dads as gay—so that children would hear it in a positive way. She was not comfortable with that. Her response was that she would deal with it if there were negative slurs.

The request of this gay father, Michael,[1] was intended to prevent the use of gay slurs in classroom discussions by using the term *gay dads* prior to negative classroom events. Michael brought materials to the teacher from Gay Lesbian Straight Educator's Network's *Lunch Box* (GLSEN). At first, the teacher, Mrs. Spencer, declined this curricular strategy, opting instead for an indirect approach. Expressing dismay, Michael stated:

> We considered Spencer's response unacceptable—she was not comfortable using the term *gay* positively and said that if the term *gay* comes up negatively she'll deal with it. Since then we have offered to do things for her on the topic. So far she has not taken us up on the offer.

In the above passage, Michael was comfortable with his out position. Comfort is different for children as well as teachers. Abigail Garner (2004) states:

> [P]arents and their children will often have different ideas about when to be out and when to be more discreet. It is an ongoing struggle to anticipate and adjust to these differences, . . . for kids, careful discretion about their parents is neither about identity nor about politics, it is about acceptance and safety (p. 121).

While parents' coming out decisions are made in the context of school safety, LGBTQ parents differ on discussing their gayness with their child; therefore, teachers must first find out how parents handle their disclosure with children. The manner in which parents discuss the issue, the age at which children come to know that their parents are gay, lesbian, bisexual, or transgender; and the terminology and emotion that is used to describe experience all matter when it comes to how comfortable children feel about themselves and their parents' sexual orientation (Garner, 2004). Such matters heighten the complexity of school experience and the tensions teachers might sense within families from either children or parents themselves. In addition, some LGBTQ parents are presented to school personnel not as co-parents or partners of parents but as other family members or friends (Kozik-Rosabal, 2000; Garner, 2004; Ryan & Martin, 2000). The implications for teachers in decision making is to help people comfortably disclose their family makeup, sexuality, and pedagogic desires for children in a safe, accepting school environment. For some teachers, this will result in shifting school curriculum and language to advocacy and activism; for others, it means keeping discussion private and discreet and looking more closely at the complexity of children's needs and the safety of the school or classroom.

In their struggles to define themselves, children search to find appropriate forms of terminology to explain their family. However, the terms they use might not always make sense to others who do not understand that the family is LGBTQ. Garner (2004) writes:

> Children of LGBTQ parents are challenged to find concise and inclusive ways to refer to themselves as a group. . . . Without a universally understood name for that relationship, children will say "other mother," and "step mother" or simply call her by a first name. In reference to the couple, a child might say "my mom and her partner," "my moms," and "my parents" all in the same conversation. These terms need to be understood within their context. (p. 11)

While children are reading safety and searching for expressions to convey their family, they are also looking for signs of acceptance in school. Peers who are accepting and school personnel who convey respect, acceptance, and openings for discussion are the safety net. This buffer-zone can also take the form of allies, visual markers of tolerance, opportunities to disclose, and verbal reminders from adult community members of the acceptability and safety of family forms. Teachers should do considerable soul-searching and individual family relationship-building to determine the best courses of action. Whether respect is shown through individual, nonintrusive acceptance or outright activism on behalf of LGBTQ parents and families, responsible teachers create ways to examine and act on their pedagogic responsibilities.

SEEKING, FINDING, AND CREATING ACCEPTANCE WITHIN SCHOOLS

While LGBTQ parents and children seek forms of acceptance, teachers' views of their roles and responsibilities toward children of LGBTQ parents have shifted. Some researchers advocate a set of widely held expectations for teachers, including age-appropriate books that feature LGBTQ families, prominent historical figures who are gay, small gestures like safety stickers with the pink triangle, and other verbal forms of tolerance, such as when teachers resist and reprimand anti-gay expressions in classrooms and in hallways, and when intake forms are parent-friendly and gender-neutral (Derman-Sparks, 1989; Kozik-Rosabal, 2000; Ramsey, 2004). Others have determined that contemporary school culture is still largely steeped in homophobic- and fear-based silences for families, teachers, and children, especially within pedagogic responses to community diversity, and rely on teacher professional decision making within cultural critique (Casper & Schultz, 1999; Kroeger, 2001, 2006a & b). Child advocates agree that regardless of personal views on homosexuality, all teachers should speak up when they hear derogatory homophobic comments and interrupt them, promoting children's well-being and safety. Additionally, anti-harassment policies that include sexual orientation and gender identity promote school climates in which teachers have policy supports to back up their decisions to intervene for all children (Garner, 2004; Ryan & Martin; 2000). If teachers work in schools without such policies, they should work to create them.

In light of the complexity, new and experienced teachers struggle with how to support children of sexual minority parents. The first steps that curriculum workers and family advocates suggest is for teachers to determine family makeup. The subtlety of homophobia in schools makes disclosure and/or safety a priority (Ryan & Martin, 2000); therefore, altering time, place, questions, and opportunities for parents to confer with teachers is important. In my research with teachers, I've also noted several important differences between new and experienced professionals (Kroeger et al., 2004; Kroeger, 2006a, 2006b).

New Teachers, New Voices

New teachers should examine their assumptions about family. Family is assumptive of heterosexual makeup; yet, new birth technologies, the preponderance of adoptive and foster-care opportunities, and the coming of age of lesbian and gays forming families of choice have increased the likeliness of encountering LGBTQ needs within the first few years of teaching. Heterosexual assumptions that children need both a father and a mother have forced different types of developmental questions. New teachers with LGBTQ families are at the apex of struggle, asking different types of questions. The authors of this book are urging us all to ask, *How do we recognize, advocate for, and change school inequities for othered types of families so to not perpetuate injustice?* New teachers work to define their perspectives on LGBTQ inclusion. After building a relationship with a family, they often struggle to find the right language to fit the situation. Beyond that, truthful conversation with children about family makeup and confronting heterosexual bias in curriculum is needed. If new teachers acknowledge recognition of intimate parent partners, they shortly also acknowledge that children are developing their own sexual identities with the gender play order being established and legitimized through school forms (Blaise, 2005; Casper & Schultz, 1999; Ramsey, 2004; Silin, 1995). New teachers quickly ask how classrooms perpetuate heterosexual assumptions, and what our role as teachers is to support children's developing questions about sexuality, gender, and the social order (Cahill & Theilheimer, 2003).

One teacher who was working in a classroom with three preschoolers who were the children of three same-sexed couples struggled with how she should address one set of parents she'd chosen to come to know through university field placements. Using terminology like *partner* or *lesbian* wasn't comfortable, nor did she know or feel comfortable asking questions about the relationship and how these moms wanted to be addressed by classroom staff and children. Only after having several conversations with a university faculty member who raised questions and then having ongoing, open-ended communication with the parents did she state (Kroeger et al., 2004):

> What I realized was that there really were no words to describe Jason's family. Regardless of the fact that they are in a same-sex household they love and take care of him and want what is best for him at school. The love in his family is enough and his Becka and MaMa are all the words there is for them. That is enough for Jason, so that is enough for me. It is all I really need to know now.

New teachers' encounters with same-sex families may not be lengthy. At times, new teachers will do what experienced teachers will not. Novice teachers bring fresh resources to field sites, are often more aware and less fearful of using anti-bias resources like children's books and videos, and have sometimes formed strong opinions about eliminating homophobia, gender bias, and sexuality oppression in wider social settings. These strategies will be noticed and valued by LGBTQ families and their children.

Experienced Teachers, Creating New Experiences

Marlene Spencer, the teacher who'd been requested by the activist parent Michael Colton to use the term *gay dads* in her conversations, taught in a first-second-grade classroom.[2] Mrs. Spencer was in her early fifties, secure in her work roles, and an inspiration to her urban school. As an experienced teacher, Mrs. Spencer listened, but did not initially endorse suggestions related to gay issues.

Mrs. Spencer's initial position when she met the two-father family involved a plan to address derogatory remarks. For Mrs. Spencer, children's exposure to Michael and his partner was a strategy, but she did not have easy comfort addressing what Michael saw as their need—to say *gay dads* in classroom conversations. Mrs. Spencer's agenda involved laying a strong foundation for academic learning and child comfort. She prioritized the acquisition of school knowledge, literacy, numeracy, elementary science, and social growth over a curriculum focused on positive gay identity or reducing homophobia among young children (Kroeger, 2006b). In the winter months of the study, Michael pressured and Mrs. Spencer acknowledged:

> Kids are beginning to realize. Just this morning Raphael asked, "How many Dads does Dimitri have?" And I said "Two." Margaret said, "How many dads

do I have?" And I said, "One, right?" No one asked more than that. Dimitri was right there. It was just a perfectly normal sort of conversation. Weiyi also asked Dimitri this the week before, and it was a request for information, not joking. Dimitri said "Two" and then, Weiyi asked, "Do you have any moms?" And he said, "Not anymore." No one reacted, and you know, I think it is just OK with them [the children]. I'm sure Weiyi is trying to figure it out, but I don't think he thinks it unusual or anything. His parents might feel differently, but we aren't dealing with that at this point in time. Victoria understands that they [Dimitri's parents] are gay and is very wise in an adolescent sort of way, and also protective of Dimitri.

Spencer's stated rationale for maintaining a low-key approach to gay and lesbian issues in the classroom was the established curriculum; a thematic 2-year cycle of content, shared with another first-second-grade classroom and peer teacher. Issues were generated after encountering specific problems with children, or raised in relation to children's questions. Mrs. Spencer's approach was supported by a respect- and community-building curriculum called "TRIBES" (Gibbs, 1999). Neither thematic units nor TRIBES dealt with the specifics of "gay" or, for that matter, the complexity of "family" (Kroeger, 2006a).

Like prolific author Abigail Garner (2004), Mrs. Spencer didn't want Dimitri to become the "poster child" of "gay families"; she didn't want Dmitri's family to become a lesson. Yet there is a fine line between what Garner calls "homophobia" and "homo-hesitant," and, at least partially, Mrs. Spencer seemed "homo-avoidant." Mrs. Spencer was certain that dealing with one child's "issues" strained others. She spoke of "unknowns." She spoke of Lars, a child from a divorce and a stepfamily, and Chantilia, a child from a single-parent family. Experienced teacher Mrs. Spencer commented:

> Lars has two fathers as well, one he lives with and a biological father who lives in town with an older brother. Lars lives with his mom, stepfather, and little brother. I just can't have a formal conversation. I hope that conversations come from the children thinking about things. "Families" isn't on our topics for the year, and to be fair I would have to cover everyone's issues. Would it be fair for Chantilia? Does Chantilia know her father? Would a discussion about fathers be fair to Chantilia?

Mrs. Spencer's response framed gay identity along with troubling issues for kids, and she had reasons not to say *gay dads* proactively. The experienced teacher seemed staunchly attentive to an education system that is responsible to all children, thereby also rendering a false but seemingly safe neutrality around community diversity. Mrs. Spencer initially believed that family issues related to sexuality, racial inequities, and social class were too problematic and emotionally laden for children, and thus should be avoided. She rationalized that the curriculum had to come from teachers to be accepted.

Examples suggest that experienced teachers need direct exposure and opportunities to supplant their existing practices with alternatives, especially in cases in which they are first encountering LGBTQ parents and children. Michael's persistence worked, but it was only after a situational crisis, larger changes in the district—including the hiring of an LGBTQ advocate—and the help of district antigay harassment policies that teacher Marlene Spencer reconsidered her pedagogical approach. Teasing in Dimitri's classroom escalated, bringing Mrs. Spencer closer to understanding the responsibility and opportunities she had as Dimitri's teacher to be his ally, and to help other children eliminate bias in their language (Kroeger, 2006b). Mrs. Spencer's position steadily shifted with time, resources, tension among children, community discussion, and district and principal supports acknowledging the ambiguities of "educational goals with political and moral consequences" (Ryan & Greishaber, 2005, p. 5). She commented at the end of Dimitri's first-grade experience:

> I think I am more confident that a gay family can work and work really well. I just haven't known any family like that in the past as well as I know this family. I still am not sure that what we are doing in the classroom is not inclusive of him. I know it is important for Dimitri but how important is it for everyone? What is the right thing to do?

As a consequence of mounting pressure and the social complexity around LGBTQ changes at the school and district level, Mrs. Spencer and her teaching team spent part of the summer planning new unit materials for young children. This change was made in light of a situation in which one of Dimitri's classmates accused another of being gay (Kroeger, 2006a). Although Michael first interpreted Mrs. Spencer as avoidant of her responsibility, the teaching materials he had been supplying throughout the year emerged as curriculum content for Dimitri during his second-grade year. The presence of Michael and his partner, their demands, parent allies within the straight community, a district hiring of two LGBTQ educators, and the nonrenewal of the Boy Scout troop conveyed a message to Marlene Spencer that she ought to (or could) change her approach to be more accepting and to demonstrate the presence and social agenda of LGBTQ families (Kroeger, 2006b).

Mrs. Spencer's actions show a willingness to engage with new knowledge; she created her own new skill set. After an in-service in which she was a speaker, she commented, "Gay happens across cultures." In reference to her curriculum, she and a co-teacher planned and altered existing thematic curriculum to include *That's a Family: A Video for Kids About Family Diversity* (Chasnoff & Cohen, 2000), and *ABC: A Family Alphabet Book* (Combs, Keane, & Rappa, 2001), and many classroom discussions about family diversity. Mrs. Spencer worked beyond the given curriculum of standards to a found and created curriculum. Overtly, she had gone farther than Michael noticed; her comfort was public, and her desire had grown to support gay families. Expecting no negative backlash from the wider community, she stated: "This is part of my job—to prevent teasing of kids whose parents are gay." In other words, she was no longer homo-avoidant but was instead accepting responsibility for creating safety before crisis emerged. Michael stated:

> I know that what Marlene and Cathy [a special education teacher] are doing this year worked. Because Dimitri is no longer coming home reporting teasing. We worked on Name it, Claim it, and Stop it. We practiced that in the van, but I know Marlene's work this year was effective. Dimitri is coming home happier and other children in the class have stopped doing whatever it was they were doing. There is no report of teasing.

Although the "improvisational" nature of Mrs. Spencer's response to Dimitri and his gay fathers allowed new notions of family in the classroom, the dilemmas faced also attest to the types of uncertainties in postmodern challenges of teaching young children (Lobman, 2005).

HISTORICAL INTERSECTIONS AS CHRONOSYSTEMS: GAY FATHERS, STRAIGHT AND QUEER ALLIES, SOCIAL MOVEMENTS

Family involvement theorists often turn to Urie Bronfenbrenner's ecological systems theory to analyze the levels and dimensions of children's lives to support family functioning and healthy child growth and development (Bronfenbrenner & Crouter, 1982; Weiss, Krieder, Lopez, & Chatman, 2005). Rarely, however, is the notion of Bronfenbrenner's chronosystem used to argue how individual people utilize public outcry, dissension, legal disputes, and societies' changing needs to leverage social change on behalf of children (Kroeger, 2006b). It is my belief that this is where our most promising work lies in changing the nature of schools for "othered" families. The chronosystem is commonly thought of as the historical time into which individuals are born, including all of the economic, technological, political, and social constraints or opportunities influencing life trajectories (Weiss et al., 2005). In the examples from my ethnographic study, however, the entire ecosystem changed in relation to the individual child within the family, school, and larger community because of dynamic historical events and people's work. What is important to this chapter is the way that Dimitri's gay fathers changed their child's social position in the school from "silenced" to visible. This action had benefits for their own child's development, as well as for other LGBTQ families and likely that of future youth (Loutzenheiser & Macintosh, 2004).

Before Mrs. Spencer's change, Michael proposed the IEP and the districts anti-harassment policies as a vehicle to address anti-homophobic strategies. "Making a bigger deal" meant taking his gay agenda beyond teacher and school to use his partner's status as a lawyer. Michael had resolved to turn to legal recourse, stating:

> We've got the district office to come in here in a minute, but we are going to wait. We are going to follow procedures. We are going to have a conversation with Marlene, January 1, and remind her that she didn't follow through. We are going to give her an opportunity, and then we are going to follow through. If prevention is not happening on a regular basis, we will be in Danielle Dumas's [the principal's] office and then downtown filing a grievance.

Forces outside of the school shifted the social sphere for Michael in a way that seemed national, allied to the concerns of straight parents, and unrelated to his son or Mrs. Spencer, but these provided tremendous shifts in Dimitri's classroom experience and Mrs. Spencer's thoughts about being his teacher. Two incidents, originating outside of the school, brought discussions of gay and lesbian discrimination to a crescendo. The first incident drawing attention was the debate about the national and local organization of the Boy Scouts on scout leadership. The second was a district- and city-wide debate over hiring an LGBTQ advocate. Both issues were part of the chronosystem or historical time (Bronfenbrenner & Crouter, 1982). Nonetheless, the concerns of Michael's community drew on his experiences to generate change for all. As an LGBTQ parent, Michael formed new networks with straights and was a bridge between queer culture and elementary school.

Michael strategically shared his views. He was careful in choosing whom he spoke with, how he talked, and when. While he activated links within groups for his purposes, others capitalized upon his gay status in the community for their own purposes. Groups sought his opinions; Michael's parent involvement turned to social activism as systems outside of his family changed. The local community's Coalition to End Homophobia supported Michael's agenda to build school environments that would support gay issues. Its members included lesbian, gay, straight, and bisexual people as well as transgendered individuals; however, these groups of people primarily wanted sexuality education, antigay harassment, drug and suicide prevention, homelessness prevention, and AIDS awareness education. In the days prior to district meetings, the Coalition to End Homophobia wrote hypothetical job descriptions, coordinated agencies to inform district board members, and recruited a cadre of hundreds of speakers to advocate positively on behalf of the proposed educational advocacy position.

At subsequent school board meetings, LGBTQ issues gained national attention. The thousands of potential clients—community members with a variety of interests: clients with HIV status, drug abuse prevention centers that served adolescents, the AIDS network, and gay families with kids—were all part of a larger movement toward school change. The group reaffirmed the connection between young children's classrooms and larger social problems. The school board passed a decision to hire an LGBTQ advocate for the district.

Concurrent with district activities, the parent teacher organization (PTO) at Dimitri's school, which had been a sponsoring agent of the Boy Scouts, had meetings about the national issue of gay Scout leaders. Parents, those serving on the PTO board and many who had children in the troop, were alarmed and upset that the national organization of Boy Scouts prohibited avowed gay members as leaders. School parents, angered by both state and supreme courts' decisions, debated whether if their school should sponsor the local Cub Scout pack. Parents from Michael and Dimitri's school orchestrated an informal gathering, and men and women on both sides of the issue shared views about the exclusionary language of the national policy. Michael was an important part of this conversation, for he shaped heterosexual parents' understandings of the intersections of sexual orientation, religion, morality, exclusionary language as homophobic, and their role with first- and second-graders. The Boy Scouts issue compelled many straight parents of boys to articulate for the first time gay and lesbian discrimination with their children. Straight parents had to reassess their roles to support gay and lesbian members of their community, and they asked Michael to work with them as they decided whether to renew the Boy Scouts charter.

Michael expressed his grief about the exclusionary Boy Scout policy, and more important, discussion allowed straight parents to see their complicit role in perpetuating homophobia. What seemed like a small matter—popcorn sales from Boy Scout fundraising in Michael's neighborhood—concurred with Michael's discussions with the superintendent about teasing in his son's classroom. Many straight parents of Dimitri's schoolmates either drove their sons around the neighborhood to sell popcorn or bought popcorn themselves, not realizing that they had solicited a LGBTQ household or endorsed a homophobic organization. Straight parents were unsettled—they didn't want themselves or their children to be complicit with homophobia; nor did they automatically understand how such issues were offensive to gay or lesbian community members.

For Michael, gay and straight friendships became more important. He'd found parents with similar desires to explore/eliminate issues of homophobia and sexuality bias. The informal PTO event gave Michael friends in the straight community. He stated:

> I felt very comfortable at that parent's house. I felt supported. . . . I was fully thrilled with the positive response from that group. The parents at Amy's house were more supportive than the gay and lesbian parents I talk to on a regular basis. I came home and told Donald [Michael's partner and Dmitri's other dad] that I felt more welcomed and supported, and I was more high after that meeting with those straight parents than I have ever felt in my life.

Though these remarkable changes were happening outside of Mrs. Spencer's classroom—at the district level and within the straight parent community— Michael described these events as a wonderful turning point. By the end of the school year, Michael joined the School Improvement Planning Committee, served on the public speaker list for the PTO, supported Mrs. Spencer with an award from Rainbow Families (2006), and stated:

> But the biggest thrill for me this year has been the allies I am developing in the straight community. Many straight parents are really behind me, and they support me. At the PTO they support me, in our neighborhood they support us, and any possible pot shots are countered. . . . We read the climate of our school. Each year we buy the teachers books, books, and more books. We come to them asking for help and push them, but we try to be empathetic. We are never rude to teachers. They are there to serve us, and they need our help.

MOVING FROM WHO AND HOW TO WHY IT MATTERS

By attending to the ways in which gay parents, straight parents, and teachers shift in response to the ambiguities of LGBTQ needs, individual actions can change school structures and rearrange experiences for children. More important, teachers should be asking themselves why it would be beneficial to think of themselves as children's allies, in a rather queer time. The gay activist father in this chapter supported long-standing school change, but it was also debates occurring nationally during the research that created openings and forced local social structure to shift (Kroeger, 2006b). Although this highly experienced teacher was initially homo-hesitant, her eventual position was advocacy. Teacher and parent activity together generated a sense of agency.

This chapter demonstrates changes within the last three decades in research, giving an account of parental activism, youth queer culture, and teacher responsiveness. By examining persons who are taking and making perspectives, the chapter demonstrates that individuals shape systemic change; therefore, a focus in teaching should be on action and perspective shaping as well as perspective taking when working with LGBTQ families with children. Teachers need to examine the values they hold toward sexual minority persons. As active agents, teachers can create new roles in their communities.

In my study, the presence of sexual minority parents ultimately allowed new opportunities to examine practice and reshape curriculum for children and community within schools to more closely match society's needs. Finally, when thinking about "other kinds" of families, a promising feature of school change was the many ways people chose to work together rather than ignore the troubling problems that LGBTQ families and their children experienced in schools. Silences were disrupted rather than maintained. Straight parents and experienced educators engaged with the concerns of gays and lesbians to provided better options for everyone.

QUESTIONS FOR REFLECTION

1. As a teacher, how can I come to know gay/lesbian parents' comforts as in/out within the community? Are there circumstances in which I should feel protective of a family member's status as LGBTQ?
2. When children's questions or confusions have come up, how have I spoken to the group about this valuable part of our learning community? Does my response to children convey acceptance and prohibit homophobic discussions among children, or is it reactive and silencing?
3. Do I recognize the intersection of racism, classism, homophobia, sexism, and gender bias in my classroom?
4. What parent-to-parent networks can the school foster in order to maintain a healthy climate for its particular community members?

NOTES

1. All proper names of informants/interviewees have been changed throughout this chapter to ensure anonymity.
2. In the rest of this chapter, the text, including quotations from Michael and Mrs. Spencer, is taken from Kroeger (2006b).

REFERENCES

Blaise, M. (2005). *Playing it straight: Uncovering gender discourses in the early childhood classroom.* New York: Routledge.

Bronfenbrenner, U., & Crouter, A. C. (1982). Work and family through time and space. In S. B. Kamerman & C. D. Hayes (Eds.), *Families that work: Children in a changing world* (pp. 39–83). Washington, DC: National Academy Press.

Butler, J. (1993). *Bodies that matter: On the discursive limits of "sex."* New York: Routledge.

Cahill, B. J., & Theilheimer, R. (2003). Can Tommy and Sam get married? Questions about gender, sexuality, and young children. In C. Copple (Ed.), *A world of difference: Readings on teaching young children in a diverse society* (pp. 120–124). Washington, DC: National Association of the Education of Young Children.

Casper, V., & Schultz, S. B. (1999). *Gay parents, straight schools: Building communication and trust.* New York: Teachers College Press.

Chasnoff, D., & Cohen, H. (1996). *It's elementary: Talking about gay issues in schools* [video and training materials]. Available through Women's Educational Media, 2180 Bryant Street, #203, San Francisco, CA 94110; (415)641–4616; WEMDH@aol.com.

Chasnoff, D. (Director & Producer), with Cohen, H., Ben-Dov, A. J., and F. Yacker. (2000). *That's a family* [video]. Available through Women's Educational Media, 2180 Bryant Street, #203, San Francisco, CA 94110; (415)641–4616; WEMDH@aol.com.

Combs, D., Keane, D., & Rappa, B. (2001). *ABC: A family alphabet book.* Ridley Park, PA: Two Lives Publishing.

Derman-Sparks, L. (1989). *The anti-bias curriculum: Tools for empowering young children.* Washington, DC: The National Association for the Education of Young Children.

Garner, A. (2004). *Families like mine: Children of gay parents tell it like it is.* New York: Harper Collins.

Gay, Lesbian, Straight Educator's Network (2006, October 30). Retrieved October 30, 2006 from http://glsen.org.

Gibbs, J. (1999). *Guiding your school community to live in a culture of caring and learning: The process called TRIBES.* Sausalito, CA: CenterSource Systems, LLC. http://www.glsen.org/cgi-bin/iowa/all/home/index.html

Harvard Law Review. (1990). *Sexual orientation and the law.* Cambridge, MA: Harvard University Press.

Hulsebosch, P., & Koerner, M. E. (1997). You can't be for children and against their families: Family diversity workshops for elementary school teachers. In J. T. Sears & W.L. Williams (Eds.), *Overcoming heterosexism and homophobia: Strategies that work* (pp. 261–271). New York: Columbia University Press.

Ireland, D. (2005). Gay teens fight back: A new generation of gay youth won't tolerate harassment in their schools. In P. Leistyna (Ed.), *Cultural studies: From theory to action* (pp. 469–474). Malden, MA: Blackwell.

Kozik-Rosabal, G. (2000). "Well, we haven't noticed anything bad going on," said the principal: Parents speak about their gay families and schools. *Education and Urban Society, 32*(3), 368–389.

Kroeger, J. (2001). A reconstructed tale of inclusion for a lesbian family. In S. Grieshaber & G. Canella (Eds.), *Embracing identities in early childhood education: Diversity and possibilities*. New York: Teachers College Press.

Kroeger, J. (2006a). Ism moments and children's becoming. *Journal of Equity and Innovation in Early Childhood Education, 4*(1), 32–47.

Kroeger, J. (2006b). Stretching performances in education: The impact of gay parenting and activism on identity and school change. *The Journal of Educational Change*. Electronic Manuscript. Retrieved October 30, 2006 from http://www.springerlink.com/content/q7j2316t2h67t443/?p=9aab90392c0c429bb07a41b025691d91&pi=0.

Kroeger, J., Lash, M., & Barbour, N., with Burns, R., Mayer-Will, M., Royski, D., Russo, S., and Tonelli, D. (2004, November). *Developing and refining teachers' models for working with and for all families of young children*. Paper presented at the annual meeting for the National Association for the Education of Young Children, Anaheim, California.

Kumashiro, K. (2001). *Troubling intersections of race and sexuality: Queer students of color and anti-oppressive education*. Landham, MD: Rowman & Littlefield.

Lobman, C. (2005). Improvisation: Postmodern play for early childhood teachers. In S. Ryan & S. Greishaber (Eds.), *Advances in early education and day care: Vol. 14. Practical transformations and transformational practices: Globalization, postmodernism, and early childhood education* (pp. 243–272). Oxford, UK: Elsevier.

Loutzenheiser, L. W., & MacIntosh, L. B. (2004). Citizenships, sexualities, and education. *Theory Into Practice, 43*(2), 151–158.

Marinoble, R. M. (1997). Elementary school teachers: Homophobia reduction in a staff development context. In J. T. Sears & W. L. Williams (Eds.), *Overcoming heterosexism and homophobia: Strategies that work* (pp. 249–260). New York: Columbia University Press.

Mercier, L. R., & Harold, R. D. (2003). At the interface: Lesbian-parents, families and their children's schools. *Children & Schools, 25*(1), 35–47.

Patterson, C. J. (1992). Children of lesbian and gay parents. *Child Development, 63*, 1021–1042.

Patterson, C. J. (1995). Families of the lesbian baby boom: Parents' division of labor and children's adjustment. *Developmental Psychology, 31* (1), 115–123.

Patterson, C. J. (1998). Family lives of children with lesbian mothers. In C.J. Patterson & A. R. D'Augelli (Eds.), *Lesbian, gay and bisexual identities in families: Psychological perspectives* (pp. 154–176). New York: Oxford University Press.

Patterson, C. J. (2000). Family relationships of lesbian and gay men. *Journal of Marriage & Family, 62*(4), 1052–1070.

Patterson, C. J. (2004). What difference does a civil union make? Changing public policies and the experiences of same-sex couples: Comments on Solomon, Rothblum, and Balsam, (2004). *Journal of Family Psychology, 18*(2), 287–289.

Patterson, C. J., & Freil, L. V. (2000). Sexual orientation and fertility. In G. Bently, & Mascie-Talor, N. (Eds.), *Infertility in the modern world: Present and future prospects* (pp. 238–260), Cambridge, England: Cambridge University Press.

Rainbow Families (2006). About Us. Contact: 711 West Lake St., Suite 210, Minneapolis, MN 55408, Telephone 612–827–7731. Retrieved October 30, 2006 from http://www.rainbowfamilies.org/about/about.htm

Ramsey, P. (2004). *Teaching and learning in a diverse world* (3rd ed). New York: Teachers College Press.

Ryan, D., & Martin, A. (2000). Lesbian, gay, bisexual, and transgender parents in the school systems. *School Psychology Review, 29*(2), 207–217.

Ryan, S., & Greishaber, S. (Eds.). (2005). *Practical transformations and transformational practices: Globalization, postmoderninsm, and early childhood education. Vol. 14, Advances in Early Education and Day Care.* Oxford, England: Elsevier.

Silin, J. G. (1995). *Sex, death, and the education of children: Our passion for ignorance in the age of AIDS.* New York: Teacher College Press.

Stacey, J., & Biblarz, J.T. (2001). (How) does the sexual orientation of parents matter? *American Sociological Review,* 66 (2) 159–183.

Weiss, H. B., Kreider, H., Lopez, M. E., & Chatman, C. M. (Eds.). (2005). *Preparing educators to involve families: From theory to practice.* Thousand Oaks, CA: Sage.

Chapter 8

What Makes a Family?
Representations of Adoption in
Children's Literature

Lesley Colabucci
Matthew D. Conley

None of Bitsy's other friends had adopted, as it happened. They were very supportive and all that, very diplomatic, but she could tell that underneath, they felt that to adopt was to settle for second-best. Oh, so many secret hurts and bruises lay behind the Arrival Party! (Tyler, 2006, p. 63)

In her recent novel, *Digging to America,* Anne Tyler tells the story of two American families who adopt Korean children. The Donaldsons are relentless in their goal of honoring their child's culture, while the Yazdons aim for assimilation. The varied approaches these families take exemplify the kinds of issues that arise for adoptive families. In a recent survey, over one-third of respondents reported believing that adopted children are more likely than their nonadopted peers to experience psychological, social, and health problems (National Adoption Attitudes Survey, 2002). Furthermore, adoption is "often perceived as a very risky venture" (Fisher, 2003b, p. 344). This is reflected in the fact that 39% of adult Americans consider—but rule out—adoption as a way to build a family (National Adoption Attitudes Survey, 2002). As Fisher (2003b) explains, adoption is something that most Americans "profess to admire in the abstract but usually avoid" (p. 356).

In his research, Fisher (2003a) examined the portrayal of adoption in college textbooks. He looked specifically at the content of books used in classes that address the sociology of marriage and family. Even in these courses, where one would expect adoption to be explored, Fisher found "little coverage" of the topic. According to this study, there is not only a lack of adequate coverage, but much of the coverage of the topic discourages students from seeing adoption as a "realistic and desirable option for forming a family" (p. 154). He also found that the *Journal of Marriage and*

Family published only six articles that addressed adoption in the past decade (Fisher, 2003a). In fact, only four references to adoption are made in the 792 pages of the *Handbook of Marriage and the Family* (Sussman, Steinmetz, & Peterson, 1999). Not surprisingly, adoption as a theme in children's literature has also been neglected and undervalued. Adoption literature is not specifically addressed in *Charlotte Huck's Children's Literature* (Kiefer, Hepler, & Hickman, 2006), *Through the Eyes of a Child* (Norton, 2006), or *Children's Books in Children's Hands* (Temple, Martinez, Yokota, & Naylor, 2005), three foundational textbooks widely used by teachers and librarians. As educators, we recognize the importance of including all kinds of diverse families in the literature we share with children and the resources we provide to professionals who work with those children.

In this chapter, we document the current state of adoption in children's literature. We investigate what kinds of stories are told, whose perspectives are represented, and which themes prevail. After describing our selection and analytic methods, we provide readers with a critical guide to adoption literature. The heart of this chapter lies in this annotated list of books in which we highlight the best of this literature. We approached each book and thus each annotation with the understanding that children's literature has both personal and educational values. As Huck, Keifer, Hepler, and Hickman (2004) explain, literature for children should "offer vicarious experiences," "develop insight into human behavior," and "present the universality of experience" (p. 69). Additionally, in accordance with reader response theory (Rosenblatt, 1993), we understand that our interpretations of each of these texts reflect our personal perspectives and professional investments.

PURPOSES AND PROCESSES OF ANALYZING STORIES

Although family is a common theme in children's literature, rarely do these books focus on explanations of family composition. However, family structure is a theme of Ada's celebratory *I Love Saturdays y Domingos* (2002), Williams's classic *Chair for My Mother* (1982), and Gonzalez's new *Antonio's Card* (2005).[1] These books feature diverse family compositions such as bilingual/bicultural families, single-parent households, and gay/lesbian families, respectively. Additionally, families in transition have, in a very limited way, been explored in children's books. Woodson's *Our Gracie Aunt* (2002) and Little's *Emma's Yucky Brother* (2001) offer long overdue images of children in foster-care settings. Although including books that represent these and other areas of diversity excited us, we decided for this chapter to keep our focus narrow in order to be able to generalize about how adoption is constructed in literature for children.

For the purpose of this study, we limited our selections to contemporary realistic fiction picture books published between 1990 and 2006. Our search for adoption literature led us to many nonfiction and fantasy selections. For instance, we discovered several examples of informational books that incorporate adoptive families. Several books with the simple title of *Families* are notable because they feature a wide array of family compositions with an emphasis on racial and ethnic diversity (Jenness, 1993; Kuklin, 2006; Morris, 2000). We also examined but eliminated several highly instructional nonfiction pieces (Gordon, 2000; Skutch, 1995; Thomas, 2003).

At the other end of the genre spectrum, *King and King and Family* (deHaan & Nijland, 2004) is a noteworthy fantasy book that features two kings who adopt a child while on their honeymoon. Similarly, many animal fantasies feature adoption, including dePaola's *A New Barker in the House* (2002) and Gray's *Our Twitchy* (2003). In the end, we eliminated nonfiction and fantasy books in order to focus on a cohesive collection. This enabled us to make comparisons across books that shared core elements. We included books about the adoption process as well as stories with a variety of adoption themes. For our purposes, we defined *adoption literature* as books that not only present a story related to adoption, but any story that included an adopted character. We eliminated books if they did not meet even minimal standards for literary quality. However, sometimes we included books with weak illustrations because of the quality and originality of the narrative. Although we are confident in the 40 books we selected, the ultimate criterion for the value of any book is an individual child's response.

A content analysis was conducted of the 40 core picture books. Engaging in content analysis enabled us to "characterize and compare documents" (Manning & Cullum-Swan, 1994, p. 464). Being systematic and intentional, we searched for themes, keywords, recurring motifs, and other trends in the literature. Books were read and reread over and over. We dialogued about the books, taking notes and brainstorming themes and issues. We documented our personal responses, then contextualized these responses through discussion and comparison. We wrote and rewrote summaries and critiques of each book in order to be more specific and detailed in our analysis. This process ultimately resulted in five overarching categories around which the annotations are organized. These include:

I. Welcoming and Waiting: Siblings and Friends Tell Adoption Stories
II. Reflecting and Reminiscing: Adult Perspectives on Adoption
III. Speaking for Themselves: Adopted Children Tell Their Own Stories
IV. Celebrating Diversity: More Stories of Adoptive Families
V. Confronting Challenges: Identity, Conflict, and Acceptance

In the sections to come, we provide descriptions of the categories, along with rationales for why books were included. The categories overlap and are not mutually exclusive. They represent our attempt to convey our findings and present meaningful descriptions for readers. Given the complex nature of any literary text and any individual's interpretation, it is only natural to expect that particular texts might occupy multiple categories. For example, we categorize *The Red Blanket* (Thomas, 2004) as a story of diversity in adoptive families (IV); however, the book certainly is also an adoption narrative from the adult perspective (II). Through analysis, we came to recognize the power of this book's representation of a single parent as its most salient contribution. The fact that the five major categories overlap in this way does not diminish their usefulness. Instead, we hope that readers will be able to use the categories to help them understand the potential of each book.

OVERVIEW OF TRENDS AND THEMES

Although it is difficult to generalize about the entire collection, there are some major trends and themes that characterize this literature. For instance, 22 of the 40 books were based on the author or illustrator's own firsthand experience with adoption. Additionally, relationships with pets are often used as a vehicle to help young children understand adoption. Recurring motifs in the literature include airplanes, ringing telephones, and photo albums. Additionally, many books mention paperwork or other technical details related to adoption. Throughout the books, the place where a child is born is usually described in some way. A specific country or town may be delineated, or it may be vague, such as "a faraway land," or "the other side of the world." The naming of the adopted children also came up repeatedly in texts. Many internationally adopted children were named in their home country before being adopted. Often, these names have cultural meaning and personal significance. However, in most of the books, American names replace these given names. It should also be noted that a preponderance of the books features children who were adopted as infants. The representations of birth parents and adoptive parents, the moments of connection between children and parents, and the ways cultural difference is depicted warrant further discussion.

Throughout the books, different terms were used to describe birth parents, their situations and feelings, and their decisions. The majority of texts refer only to the birthmothers. Referencing birthmothers poses a unique challenge since "most people still consider it unnatural for birthmothers to give up their child" (Freundlich, 1998, p. 22). Perpetuation of this negative connotation should be avoided. Some authors were deliberately vague in how they characterized birthmothers, while others went into great detail about them. We found that less detail-oriented explanations worked just as well as some of the highly specific ones. For instance, in *How I Was Adopted* (Cole, 1995), the narrator explains that "Many children stay with the woman who gave birth to them. Some children do not. Some children need to be adopted." This more direct language serves the purposes of the text and answers questions that may arise without making any assumptions about the birth parents. This type of language keeps the focus on the child. Similar but somewhat more subtle descriptions of birth parents include: "somewhere in the world a mother gave birth to you, a father gave life to you," and "she started your life." Several books simply explain that the child "needed" a family or that a "little girl was waiting for a mommy." These latter two render birthmothers nearly invisible, but in some selections birthmothers are described almost critically—too young or too poor or lacking a husband. Readers of adoption literature learn quickly that many birthmothers were not "ready" to take care of a child or that they would not be able to take care of a baby "properly." They are not demonized but are also not fully recognized for their courage and humanity. These variations in the language used to describe birth parents are indicative of the range in tone and attitude of the collection. Regardless of these descriptive differences, the books overwhelmingly portrayed birth parents sensitively, reassuring adopted children that they were loved and that their biological mothers wanted what was best for them.

Adoptive parents are also described in varying ways throughout literature. Basically, the adoptive parents are described as wanting a child to love and desiring to be a family. Unfortunately, most of the single women who adopt are also characterized as "missing something" or "being lonely," or having an "empty place." If the audience for these books is indeed young children, then some of these descriptions are too adult-centered and perpetuate sex-role stereotypes. In contrast, other authors chose not to make any sort of heavy-handed statement about the lives of the adoptive parents. For instance, one of the fathers in *Beginnings* (Kroll, 1994) simply explains that he "knew our family wasn't finished yet." In another book (Koski, 2002), the parents explain in a straightforward way that "we chose some children to be a part of our family." In this way, the authors keep the focus on the adopted child and keep the text interesting to young readers.

Of the 40 books, 27 involve adoptive parents meeting their children. Descriptions of these first moments together range from quixotic to painfully realistic. Some parents fall in love with their adopted child immediately, as soon as they see or hold the child. One mother is so sure of her bond with her adopted child that she wonders if the people of China had a "window to my soul" (Lewis, 2000). The parents in *White Swan Express* (Okimoto & Aoki, 2002) feel similarly certain, describing knowing that the children had "always been theirs." On the other hand, in some stories, both parents and babies cry and need time adjusting to each other. In one story, the parent uses a blanket to comfort the child while in another a soothing lullaby does the job. Siblings also struggle to connect with adopted children. Often, the turning point for siblings depends on a tender moment. For instance, David is able to make his new brother, Jin Woo, laugh (Bunting, 2001). The wide spectrum of portrayals of how adoptive parents and children connect is realistic and reassuring. The narratives that feature a "perfect match" are quite different from ones that address an adopted child's potential fear or an adoptive parent's insecurities.

Since so many of the families we encountered in adoption literature are interracial, tensions related to cultural and ethnic differences arise. This reflects the U.S. Census Bureau's 2004 report that 13% of all adopted children are foreign-born. Clearly, significant internal tensions occur for international adoptees because "color and ethnicity add layers of complexity to a process that is complicated to begin with" (Pertman, 2001, p. 92). In the books we examined, responses to cultural differences ranged from denial of its existence to acceptance of its significance.

CRITIQUES OF BOOKS IN THE COLLECTION

In this chapter, we have attempted to give readers access to both general and specific information about adoption literature. Figure 8.1 documents the literature we reviewed, highlighting several trends and issues presented in the books. Readers may find this chart helpful as they consider the usefulness of these books for young children. They can consult this reference to find out if a book has the following characteristics: mentioning adoption in the title or subtitle, having a plot based on the adoption narrative, featuring an open adoption or interracial adoption, being based on personal experience, or being published by a small press rather than a major publishing house.

In the sections below, we offer readers a chance to acquaint themselves with adoption literature. In each category, the books are not organized alphabetically or chronologically but rather according to literary quality and aesthetic value. Therefore, the highly recommended texts are first and have received extended critique. Full bibliographic information for each title can be found in the list of adoption literature at the end of the chapter.

FIGURE 8.1. Characteristics of Adoption Books Selected

Title/ Subtitle	Adoption	Plot: Adoption Story	Open Adoption	Interracial Adoption	Personal Experience	Publisher: Small Press
Allison				•		
An American Face				•		•
An Mei's Strange and Wondrous Journey		•		•	•	
Beginnings		•	•	•		•
Best Single Mom in the World	•	•		•		•
Bonesy and Isabel				•		
Borya and the Burps	•	•		•	•	•
The Coffee Can Kid		•		•		•
The Day We Met You		•			•	
Families Are Different		•		•	•	
Felicia's Favorite Story		•		•		•
Happy Adoption Day	•	•			•	
Heart of Mine	•	•		•	•	•
How I Was Adopted	•	•				
How My Family Came to Be	•	•		•	•	•

FIGURE 8.1. Continued

Title/ Subtitle	Adoption	Plot: Adoption Story	Open Adoption	Interracial Adoption	Personal Experience	Publisher: Small Press
I Don't Have Your Eyes				●	●	●
I Love You Like Crazy Cakes		●		●	●	
Impatient Pamela						
Jin Woo		●		●	●	
Just Add One Chinese Sister	●	●		●	●	
A Koala for Katie	●	●				●
Lucy's Family Tree				●		●
Megan's Birthday Tree	●	●	●			●
My Mei Mei		●			●	
Molly's Family						
My Family Is Forever		●		●	●	
Over the Moon	●	●		●	●	
Pablo's Tree						

FIGURE 8.1. Continued

Title/ Subtitle	Adoption	Plot: Adoption Story	Open Adoption	Interracial Adoption	Personal Experience	Publisher: Small Press
The Red Blanket		•		•	•	
Sam's Sister		•	•		•	•
Sisters		•		•		
Tell Me Again About the Night I Was Born		•				
Through Moon and Stars and Night Skies		•		•		
Waiting for May		•		•	•	
We See the Moon				•	•	•
We Wanted You		•		•		•
When I Met You	•	•		•	•	•
When Joel Comes Home		•			•	
The White Swan Express	•	•		•	•	
You're Not My Real Mother				•	•	

Category I. Welcoming and Waiting:
Siblings and Friends Tell Adoption Stories

The books in this category all feature young children preparing for or coping with a change in family structure. These books all value the voice of the "waiting" children who, as the main characters, address some aspect of adoption from their perspective. The characters describe varying levels of anticipation, but many of them experience anxiety as well. The protagonists in *Just Add One Chinese Sister* (McMahon & McCarthy, 2005) and *Waiting for May* (Stoeke, 2005) travel with their families to China to meet their new sisters. In *My Mei Mei* (Young, 2006), a child adopted from China awaits her sister, who is being adopted from the same country. David in *Jin Woo* (Bunting, 2001) waits with his parents at the airport as his new brother arrives from Korea. Similarly, the young narrator in *When Joel Comes Home* (Fowler, 1993) joins a group of friends as they greet a newly adopted child. In *Sisters* (Caseley, 2004), Melissa describes being a sibling of an adopted child. This book features a child who was adopted when she was older—a rare representation. We discovered another rare portrayal in *Sam's Sister* (Bond, 2004). This important book fills a troubling gap in the adoption literature by focusing on a birthmother and her 5-year-old daughter. This story of a birthmother choosing to give her child up for adoption is told from the point-of-view of the would-be sibling.

My Mei Mei

Ed Young has written and illustrated a story of international adoption and sibling dynamics. This book stands out in this collection because the story focuses as much on the sibling relationship as on the adoption itself. The young narrator, Antonia, describes her own adoption by explaining how she "joined" her Mommy and Baba. As Antonia grows up, she yearns to be a *Jieh-Jieh* (big sister). When she is 3, she travels with her parents to China to bring home a real *Mei Mei* (little sister).

Just Add One Chinese Sister

This story of international adoption is written in two voices, as Claire Guan Yu's mother and brother, Conor, tell the story of her adoption. Conor contributes to the telling through a journal while the mother shares a scrapbook with Claire. Readers get two perspectives on the journey and the process. The title may seem trivializing, but the voices of the mother and son ring true creating a heartfelt story.

Jin Woo

This story is told exclusively from a young boy's perspective as he awaits his adopted sibling from Korea. As an adopted child himself, David conveys his fears and his eventual love and acceptance of his new brother. Although the family does not travel to Korea for the adoption, culture is still acknowledged and explored. In this way, culture is recognized as important but does not function as a crisis or problem.

When Joel Comes Home

Friends and neighbors go to the airport to join Jean and George in welcoming their newly adopted son, Joel.

Waiting for May

A young boy describes waiting for his new sister. He travels to China with his family to bring May home.

Sam's Sister

Five-year-old Rosa tells the story of how her mother decides on an open adoption. Rosa comes to understand that she will be a sister but that her brother will live with another family. However, because it's an open adoption, Rosa and her mother will be able to visit the adopted child.

Sisters

Melissa and Kika adjust to becoming sisters after Kika is adopted as an older child. The story is told from the perspective of both characters.

Category II. Reflecting and Reminiscing: Adult Perspectives on Adoption

In the books in this category, adults share their experiences as adoptive parents. The narrators describe the waiting, the joy of meeting their child, and the fulfillment they experience. In *We Wanted You* (Rosenberg, 2002), the illustrations document the life of an adopted child, while the text captures salient moments and fond memories from the parents' point of view. The parent in *When I Met You* (Bashista, 2004) describes changes that her Russian-adopted daughter experiences living in the United States. The memories captured in *Heart of Mine* (Hojer & Hojer, 2000) and *Over the Moon* (Katz, 1997) relate more specifically to the adoption process. They both provide a detailed synopsis of the entire adoption process, from anticipation to preparations to first encounters. *The Day We Met You* (Koehler, 1990) also focuses on preparations from the parent's perspective, but in a simple format geared for young children. *Happy Adoption Day* (McCutcheon, 1996) is a celebration of adoption in the voice of excited parents.

We Wanted You

This book offers a simple and tender presentation of the life of an adoptive family from the perspective of the parents. The book feels almost like a photo album as a backward chronology unfolds. Catalanotto's illustrations depict turning points in the life of the adopted child (a new car, graduation, and so forth). What is most impressive about this book is the simple and accessible explanation of adoption it conveys, making it an ideal read-aloud for school or home.

When I Met You

Using repetitive elements, a mother recounts for her daughter the changes that have occurred since she was adopted from Russia. On one side of each page, the daughter's cultural roots are explored, while on the other side her new American customs are featured. Examples related to food, clothing, climate, and landscape are mentioned. Although the book may simplify and dichotomize Russian and American culture, the author maintains a respectful tone that emphasizes the importance of cultural connections.

The Day We Met You

In this warm and comforting picture book, parents describe how they prepared for their seemingly internationally adopted child. This simple text conveys a universal theme and is ideal for read-aloud for the very young.

Happy Adoption Day

Grammy-nominated singer/songwriter John McCutcheon wrote the lyrics that constitute the text for this festive, multicultural book.

Heart of Mine

In this book translated from Swedish, adoptive parents describe their experience adopting a child from Vietnam.

Over the Moon

The adoptive parents in this book dream of the child they will adopt, then tell the tale of their journey to Central America to meet her.

Category III. Speaking for Themselves: Adopted Children Telling Their Own Stories

The adopted children in these books tell their own stories. As in Category I, the voice of the child is dominant. The children either pursue the retelling of their adoption stories or are positioned as experts on their own lives. As the child narrators recount their personal adoption stories, readers gain insight into their fears, questions, and confusions. The adopted children powerfully convey their experiences of love, acceptance, and affirmation. In each book, the adopted child is empowered through the retelling of his or her story. The adopted daughters in *The Coffee Can Kid* (Czech, 2002) and *The Best Single Mom in the World* (Zisk, 2001) both initiate the recounting of their adoptions, but rely on their parents for elaboration. In *An Mei's Strange and Wondrous Journey* (Molnar-Fenton, 1998), the title character tells the story of her life as an adopted child from birth to age 6. In *Tell Me Again about the Night I Was Born* (Curtis, 1996), the protagonist asks for the story of her adoption to be retold, but then delights in telling it herself. *Through Moon and Stars and Night Skies* (Turner, 1990) has a similar format. The narrators in *How I Was Adopted* (Cole, 1995), *Families are Different* (Pellegrini, 1991), and *My Family Is Forever* (Carlson, 2004) speak authoritatively about their experiences as adopted children, sharing details of their unique families and reflecting on what being adopted means to them. Similarly, the narrator in *We See the Moon* (Kitze, 2003) offers insights into what being adopted means, but this time with a focus on connections to the child's birth country.

The Coffee Can Kid

Six-year-old Annie asks her father to tell her once again the story of her adoption. Items stored inside a coffee can set the stage for the shared retelling. By positioning the father as the central adult in the story, the author diverges from the typical adoption narrative and offers a refreshing portrayal of father-daughter relationships. The author is deliberately respectful to both birthparents and adoptive parents.

Tell Me Again About the Night I Was Born

A young girl asks her parents to recount the story of her birth. Details of her adoption are shared through the repeated phrase, "Tell me again how . . ."—revealing that she already knows the story by heart. This adoption story is firmly grounded in what is interesting to the child, as opposed to some more nostalgic adult retrospectives.

We See the Moon

Through Chinese folk art paintings and simple text—including a familiar poem—*We See the Moon* explores the complex relationships that exist between adopted children and their birthparents. By turning to the moon for answers, readers are reminded of our connectedness across time and space. This book would be suitable for a bedtime story.

How I Was Adopted

This book is cheerful and informative, much like Cole's *Magic School Bus* books. Readers learn how Samantha became her parent's child. The text is age-appropriate, offering help to parents, teachers, and others who are struggling with how to talk about adoption with children. The narrator seems to talk directly to the reader. She uses scientific terms and adult language in a way that seems natural.

An Mei's Strange and Wondrous Journey

The journey from China to America is the theme of this poetic story of adoption.

The Best Single Mom in the World

A young girl and her single mother share in telling the story of how they came to be a family.

My Family Is Forever

A young girl tells the story of her adoption and describes the joys of being in a family like hers.

Through Moon and Stars and Night Skies

A child chronicles the fear and excitement he experienced when he was adopted and brought to his new home in a new country.

Families Are Different

A child adopted from Korea compares her family to those of her classmates.

Category IV. Celebrating Diversity: More Stories of Adoptive Families

These books feature a broad range of representations of adoptive families. The dominant images and definitions we have of families are generally also reflected in adoption literature. However, we found several books that feature nontraditional portrayals, including books about single mothers and gay and lesbian parents. The books in this category offer a wide range of diversity in terms of race and ethnicity. The multicultural elements add value and importance to these pieces. The adoptive mothers in *The Red Blanket* (Thomas, 2004) and *I Love You Like Crazy Cakes* (Lewis, 2000) both travel to China to adopt a daughter. As single women, they offer their unique perspective on the journey to motherhood. The adoptive mother in *Pablo's Tree* (Mora, 1994) is also single, but this tale focuses on the relationship between Pablo and his grandfather. In two of the books in this category, same-sex families are featured. *Felicia's Favorite Story* (Newman, 2002) portrays lesbian parents who adopt internationally, while *How My Family Came to Be* (Aldrich, 2003) features gay fathers who adopt an African-American child. *The White Swan Express* (Okimoto & Aoki, 2002) and *Beginnings* (Kroll, 1994) offer portraits of multiple kinds of families. Both of these books are deliberate in their effort to present diversity in a positive light. Another unique book in this category is *Impatient Pamela* (Koski, 2002), which discusses family size and composition. In this book, adoption is normalized as Pamela learns how her family is different from her friend's family.

The Red Blanket

The story begins with the preparations a single mother makes once she learns she will be journeying to China to adopt a daughter, PanPan. She purchases a red blanket that becomes a source of comfort and basis for bonding. The red blanket that comforted PanPan and connected mother and daughter in the beginning grows threadbare while the relationship between mother and daughter grows stronger. The story is written from the mother's perspective and may be more appealing to adoptive parents than their children.

The White Swan Express

Readers travel with four sets of parents as they set off to China to adopt daughters. The four Chinese babies are adopted respectively by a married couple from Miami, a lesbian couple from Seattle, a single mother from Minnesota, and a Japanese couple from Toronto. These simultaneous stories create a delightful layering of families. Culture and ethnicity are acknowledged and portrayed respectfully, as are the technical dimensions of the process.

Pablo's Tree

Pablo's grandfather, Lito, buys a tree to mark the child's birthday and decorates it every year in his honor. The book centers around the loving relationship between Pablo and Lito, and tells the story of how Pablo came to be adopted. Pablo's affection for his grandfather, pride in his culture, and comfort with his identity as an adopted child are all themes of this book.

How My Family Came to Be

This is one of only a handful of books about children adopted by same-sex parents—a growing trend in the United States (Fisher, 2003b). Additionally, it features a domestic adoption, another topic that is neglected in this literature. This interracial family is created when two White dads adopt an African-American child. The child narrates the story from a retrospective position, celebrating both his family and other kinds of families, even ones with "just plain old one mom and one dad." The illustrations should be critically examined before sharing it with children, due to some racial stereotyping.

Beginnings: How Families Come to Be

Although it is clearly a piece of fiction, this book reads almost like non-fiction. Six families are featured, and each child has his or her own mini-chapter. The book opens with Ruben, a biological child, asking his mother how he "began." Then, readers meet children whose family beginnings are quite different. This book offers a broad range of possible scenarios for families. It celebrates different kinds of adoptions, as well as family diversity in regard to size, composition, and racial and ethnic diversity.

I Love You Like Crazy Cakes

This book offers a tender and intimate portrait of a single woman who travels to China to adopt a child.

Impatient Pamela Wants a Bigger Family

This book is one of many in a popular series for early readers. In this one, Pamela learns about the differences between her family and her friend Sam's larger, more diverse family.

Felicia's Favorite Story

Lesbian parents, one of whom is Puerto Rican, adopt a child from Guatemala.

Category V. Confronting Conflict: Stories of Identity and Acceptance

The books in this category address the ways that adopted children and their families come to terms with conflict and explore identity. In each book, the adopted child is struggling to understand some aspect of adoption. These books include diverse angles on the adoption theme, taking on dilemmas related to race, family identities, and open adoption. In several of these selections, the protagonists face the realities of racial differences. In *You're Not My Real Mother* (Friedrich, 2004), a White adoptive mother helps her Vietnamese daughter understand that she is her real mother despite their racial differences. *I Don't Have Your Eyes* (Kitze, 2003) and *Allison* (Say, 1997) further explore this potential concern of adopted children. Jessie from *An American Face* (Czech, 2000) is Korean and yearns to look "American" like his friends and parents. For *Bonesy and Isabel* (Rosen, 1995), the love of a family pet helps bridge cultural differences. In *A Koala for Katie* (London, 1996), the young adopted child finds comfort in "adopting" a stuffed toy given to her by her father. The characters in *Molly's Family* (Garden, 2004) and *Lucy's Family Tree* (Schreck, 2001) experience conflict and confusion about adoption based on experiences at school. The adopted baby in *Borya and the Burps* (McNamara, 2005) is nervous about his new family until he discovers something that he and his new father have in common. Finally, in *Megan's Birthday Tree* (Lears, 2005), the source of conflict revolves around the complexities of open adoption as Megan struggles with her birthmother's relocation.

You're Not My Real Mother

Despite its misleading title, this book celebrates the loving bond between an adoptive mother and her daughter. The spark for the good-natured and endearing conversation that takes place in the book is the daughter's questioning of why she does not look like her mother. The mother transforms this moment of potential crisis into a playful exchange, resulting in a text with patterned dialogue and realistic language.

I Don't Have Your Eyes

The playful repetition and conversational style of this book will make it appealing to young readers. Throughout the book, adopted children ask questions about the physical differences between them and their caregivers. Parents and children from various racial and ethnic backgrounds are featured. Fathers and older parents are included in this uplifting book.

Allison

The title character receives a gift of a red kimono—just like the one her doll wears—from her grandmother. When she sees herself and the doll in the mirror, she realizes they share other traits, traits she does not share with her adoptive parents. This realization leads to a discussion of her adoption and to loneliness, confusion, and anger for Allison. Ultimately, the reader is assured that Allison has come to understand and appreciate her family.

Molly's Family

A young girl gains a better understanding of why she has two mothers. She lives with both her birthmother, Mommy, and her birthmother's partner, Mama Lu. Molly is confused when her classmates tease her, arguing that no one can have two moms. While this experience is traumatic for Molly, readers benefit from learning about the varied family compositions in her classroom.

Megan's Birthday Tree

This story mainly focuses on Megan's relationship with her birthmother, Kendra. Each year on Megan's birthday, Kendra decorates and mails photos of a "birthday tree" that she planted when Megan was born. Megan becomes worried and insecure when she learns that Kendra is moving away.

Megan's first-person narration helps readers gain a better understanding of open adoption.

Lucy's Family Tree

Mexican-born Lucy was adopted by a White, American couple. She struggles with feeling different when she has to complete a family tree for school. Advice for adapting such projects is provided in an endnote.

An American Face

Having been adopted from Korea, Jessie experiences confusion about racial appearances while waiting to become an American citizen.

Bonesy and Isabel

A family pet helps an adopted child adjust to her new life. Isabel, who is from El Salvador, was adopted as an older child.

A Koala for Katie

Katie resolves some insecurity about her adoptive parent's love for her after "adopting" a stuffed koala herself.

Borya and the Burps

Borya is happy with the other babies in his orphanage and is anxious when he is adopted by a couple who "do not talk right."

CONCLUSION

> *Adoption continues to function as a site on which the culture at large works out its understandings about "family", including the issues of who should be in a family, what roles family members [including both birth parents and adoptive parents] should play, and what function (both public and private) the family should fulfill.* (Berebitsky, 2000, p. 168)

Understandings and beliefs about families are also being "worked out" in children's literature about adoption. Through our review of this literature, we came to appreciate the narratives of parents and children coming together. Additionally, we were moved by the images of diversity that we discovered and the stories of children struggling to understand their histories and identities. Teachers, parents, and other concerned professionals should give careful attention to the selections we have described in this chapter. Once they are aware of this literature, they can make informed decisions about incorporating these books into their classrooms and homes. However, several challenges will need to be overcome if quality books about adoption are to make their way into children's hands. Through our review, we learned that the availability of these books is limited. Many are produced by small presses that rarely have the funding to effectively promote their books and recruit well-known authors or illustrators. Accordingly, the books do not seem to land on library or bookstore shelves, and the overall quality sometimes suffers. This is further evidence of how adoption continues to be undervalued in society.

It is also clear from this review that there are still gaping holes in the literature. Single fathers, for instance, are not the focus of any of these books. Similarly, more high-quality stories of gay and lesbian families are necessary. Although international adoptions dominate in children's literature, the voices of families who adopt domestically through foster care, open adoption, or related adoption need to be heard, particularly since this is more common among the poor and people of color. Neglecting these stories further perpetuates the dominance of the White, middle-class experience in children's literature.

One of our most profound discoveries concerns how race and gender are constructed in adoption literature. These areas warrant further discussion and research. Expectations of women and mothers are conveyed in subtle but powerful ways through these stories. Similarly, assumptions about the role of race and ethnicity and the nature of difference pervade these books. Although we would like to see more books that take on some of these complex issues, there is also a need for books that feature adopted children in stories that are not *about* adoption. Currently, the literature available does not adequately capture the everyday life experiences of adopted children in a normalizing way. We look forward to the day when children's literature offers a more complete picture of adopted children and their families.

QUESTIONS FOR REFLECTION

1. What criteria might parents or other educators develop to guide them in selecting adoption literature to share with children?
2. What trends in this literature are worth celebrating and which warrant concern? What other kinds of stories do you hope will be told as this body of literature expands?

3. How might the books that feature international adoption present opportunities for cross-cultural learning, including discussions of social justice?

4. According to this review of the literature, most adoption stories focus on the role mothers rather than fathers. What is the significance of this bias? Similarly, most adoption books feature international adoptions rather than domestic ones. What are the implications of this?

5. This body of literature is important because it serves to affirm the life experiences of readers who may otherwise be denied that privilege. What are some of the benefits and risks of sharing this literature with adopted children?

NOTE

1. For bibliographic information about children's books cited, see the separate reference list at the end of the chapter.

REFERENCES

Berebitsky, J. (2000). *Like our very own: Adoption and the changing culture of motherhood, 1851–1950.* Lawrence: University Press of Kansas.

Fisher, A. (2003a). A critique of the portrayal of adoption in college texts and readers on families, 1991–2001. *Family Relations, 52,* 154–160.

Fisher, A. (2003b). Still "not quite as good as having your own"? Toward a sociology of adoption. *Annual Review of Sociology, 29,* 335–361.

Freundlich, M. (1998). Supply and demand: The forces shaping the future of infant adoption. *Adoption Quarterly, 2,* 13–46.

Huck, C., Kiefer, B., Hepler, S., & Hickman, J. (2004). *Children's literature in the elementary school* (8th ed.). Boston: McGraw-Hill.

Kiefer, B., Hepler, S. & Hickman, J. (2006). *Charlotte Huck's children's literature* (9th ed.). Boston: McGraw-Hill.

Manning, P., & Cullum-Swan, B. (1994). Narrative, content, and semiotic analysis. In N. Denzin & Y. Lincoln (Eds.), *Handbook of Qualitative Research* (pp. 463–478). Thousand Oaks, CA: Sage.

National Adoption Attitudes Survey: Research Report. (2002). Harris Interactive Market Research. Sponsored by Dave Thomas Foundation for Adoption, in cooperation with Evan B. Donaldson Adoption Institute.

Norton, D. (2006) *Through the eyes of a child* (7th ed.). New York: Prentice Hall.

Pertman, A. (2001). *Adoption nation: How the adoption revolution is transforming America.* New York: Basic Books.

Rosenblatt, L. (1993). *Literature as exploration* (4th ed.). New York: Modern Language Association.

Sussman, M., Steinmetz, S. K., & Peterson, G. W. (Eds). (1999). *Handbook of marriage and the family.* New York: Plenum.

Temple, C., Martinez, M. Yokota, J., & Naylor, A. (2005). *Children's books in children's hands* (3rd ed.). Boston: Allyn & Bacon.

Tyler, A. (2006). *Digging to America.* New York: Knopf.

U.S Census. (2004, September 20). Facts for features: National adoption month. Retrieved July, 20, 2006, from http://www.census.gov/Press-Release/www/ releases/archives/fact_for_features_special_editions/002683.html.

CHILDREN'S LITERATURE

Adoption Literature

Aldrich, A. (2003). *How my family came to be.* Oakland, CA: New Family Press.

Bashista, A. E. (2004). *When I met you.* Pittsboro, NC: DRT Press.

Bond, J. (2004). *Sam's sister.* Indianapolis: Perspectives Press.

Bunting, E. (2001). *Jin Woo.* New York: Clarion.

Caseley, J. (2004). *Sisters.* New York: Greenwillow Books.

Carlson, N. (2004). *My family is forever.* New York: Penguin.

Cole, J. (1995). *How I was adopted: Samantha's story.* New York: Morrow.

Curtis, J. L. (1996). *Tell me again about the night I was born.* New York: HarperCollins.

Czech, J. (2000). *An American face.* Washington, DC: Child & Family Press.

Czech, J. (2002). *The coffee can kid.* Washington, DC: CWLA Press.

Fowler, S. G. (1993). *When Joel comes home.* New York: Greenwillow Books.

Friedrich, M. (2004). *You're not my real mother.* New York: Little Brown.

Garden, N. (2004). *Molly's family.* New York: Farrar Straus & Giroux.

Hojer, D., & Hojer, L. (2000). *Heart of mine.* New York: R & S Books.

Katz, K. (1997). *Over the moon.* New York: Henry Holt.

Kitze, C. (2003). *I don't have your eyes.* Warren, NJ: EMK Press.

Kitze, C. (2003). *We see the moon.* Warren, NJ: EMK Press.

Koehler, P. (1990). *The day we met you.* New York: Bradbury Press.

Koski, M. (2002). *Impatient Pamela wants a bigger family.* Duluth, MN: Trellis Publishing.

Kroll, V. (1994). *Beginnings: How families come to be.* Morton Grove, IL: Albert Whitman.

Lears, L. (2005). *Megan's birthday tree: A story about open adoption.* Morton Grove, IL: Albert Whitman.

Lewis, R. (2000). *I love you like crazy cakes.* New York: Little Brown.

London, J. (1996). *A koala for Katie.* Morton Grove, IL: Albert Whitman.

McCutcheon, J. (1996). *Happy adoption day.* New York: Little Brown. McMahon, P. & McCarthy, C. (2005). *Just add one Chinese sister.* Honesdale, PA: Boyds Mills Press.

McNamara, J. (2005). *Borya and the burps*. Indianapolis: Perspectives Press.

Molnar-Fenton, S. (1998). *An Mei's strange and wondrous journey*. New York: DK Publishing.

Mora, P. (1994). *Pablo's tree*. New York: Macmillan.

Okimoto, J., & Aoki, E. (2002). *The white swan express*. New York: Clarion.

Newman, L. (2002). *Felicia's favorite story*. Ridley Park, PA: Two Lives Publishing.

Pellegrini, N. (1991). *Families are different*. New York: Holiday House.

Rosen, M. (1995). *Bonesy and Isabel*. New York: Harcourt Brace.

Rosenberg, L. (2002). *We wanted you*. Brookfield, CT: Roaring Brook Press.

Say, A. (1997). *Allison*. Boston: Houghton Mifflin.

Schreck, K. H. (2001). *Lucy's family tree*. Gardiner, ME: Tilbury House.

Stoeke, J. M. (2005). *Waiting for May*. New York: Dutton.

Thomas, E. (2004). *The red blanket*. New York: Scholastic.

Turner, A. (1990). *Through moon and stars and night skies*. New York: Harper & Row.

Young, E. (2006). *My Mei Mei*. New York: Philomel Books.

Zisk, M. (2001). *The best single mom in the world*. Morton Grove, IL: Albert Whitman.

Books with Diverse Family Representations

Ada, A. F. (2002). *I love Saturdays y domingos*. New York: Atheneum.

deHaan, L. & Nijland, S. (2004). *King and king and family*. Berkeley, CA: Tricycle Press.

dePaola, T. (2002). *A new Barker in the house*. New York: Putnam.

Gonzalez, R. (2005). *Antonio's card*. San Francisco: Children's Book Press.

Gordon, S. (2000). *All families are different*. Amherst, New York: Prometheus Books.

Gray, K. (2003). *Our Twitchy*. New York: Henry Holt.

Jenness, A. (1993). *Families*. Boston: Houghton Mifflin.

Kuklin, S. (2006). *Families*. New York: Hyperion.

Little, J. (2001). *Emma's yucky brother*. New York: HarperCollins.

Morris, A. (2000). *Families*. New York: HarperCollins.

Skutch, R. (1995). *Who's in a family?* Berkeley, CA: Tricycle Press.

Thomas, P. (2003). *My new family: A first look at adoption*. Hauppauge, New York: Barrons.

Williams, V. (1982). *A chair for my Mother*. New York: HarperTrophy.

Woodson, J. (2002). *Our Gracie Aunt*. New York: Hyperion.

Chapter 9

Emerging Faces of Homelessness: Young Children, Their Families, and Schooling

Tracy Thoennes

What comes to your mind when you think of homelessness? Do families with young children enter into your view of homelessness? If you neglected to consider young children and their parents as comprising part of this population, you may be alarmed to know that families with children under the age of 5 are the fastest-growing segment of the homeless population in the United States. In fact, the average age of all homeless persons nationally is 6 years. Family homelessness has now emerged as a serious problem at the national and state levels, as well as within small communities. This chapter will explore some of the evolution of views and policies toward the homeless, their impacts, what resources school personnel have at their disposal to assist homeless students and families, and what teachers and administrators can do to provide support for their homeless students.

RECOGNIZING THE PROBLEM OF UNHOUSED FAMILIES

The commonly held notion that homeless families are concentrated in urban areas and are limited to troubled alcoholic adult men keeps the rural and suburban homeless virtually invisible and makes the problem of homelessness easier to ignore. Yet, in a given year in the United States, 3.5 million people, 1.35 million of them children, experience homelessness.

Family homelessness is a broad problem, existing in both urban and rural settings. In urban areas, homeless families may remain invisible, as being homeless doesn't necessarily mean that they are living on the streets.

Urban unhoused families are commonly known to double up with friends or relatives, reside in transitional housing or shelter programs, or live in cars. Unhoused rural families are less likely to be found living on the streets or in shelters. Instead, they most often find refuge by doubling up with family members or friends or by living in cars or campers. Both urban and rural homelessness are a result of unaffordable housing and severe poverty and are complicated by a lack of awareness of resources. DaCosta Nunez (1996) warns that although family homelessness is often invisible to larger society, it will likely impact the next generation as they may age into this nomadic lifestyle.

Homelessness disrupts every aspect of family life, damaging the physical and emotional health of family members, interfering with children's education and development, and frequently resulting in the separation of family members. Though a tumultuous experience, homelessness is not fixed or static; instead, it is a fluid state. A family can move back and forth between being housed, nonhoused, doubling up, tripling up, staying in shelters, and so forth. Because homelessness causes families to move frequently, the high mobility rate can negatively affect children's ability to attend school and to experience education in a stable and consistent manner.

According to the Institute for Children and Poverty (2001), it is estimated that in the United States, one in five school-age homeless children will repeat a grade in school—twice the national rate for all children—and as they get older, children who repeat a grade are more likely to develop a negative self-image, drop out of school, and get into trouble with the law than those who are not left back. The institute also reports that over half of homeless children transfer schools at least once in a given year, that frequent moves decrease the likelihood that homeless children will receive the special education classes they need, and that the impact of such absenteeism is devastating: Two-thirds of students (68%) who miss 20 or more school days in one year during first, second, or third grade eventually drop out.

So, although homelessness is typically a temporary experience, it can have lasting and damaging consequences for children. Homelessness creates for children and families a loss of housing, neighborhood, friends, family, and possessions (Duffield, 2001). Unhoused children experience poor health at twice the rate of their housed peers, are twice as likely to experience hunger, and are known to have higher rates of ear infections, stomach problems, speech problems, and asthma. They are twice as likely to have learning disabilities, and four times as likely to have delayed development. Problems of this nature clearly have an influence on children's health and well-being. What policies are in place to provide support and assistance?

EXAMINING POLICIES TOWARD HOMELESSNESS

Several factors related to policy (or lack of it) toward the homeless have historically contributed to the conditions of homelessness with which we continue to struggle today. In fact, during the Reagan administration of the 1980s, homelessness was not even considered a problem requiring federal intervention. The conservative political agenda during this administration severely limited the formation of policy on this issue. Eventually, thanks to the tireless work of advocacy groups, critical contributions were made toward policy development regarding poverty and homelessness.

A Brief History of U.S. Policies

In 1983, the first task force on homelessness was created, but actually addressing the issue was taken up by advocacy groups such as the National Coalition for the Homeless, the National Housing Institute, and the Welfare Center. The Welfare Center works on behalf of low-income people to ensure that adequate income support is available, and the National Housing Institute examines the key issues causing the crisis in housing and community in the United States. The National Coalition for the Homeless, a national advocacy network of homeless persons, activists, service providers, and others, is committed to ending homelessness through public education, policy, advocacy, grassroots organizing, and technical assistance. This organization served as a key player in the formation and passage of the Stewart B. McKinney Act of 1987.

As advocates throughout the country began demanding that the federal government acknowledge the scope of the state of homelessness, the Homeless Survival Act was introduced into both houses of Congress in 1986. According to Bogard & McConnell (1998), this act consisted of emergency relief, preventive measures, and long-term solutions to homelessness, but unfortunately, only portions of the proposal were signed into law. The Homeless Eligibility Clarification Act of 1986 removed permanent address requirements and other barriers to existing programs such as Supplemental Security Income, Aid to Families with Dependent Children, Veteran's Benefits, Food Stamps, and Medicaid (Bogard & McConnell, 1998).

The Homeless Housing Act, passed in the Senate and the House in 1987, resulted in the provision of an Emergency Shelter Grant Program as well as a transitional housing demonstration program. After the death of its chief Republican sponsor, Representative Stewart B. McKinney of Connecticut, the act was renamed the Stewart B. McKinney Homeless Assistance Act and signed into law by a reluctant President Ronald Reagan in 1987 (National Coalition for the Homeless, 2003).

Because the concept for the McKinney Act originated from a Republican, right-wing platform, and because Reagan and his administration were known not to favor social policy for the benefit of the poor, the act's passage came as a surprise to advocacy groups. However, as advocacy groups such as the National Coalition for the Homeless began to further identify homelessness in the 1980s, the Reagan administration was forced to respond to the dilemma of homeless families. Another notable surprise came when the McKinney Homeless Assistance Act was adopted with almost no modification under the Clinton administration, except to add the name of the late Representative Bruce Vento, a leading supporter of the act since its original passage. Though Democrats have a long history of developing poverty programs, this policy on homelessness, which President Bill Clinton reactivated into law, was defined by a conservative agenda. In 2001, the law was reauthorized by Congress as the McKinney-Vento Homeless Education Assistance Improvements Act in the No Child Left Behind Act signed by President George W. Bush on January 8, 2002 (Institute for Children and Poverty, 2001).

Provisions of the McKinney-Vento Act

In spite of the proliferation of homeless families, and likely in response to stereotypes surrounding the discourse on homelessness, the sole legislative response to homelessness in the United States has been the McKinney-Vento Act (PL100-77). This act addresses the educational rights of the homeless student in order to remove barriers to a free and appropriate public school education. This federal legislation requires all school districts to appoint a federally funded liaison to communicate with homeless families, publicize the rights of homeless parents at schools and other agencies that work with families in transition, and oversee district programs for identifying and promoting the enrollment of homeless students (Berliner, 2002). School liaisons work to ensure that nonhoused students secure the educational services to which they are entitled (see also Chapter 5, this volume). The revised McKinney-Vento Act also required that each state make plans to ensure that homeless children be given the opportunity to achieve the same newly created academic standards as other children in the state. Though the act required the federal government to provide funding to the states to carry out those mandates, the availability of sufficient funds has depended on the budget passed by Congress and signed by the president. The funding available federally can be secured through grant writing on the part of school district administrators. Monies are available to financially support after-school programs, tutoring services, outreach committees, and so on.

It is important to note that in the McKinney-Vento Act, a homeless child is defined as one who lacks a fixed, regular, and adequate nighttime residence, and who is sharing the housing of others, abandoned in hospitals, awaiting foster-care placement, or who is living in motels, hotels, trailer parks, camping grounds, cars, public places, abandoned buildings, substandard buildings, bus or train stations, or emergency or transitional shelters (National Coalition for the Homeless, 2006). The National Association for the Education of Homeless Children and Youth bring some clarity to the wording fixed, regular, and adequate nighttime residence (National Association for the Education of Homeless Children and Youth, 2004). A fixed residence is one that is stationary, permanent, and not subject to change. A regular residence refers to one which is used on a regular (i.e., nightly) basis, and an adequate residence is one that is sufficient for meeting both the physical and psychological needs typically met in home environments. In a U.S. Department of Education Report to Congress in 2000, provisions of the reauthorization of the McKinney-Vento Act are described that recognize that students in many different living situations are homeless. In the report, the Department of Education points out that many homeless children and their parents may be living in motels or other temporary facilities, or may live on the streets, in abandoned cars, and in woods and campgrounds (Homes for the Homeless, 2005).

The Impact of Social Policy upon Homeless Families

Understanding events in the history of welfare legislation can assist one in grappling with how the poor have been affected by policy decisions. The most vulnerable citizens in the United States today are poor mothers and their children. Today families, typically women with two children under the age of 5 years, make up 30% of the homeless population (DeAngelis, 1994). The widening gap between the poor and the rich and the increasing cost of raising children are key factors (Coontz, 1992). The 1996 welfare law, the Personal Responsibility and Work Opportunity Act (PRWORA), denied poor families needed resources, plummeting a majority of them into homelessness. The immediate impact of PRWORA cut $55 billion of support to low-income programs and eliminated Aid to Families with Dependent Children (AFDC), Job Opportunities and Basic Skills (JOBS), and Emergency Assistance (EA). Families that had been receiving benefits now faced time limits on assistance, were required to work as a condition for cash assistance, and experienced a grave reduction in food and medical assistance. As a result of this welfare law, the number of children living below the poverty line (defined as an income of less than $6,800 per year for a three-person family) grew by half a million (Piven, 2002).

Many of the issues discussed in the literature on families and support policies include, but are not limited to, cultures of poverty, child care, non-traditional family types, low minimum wage, and lack of affordable housing. Much of the literature focuses on the culture of poverty theory, first given a name by Oscar Lewis in 1961. According to this theory, it is the material circumstances and practical hardship of poverty (i.e., low incomes, few job prospects, and substandard living conditions) that initially produce the cultural response of deviant values among the poor (Hays, 2003). Culture of poverty generalizes that once deviant values and practices take hold in a community, they are passed down from generation to generation. Conservatives interpret the cultural dimensions of poverty as being the result of moral failings on the part of the poor. Liberals, in contrast, often subscribe to the belief that the cycle of poverty can be broken through social work intervention, retraining, and therapy. Current welfare policy reaffirms and strengthens the dynamic polarization of racial privilege and disadvantage (Burnham, 2002). The cultural demonization of the poor is widely recognized and persistent (Howard, 1999), and further oppresses young families with children living below the federal poverty guidelines. As Kozol (2000) explains, while public policies to protect children from the crisis of homelessness are shamefully absent in the United States, there is, nevertheless, much that can be done to prevent homelessness from robbing children of their rights to an education—a vital necessity if they are to escape poverty and face their futures with any measure of hope.

CONSIDERING HOMELESSNESS AND SCHOOLING

Currently, U.S. public schools are witnessing an alarming increase in the numbers of homeless children in the student body. Homeless students are the most identifiable at-risk group served in America's schools (National Coalition for the Homeless, 1999). School administrators and teachers are now being presented with a new population of students with unique needs.

The Child's Perspective: Sofie

As an illustration of these homeless students, I offer a portrait of a child I call Sofie. She is a composite of children I have come to know during my year-long study of five homeless families. The portrait is also based on my research of the literature and conversations with various advocates for the homeless. When I first met her, Sofie was living with her mother and two younger brothers in a shelter-sponsored transitional housing program. They were enrolled in the program for the entire time allotment, about 20 months.

With her mother and father divorced, Sofie resided with her mother and two brothers, visiting her dad on alternate weekends. Previously, before living in transitional housing, the family had been living in a rented apartment, but following the divorce of her parents, her mother, Elizabeth, became strapped with debt and with her single income, could no longer afford to pay the monthly rent there.

Elizabeth qualified for and moved into a shelter-sponsored transitional housing program that assisted families in working toward economic self sufficiency. Elizabeth was working full-time as a dental assistant and utilized the shelter program's child-care center to arrange care for her youngest son. The assistance program offered an individualized approach to facilitating the process of becoming permanently housed and economically self-sufficient. Each family was assigned a case worker who assisted parents in planning and implementing short- and long-term goals that would provide the greatest success for the entire family. In addition to having opportunities to attend professional counseling services, residents had access to parenting classes, finance management counseling, educational opportunities, and employment training. From what I observed while visiting with the families there throughout a year's time, these women in the shelter were willing to help one another and genuinely cared about the well-being of all of the residents. They helped each other out with child care in a pinch, shared dinners together, and spent time each day talking with one another, sharing thoughts, ideas, and frustrations. There were sometimes disagreements or arguments over discipline of the children in the courtyard play area, but the women managed to resolve their differences agreeably.

I visited with these families one evening per week, and when it became too cold to stay outdoors and talk, many of the mothers invited me into their kitchens to visit. Sofie's mother, like the other mothers, impressed me as being conscientious about parenting and as being a loving, nurturing, and responsible mother.

Enrolled in a nearby public school, Sofie and her other brother attended an after-school program there that provided care for them until Elizabeth completed her work shift for the day. The older brother attended public school and, although he applied a great deal of effort, he seemed to struggle with completing academic tasks, as did Sofie.

At the time I met her, Sofie was in the fourth grade. She was one of those kids whom I worry might, in the future, easily lose interest in school, as she found so much of it "boring" and "not fun." She was much more positive about her social endeavors, her friends, and her free time. This is typical of many children, but with Sofie, I was consistently concerned about her prospective success in the institution of schooling.

Sofie, herself, was an exuberant, fun-loving child with bright eyes and a fascination for pop music, dancing, singing, and cheerleading. At a moment's notice, Sofie might jump onto one of the picnic tables in the courtyard where she lived and start singing and dancing enthusiastically. She seemed to generally enjoy going to school, and she had a good rapport with her teacher, but she faced struggles in completing all of her work in a timely manner. Sofie told me that she enjoyed social studies, music, physical education, and reading novels. She emphasized that math, English, and reading were her least favorite subjects. It was tough for her to get started on her schoolwork, but once she got started, she usually completed her assignments and homework, although begrudgingly. Her mother reported that she was not performing at grade level. Sofie experienced difficulty concentrating and staying on task, and some of that could have been attributed to her high energy levels.

Often, while seated at the kitchen table in Elizabeth's place, I would help Sofie and her brothers with schoolwork and do art activities with them. I often got the feeling that Elizabeth wished I would stick strictly to the academic work, but I also wanted to provide them with fun and engaging activities. Over a year's worth of visits, we worked out math problems, read aloud, stumbled around with spelling, and created paintings, multimedia collages, sculptures, and drawings.

I often felt very out of place, as though I were encroaching upon their privacy as a family. As I worked with the children one night per week, Elizabeth would be trying to prepare dinner while at the same time keeping the kids from snacking too much before their evening meal could be prepared. Elizabeth would be forced to multitask, as many parents are. After starting dinner, I would see her washing dishes, folding clothes, caring for her 4-year-old son, fielding questions from her children, and talking with her case worker and neighbors when they stopped in.

At home, Sofie sometimes presented her mom with resistance and defiance. Highly emotional, Sofie would argue with her mom about when to start homework. She was generally an enthusiastic child with a great deal of energy; however, when her mother would try to redirect Sofie to complete her homework, Sophie would react with opposition, tears, and screaming. Sofie did struggle with transitions between tasks and with having to finish too much homework. Usually, by the time I had to leave each evening, Sofie would still be attending to her homework. Instead of doing her schoolwork, Sofie preferred to play in the courtyard with the other children who resided there. I would feel guilty about pulling her away from her favorite activities, but usually when I arrived she would run up to my car, beaming, and ask, "What are we doing tonight?" She would sing songs for me, ask me for advice, and make me feel very welcome in her home environment.

I recall one evening that Sofie and I were preparing to do some reading activities, when she suddenly remembered that she had an unfinished homework assignment to complete. It was an assignment that required researching a topic using the Internet. She had begun working on the task at her after-school program, but told me that she ran short of time to finish it. Since the family did not have a computer in the home, and it was too late for her to go to the library, the assignment would have to wait until the next school day.

Sophie and her family's story brings to light many of the real-life issues that affect the quality of a homeless student's educational experiences and successes. For example, if children are residing in a shelter, there may not be a quiet place for them to complete schoolwork. Even in the transitional housing program, some of the living quarters were shared spaces, so many of these children did not have a desk or a specific place to do their work. The next section of this chapter moves us beyond the challenges of home life and into the realities that homeless children face within the school culture itself.

Homeless Students in School Culture

Employing curriculum theory can assist in understanding how certain student populations are marginalized in school culture. Key theories addressing students' educational experiences, such as critical theory, reproduction theory, social stratification theory, and concepts such as hegemony (McLaren, 1989; 1988), cultural capital (Bourdieu & Passeron, 1977), ideology (McLaren, 1989), and hidden curriculum (Jackson, 1968), connect us to some of the systemic issues of school and societal control that a homeless child such as Sofie will face in her educational journey. To get a clearer picture, we must consider how being from nondominant social classes can affect the ways in which homeless children such as Sofie are received in the school culture.

Reproduction theorists (Giroux, 1985, 1988) argue that schools as institutions reproduce the values, social practices, and skills needed for the continuation of the existing dominant social culture. Homeless students coming from a lower social class will face challenges in assimilating to that dominant social culture. Schools commmonly and routinely make available different types of educational experience and curriculum knowledge to students in different social classes (Anyon, 1995), further setting homeless children apart from their middle-class peers. Bourdieu (1977) explains that cultural patterns (the ways of talking and acting, moving, dressing, and socializing; likes and dislikes; competencies; and forms of knowledge that distinguish one group from another) constitute the cultural capital of a group. A highly valued cultural capital is one that is possessed by the dominant culture. Translating this concept to the experience of homeless students in public school means that because they do not meet the school's standards for myriad reasons, whether it is dialect, communication style, or manners, they may be perceived as less capable than those who possess the dominant culture's forms of cultural capital.

This lack of cultural capital provides yet another indication to homeless students of their lack of social mobility, because in a meritocratic society, education has historically been seen as the key to upward mobility. According to deMarrais and LeCompte (1999), social class, rather than occupation, family background, or education, forces the most intense level of marginalization upon a student. Young homeless students face a unique struggle in that they are victims of poverty left with no power to change their family's situation and, as result of their economic disadvantage, they face discrimination in society and school culture.

Ideology (McLaren, 1989), a way of thinking about and interpreting the world, plays a central role in establishing and maintaining power within institutions such as schools. The hidden curriculum (Jackson, 1968) refers to implicit messages used in schools to convey "appropriate" values, beliefs, and behaviors to children (see also Chapter 10, this volume). Homeless children in public schools are particularly vulnerable to types of social control and marginalization manifested through such practices. They will not necessarily come to school with the "norms" of acceptable behavior, such as linguistic ability or behaviors to be able to fit into a dominant social group.

Very briefly introduced and discussed here, these theoretical concepts help us to conceptualize how economic, political, and sociocultural influences can marginalize students of less dominant groups, but practical work is needed to specifically examine the perspective of the child and what can be done in schools to support homeless students and their families.

What Teachers, Administrators, and Schools Can Do

How do homeless students and their families fare in the public school culture? My hope is that awareness will be heightened regarding the experience of the homeless student and his or her family. Schools aren't responsible for solving homelessness, but they certainly can take some steps to alleviate its effects on children. School districts can provide professional development sessions for teachers and other school personnel to build awareness of the specific educational needs of homeless students. School administrators, teachers, and support staff can create an educational environment that is supportive, promotes tolerance, and draws on the resources provided through the McKinney-Vento Act. On a macro level, schools can work with shelter directors, McKinney-Vento district liaisons, and Title 1 staff. School personnel can make attendance a priority by ensuring that their district is aware of address changes for each family and that adequate transportation is being provided (National Coalition for the Homeless, 2003).

Federal grant monies are available to schools for implementation of programs such as before- and after-school care, meals, homework assistance, and establishment of clothing supplies. Advocating for programs that better the lives and well-being of homeless students and their families is a first step that communities can take, and remaining aware of current legislation and McKinney-Vento updates is critical.

Teachers can be aware that homeless students face a lack of opportunities to complete assignments and see projects come to completion and evaluation. Often, if children are residing in temporary shelters or doubling up with family members or friends, they can easily lack an adequate and appropriate space for completing assignments. Portable desks such as clipboards with pencils attached can be helpful for students completing homework in their temporary living space.

Berliner (2002) provides five principles for educators in teaching homeless students:

1. Do not stigmatize homeless children. Think of them as children temporarily without a home due to a complex set of circumstances beyond their control, and often beyond their understanding.
2. Make schools safe havens.
3. Think of the needs of the whole child, including physical health, mental health, and food and nutritional needs.
4. Actively work with parents and guardians to develop concrete goals and programs.
5. Collaborate with community members and develop a network to undertake a comprehensive effort to helping children who are homeless.

In conclusion, perhaps most important, within society and the school culture, homeless children and their families should not be viewed monologically. As Rossi (1994) indicates, homelessness is not just about the absence of a physical shelter. Homelessness affects children in multiple ways, including socially, emotionally, academically, and physically. In the school culture, homeless children should have the same opportunities as their housed peers to enjoy success in their educational endeavors.

In society, one hopes that children experiencing homelessness can feel valued and be included in child culture. Once again, it is critical to allow the descriptions of homeless life to originate from the voice of the individual and not from that of a monolithic definition of a group of people. We can reach out to homeless families by ignoring societal constructs of homeless individuals and by acknowledging their perspectives and respecting their voices, such as that of a 9 year-old homeless child in New York City. Her poem is both powerful and moving.

Been No Crystal Ball

Well rock life for me has
Been no crystal ball
It's been bugs on top
And snakes on the bottom
But still I rise
Well, rock, you say
You can't go on
Because you been kicked on
Sat on
The World is too big for you to give up on
Life is too small to just stop going on
Life for me has been no crystal ball

QUESTIONS FOR REFLECTION

1. Discuss the societal constructs of the typical homeless person. Compare and contrast that image with the demographics regarding the homeless.
2. Why is there such an increase in homeless families, especially those with children under the age of 5? Discuss the economic factors and social policies that have had an impact on increasing numbers of homeless families.
3. What types of legislation are currently and still need to be in place to advocate for the *educational rights* of homeless students?
4. How can teachers and schools avoid stigmatizing students who are living in poverty and who may also be homeless? How can school communities reach out to economically disadvantaged students and their families?
5. What can teachers do specifically to assist homeless students? What is the responsibility of school districts in addressing the needs of homeless students?

REFERENCES

Anyon, J. (1995). Race, social class, and educational reform in an inner city school. *Teachers College Record, 97*(1), 69–94. In R. Lyons, J. Rodriguez, J. Catallozzi, & N. Benson (Eds.), *Struggles over schooling in a democratic state*. Lanham, MD: University Press of America, 2001.

Berliner, B. A. (2002). Helping homeless students keep up. *Education Digest, 68*(1).

Bogard, C. J. & McConnell, J. J. (1998). Rhetoric, recision, and reaction. In C.Y.H. Lo & M. Schwartz (Eds.), *Social policy and the conservative agenda*. Oxford, UK: Blackwell.

Bourdieu, P. (1977). Cultural reproduction and social reproduction. In J. Karabel & A. H. Halsey (Eds.), *Power and ideology in education* (pp. 487–511). New York: Oxford.

Bourdieu, P., & Passeron, J. (1977). *Reproduction in education, society, and culture*. Beverly Hills, CA: Sage.

Burnham, L. (2002). Welfare reform, family hardship, and women of color. In R. Albelda & Withorn (Eds.), *Lost ground* (pp. 43–56). Boston: South End.

Chase-Lansdale, P. L. & Brooks-Gunn, J. (1995). *Escape from poverty: What makes a difference for children?* Cambridge, MA: Cambridge University Press.

Coontz, S. (1992). *The way we never were: American families and the nostalgia trap*. New York: Basic Books.

DaCosta-Nunez, R. (1996). *The new poverty: Homeless families in America*. New York: Plenum.

Daskal, J. (1998). *In search of shelter: The growing shortage of affordable rental housing*. Washington, DC: Center on Budget and Policy Priorities.

DeAngelis, T. (1994). Homeless families: Stark reality of the 90's. *American Psychological Association Monitor*, (1), 38.

DeMarrais, K. B., & LeCompte, M. D. (1999). *The way schools work: A sociological analysis of education* (3rd ed.). New York: Addison Wesley/Longman.

Department of Housing and Urban Development (2004). Fiscal year 2004 HUD budget executive summary. Retrieved on March 12, 2006, from http://www.hud.gov/about/budget/fy04/execsummary.cfm

Duffield, B. (2001). The educational rights of homeless children: Policies and practices. *Educational Studies, 32*(3), 1–10.

Giroux, H. (1985).Toward a critical theory of education; beyond a Marixism with guarantees. A response to Daniel Liston. *Educational Theory, 35*(3), 313–319.

Giroux, H. (1988). *Schooling and the struggle for public life*. Minneaplois: University of Minnesota.

Hays, S. (2003). *Flat broke with children: Women in the age of welfare reform*. New York: Oxford University Press.

Homes for the Homeless. (2005). Miles to go: The flip side of the McKinney-Vento Homeless Assistance Act. A report of the Institute for Children and Poverty. Retrieved February 2, 2007 from http://www.homesforthehomeless.com/.

Howard, C. (1999). The American welfare state, or states? *Political Research Quarterly, 52*, 421–442.

Jackson, P. (1968). *Life in classrooms*. New York: Holt, Rinehart, & Winston.

Kozol, J. (2000). *Ordinary resurrections: Children in the years of hope*. New York: HarperCollins.

Institute for Children and Poverty. (2001). Been no crystal ball. *Homeless in America: A children's story*. New York: Author.

McLaren, P. (1988). Our ideology and education: Critical pedagogy and the politics of education. *Social Text, 19–20*.

McLaren, P. (1989). *Life in schools: An introduction to critical pedagogy in the foundations of education*. New York: Longman.

Moore A., & Driscoll, A. K. (1997). Low wage maternal employment and outcomes for children: A study. *The Future of Children*, 7 (1), 122–127.

National Association for the Education of Homeless Children and Youth. (2004). Reauthorizing No Child Left Behind Act. Retrieved February 10, 2007 from http://www.naehcy.org.

National Coalition for the Homeless. (1999). *Facts about homelessness: Who is homeless*. Retrieved November 2, 2002, from *http://nationalhomeless.org*.

National Coalition for the Homeless. (2003). *Facts about homelessness: Who is homeless*. Retrieved February 10, 2005 from *http://nationalhomeless.org*.

National Coalition for the Homeless. (2006). *Facts about homelessness: Who is homeless*. Retrieved March 23, 2007, from *http://nationalhomeless.org*.

Newman, J. (1995). Socioeconomic class and education: In what ways does class affect the educational process? In J. L. Kinchloe and S. R. Steinberg (Eds.), *Thirteen questions: Reframing education's conversation*. New York: Peter Lang.

No Child Left Behind Act. (2002). PL 107-110 No Child Left Behind Act of 2001. Education. Intergovernmental relations, 20 USC 6301.

Piven, F. (2002). Welfare policy and American politics. In G. Delgado (Ed.), *From poverty to punishment: How welfare reform punishes the poor*. Oakland, CA: Applied Research Center.

Rafferty, Y. & Shinn, M. (1991). The impact of homelessness on children. *American Psychologist*, 46, 1170–1179.

Rossi, P. (1994). Troubling families: Family homelessness in America. *The American Behavioral Scientist, (37)*3, 342.

Stewart B. McKinney-Vento Homeless Assistance Act (1987).

Stewart B. McKinney-Vento 2001. Law into practice. (2002). The educational rights of students in homeless situations: What LEA administrators must know. Retrieved June, 2005, from www.naehcy.org. Report collaboratively developed by National Center for Homeless Education (NCHE) (Sec. 11431).

Chapter 10

From Textbooks to the Teachers' Lounge: The Many Curricula of Family in Schools

Tammy Turner-Vorbeck

It may be somewhat surprising to many of us involved in schooling that there are multiple forms of school curriculum that commonly address several dimensions of family. Among such dimensions are the structure, psychological soundness, ethnicity, and morality of various forms of family. Because these considerations of family often lie beyond the explicit curriculum, this chapter focuses upon an examination of the more elusive, yet highly impactful, null and hidden curricula of family in schools. The curriculum we are most familiar with, the explicit curriculum, is based upon what is *present* in multiple discourses through what we traditionally consider to be the primary vehicles of learning such as textbooks, lessons, and activities. The null curriculum on family is constituted inversely through what is *absent* in curriculum on family and signifies what is not allowed to represent family. Less familiar to us, yet coexisting alongside the explicit curriculum, is the hidden curriculum on family. The hidden curriculum is created by what is *implied* as either legitimate or illegitimate knowledge about family within school discourses not usually identified as "curriculum." By allowing for the narrow definition of a natural and normal family, the hidden curriculum supports the creation of othered forms of family. This chapter will reveal that when curricular conceptions of family are restricted to typical family structure, other forms of family are omitted and, thus, devalued. Moving the critique from the theoretical to the practical, the chapter concludes by addressing the question of what can be done, providing suggestions based on the nexus: Awareness-Reflection-Action.

As a curriculum researcher and scholar, teacher educator, advocate for family diversity within a multicultural education framework, and mother of three children adopted when older from the state of Indiana's foster-care system, I bring both my academic knowledge and personal experiences to bear upon the dual questions: How *is* and how *should* the construct of family be represented within curriculum? Supporting the theoretical with the experiential, it is the intent of this writing to provide the reader with an understanding of the complex relationship between the primary forms of curriculum at work in schools in order to fully illuminate the real-life consequences that various curricular messages about the concept of family create for students.

FORMS OF CURRICULUM: EXPLICIT, NULL, AND HIDDEN

The term *curriculum,* as it is conceived of in this writing, refers to the formal curriculum, such as lessons, textbooks, and activities, as well as the informal curriculum, present in school culture (such as school functions and paperwork) and popular culture (such as movies, television, and books). deMarris and LeCompte (1999) explain that

> A curriculum, usually thought of as a course of study or a plan for what is to be taught in an educational institution, is composed of information concerning what is to be taught, to whom, when, and how. Consideration of the curriculum must also include its purpose, content, method, organization, and evaluation. . . . A simpler but more comprehensive way to think about curriculum is that it is *what happens to students in school.* More than the formal content of lessons taught—which is what people normally think of when they envision a curriculum—it is also a method of presentation, the way in which students are grouped in classes, the manner in which time and tasks are organized, and the interaction within classrooms. The term *curriculum* refers to the total school experience provided to students, whether planned or unplanned by educators. By conceptualizing the curriculum this broadly, we are able to include its intended as well as unintended outcomes. (p. 223)

Cortes (1981) also provides a useful, broad, and inclusive definition of *curriculum* that incorporates the idea of the existence of many agents and locations of education in students' lives, such as peer groups, neighborhoods, families, church organizations, occupations, mass media, and "other socializing forces that 'educate' all of us throughout our lives" (p. 24). In terms of both formal and informal curriculum, several scholars (Jackson, 1968; Peshkin, 1992) have endeavored to define the various forms of curriculum, with the most commonly defined and explored forms being the *explicit* (also called *overt* or *written*) curriculum, the *null* curriculum, and the *hidden* (also called *implicit* or *covert*) curriculum. It is important to note that the unifying construct foundational to these various forms of curriculum is this: *Curriculum sends messages to students.* Some messages are acknowledged and openly sanctioned, some are implicit and silently supported, and others are unrecognized or even subliminally suggested.

The Explicit Curriculum of Family

The most commonly considered form of curriculum, the explicit curriculum, is based upon what is *present* in curriculum. This form of curriculum consciously and purposefully addresses knowledge of family. It is represented by intentional instruction. deMarris and LeCompte (1999) discuss the explicit curriculum and its most influential stakeholders:

> Since schools are highly political institutions, the content and form of instruction depend in part upon which socioeconomic interests wield power in society.... [P]articular textbooks chosen determine what curricula will dominate a school system, since textbooks often serve as the curriculum. These choices are powerfully influenced by negotiations among the textbook publishing industry, state and federal educational policymakers, special-interest groups (teachers' unions, associations of school administrators, parent-teacher associations, religious organizations, etc.), and corporations. All of these interest groups differ radically in their beliefs about the purpose of schooling, its role in transmitting ideas and values, and which ideas and values should be taught. (p. 228)

The struggle over the selection of textbooks used in the explicit curriculum represents a struggle for control over the messages within those textbooks. Textbook representations of family are among those messages most contested.

The traditional, nuclear family continues to be the primary focus of textbook depictions of families and family life. Library and supplemental books can be used to help broaden the definition of family, as pointed out in Chapter 8 of this book, but many still feature misconceptions or narrowly defined normative assumptions. In addition to the "gaping holes in the literature" that they identify, Colabucci and Conley also report that normatively, "Expectations of women and mothers are conveyed in subtle but powerful ways through these stories. Similarly, assumptions about the role of race and ethnicity and the nature of difference pervade these books." Such normative expectations of the roles of family members based on particular gender, race, and so forth are another area of family diversity that is often even more subtle.

Adding yet another dimension is the common expectation held for physical sameness among all members of a family, as Heilman explored in Chapter 1 of this book. The danger in providing these restrictive definitions and representations of family, the roles allowed (or disallowed) within them, and the expected appearance of members is that by doing so, we are condoning an implied standard that becomes constituted as the normal conception of family, leaving alternate forms and enactments of family and family roles to be judged as different or even, abnormal.

Classroom lessons, activities, and assignments are also a form of the explicit curriculum. As I have discussed elsewhere:

> The common K–3 curriculum introduces and defines concepts of family with lessons and activities which belong to variants within the familiar "family tree" genre. Even the most well-meaning teachers can be unintentionally exclusive when using such familiar activities by not realizing that if students are being raised by single parents, step-families, grandparents or other relatives, gay parents, or in adoptive or foster families they will likely have some background that is missing, complicated, or even kept secret. The family tree activities have restrictive and pre-defined branches to be filled by the biological family members and the projects of students from other forms of family often result in "funny-looking, unbalanced trees". Students from nontraditional and othered families often also feel awkward and excluded when asked to write an autobiography or bring baby photos to class. Even doing genealogy studies in middle and secondary school classes can make older students extremely uncomfortable. (Turner-Vorbeck, 2006, p. 165)

My own three children have all been asked to do the family-tree, baby photo, early autobiography, and genealogy assignments at various times in their public school years. Just last year, my youngest daughter, who was then 12 years old and in the seventh grade at her middle school, arrived home in tears because her "very strict" new language arts teacher told students that they must go home and interview both parents on why they gave their child his or her first name. She was long accustomed to being put on the spot about being an adopted child, but for reasons undoubtedly related to the unique peer-group pressures of middle school, along with her own fragile, developing adolescent identity, she was distressed about the ignorance of yet another well-meaning teacher and the burden of once again having to explain her difference to her classmates. Of course, these circumstances do produce teachable moments. It gave me another opportunity to contact a teacher about the need for sensitivity and inclusion in the curriculum to diverse forms of family. It also gave my daughter a chance to decide creatively how she could meet the requirements of the assignment, which she did. She decided to write and orally report about a nickname she was given by me shortly after her adoption at age 4.

There are hundreds of similar examples of restrictive classroom activities and assignments that frustrated family members have communicated to me across the last 12 years, and although, if handled appropriately, they can become opportunities for learning and growth, they are also often unnecessarily painful and are usually perpetuated out of habit or ignorance.

Popular culture provides another form of curriculum, as the lessons that its books, movies, and music impart upon youth become a larger and larger part of their out-of-school education. Cultural and media scholars have been bearing witness to the increasingly powerful impact that popular culture is having on the education and socialization of youth, perhaps even eclipsing that of formal schooling (Cortes, 2000; Kellner, 1998). Popular culture artifacts are also becoming more widely utilized by classroom teachers as tools to support the official school curriculum because of the increased student interest and motivation attributed to their classroom use. Although this chapter does not provide an analysis of such items of popular culture, one example is useful to briefly explore due to its enormous prevalence as an item from popular culture that has been adopted for use as classroom material: the *Harry Potter* books. In the critical book *Harry Potter's World*, several authors explore the series for messages of family and family roles and identities, coming to similar conclusions:

> We see echoes of the same [stereotypical] roles throughout the *Harry Potter* series. Domineering fathers head the Crouch and Malfoy families (in fact, the Malfoy family seems like a magical world version of the Dursleys), while nurturing mothers in the Crouch and Potter families literally die to save their sons. . . [families] are comical, conventional, superficial, predictable—and totally misrepresentative of the diversity of family structures in contemporary society. (Kornfeld & Prothro, 2003, p. 191)

The disturbing conclusion about representations of family in the explicit curriculum in all of its various forms (textbooks, library/supplemental books, classroom lessons, activities, and assignments, as well as popular culture) is that the images of all the real families of the actual students in our classrooms are not visible, but rather, many are invisible.

The Null Curriculum on Family

Curriculum scholars have been attempting to define and address the existence and importance of a null curriculum for a number of years. The term *null curriculum* has been most widely associated with curriculum scholar Eliot Eisner (1994), who observes:

> There is something of a paradox involved in writing about a curriculum that does not exist. Yet, if we are concerned with the consequences of school programs and the role of curriculum in shaping those consequences, then it seems to me that we are well advised to consider not only the explicit and implicit

curricula of schools but also what schools do not teach. It is my thesis that what schools do not teach may be as important as what they do teach. I argue this position because ignorance is not simply a neutral void; it has important effects on the kinds of options one is able to consider, the alternatives that one can examine, and the perspectives from which one can view a situation or problems. (p. 9)

Kincheloe, Slattery, and Steinberg (2000) explain the null curriculum as that which "gets left out of the curriculum—those authors, ideas, topics, and issues that go undiscussed" (p. 324). The null curriculum results from decisions made about what to teach and what not to teach, about what gets in and what gets left out of the curriculum. The lack of inclusion in the explicit curriculum of diverse forms of family, either through materials or through lessons themselves, is an example of a null curriculum. Because non-nuclear forms of family are considered controversial by many people, it fits the description of a null curriculum, as "many school districts and teachers ignore or gloss over these controversial topics, which is the null curriculum in action" (p. 324). They attribute to Goodson (1997) this description of the significance of the null curriculum, stating that, "Like the hidden curriculum, the null curriculum has a greater impact on students than the overt curriculum. The null curriculum and the hidden curriculum affect students forever; whereas students often forget the overt curriculum shortly after they complete their proficiency tests" (p. 325).

In researching the representations of family in social studies curriculum, where the explicit curriculum commonly addresses the concept of family, I was disheartened to find that

> Non-traditional forms of family are more often than not simply absent from most forms of curriculum and also from most educational standards, ruling them irrelevant. Gay families, adoptive families, and families headed by grandparents and single parents are prominently absent in the language of the typical. (Turner-Vorbeck, 2006, p. 166)

These common, diverse forms of family are missing from school curriculum on family in spite of the substantial claims from cultural and family scholars that diverse forms of family represent the majority of families and what is typical, as opposed to what they call the "myth" of the nuclear family (Chambers, 2001; Coontz, 1992, 1997, 1999, 2000, 2003; Giddens, 2003; Stacey, 1990, 1996, 2000; Thomas & Wilcox, 1987). This begs the question: What is a *normal* family?

As argued by the authors in this book and many family scholars, what is a *normal* family and what is an *ideal* family may be commonly understood and agreed upon by the majority of members in a society, but these conceptions are not built upon fact. Nor do these conceptions represent the reality of the majority of families today. In fact, they may never have represented reality.

The Hidden Curriculum on Family

Coexisting alongside the explicit curriculum is the hidden curriculum on family. Curriculum scholars examining this form of curriculum generally agree that the hidden curriculum is latent, created by what is *implied* as either legitimate or illegitimate knowledge about family within school discourses not usually identified as "official curriculum" (Blumberg & Blumberg, 1994; Lynch, 1989; Portelli, 1993; Seddon, 1983). The hidden curriculum is constituted by what students learn in school that is not a part of the intentional, explicit curriculum. According to Longstreet and Shane (1993), the hidden curriculum "refers to the kinds of learning children derive from the very nature and organizational design of the public school, as well as from the behaviors and attitudes of teachers and administrators" (p. 46). The hidden curriculum, therefore, includes the structure of the school itself (schedules, class periods, discipline policies, forms of assessment), the physical organization of schools and classrooms, teacher-student interactions, teachers' subjective expectations of students and interpretations of their behaviors and motivations, and identity development and group assimilation of individual students, among other dimensions.

This conceptualization of curriculum reconciles well with the prevalent idea that education is a socialization process and that schools function as a primary socializing institution within society, reflecting the dominant power structure in society. From a neo-Marxist perspective, the hidden curriculum considers the dominant role structures of society and the power they imbibe as most valid, while it seeks both to legitimate and reproduce them. In classic studies on curriculum, scholars and researchers have addressed the hidden curriculum and issues related to it, such as power, control, and hegemony. Two prominent theorists who have each deeply explored the concept of "a hidden curriculum" include Michael Apple and Henry Giroux.

Apple (1979) calls our attention to a need for teachers to be reflective about their roles in the hidden curriculum by stating that

> Since schools as institutions are so interconnected with other political and economic institutions which dominate a collectivity and since schools often unquestioningly act to distribute knowledge and values through both the overt and hidden curriculum that often act to support these same institutions, it is a necessity for educators to engage in searching analyses of the ways in which they allow values and commitments to unconsciously work through them. (p. 120)

The concept of a hidden curriculum of family operating in schools is critically important as we examine its connection to the "othering" of families that fall outside of the parameters of discourse defining the *normal* family and the *ideal* family. As pointed out in the Introduction, critical multiculturalist Arturo Madrid (2001) has written about the negative personal dimensions of *othering*. Relatedly, Apple (1982) considers the notion of the labeling of deviance with that of the hidden curriculum in schools:

> It should be clear that there is a danger in even employing a concept such as deviance. Its traditional usage tends to bring out conceptions of people who are different *and* inferior. In this accepted view, schools are basically meritocratic institutions. They lead to large-scale mobility among groups and individuals in a population. Any lack of mobility, any failure in achievement, is defined as a lack within the individual or group who has failed. One might say here that deviance is "earned" by the deviant, since the overt and hidden curriculum, the social regulations of the classroom, and the categories by which educators organize, evaluate, and give meaning to the activities found in schools are perceived as being basically neutral. This claim of neutrality is, of course, less accurate than its proposition would have us believe. (p. 37)

Apple's (1979) concern is that "the labeling of students, and the school's ameliorative ideology that surrounds its decision to use particular social labels, has a strong impact on which students accept which particular distinctions as natural" (p. 134). If distinctions are uncritically accepted as natural, then they remain unexamined and unchallenged, destined to be repeated and reproduced.

Giroux (1981) focuses us upon the interrelatedness of forms of curriculum as he describes how one level of the hidden curriculum is actually embedded within the formal, explicit curriculum:

> As we have seen, the hidden curriculum of schooling operates at two levels of classroom experience. On one level, specific ideological assumptions and norms are embodied in the cultural capital and modes of reasoning institutionalized by school and used by teachers in the formal curriculum. On another level, students also learn roles, feelings, norms, attitudes, and social expectations from the social context, interpersonal relations, and organizational structures of the classroom. (p. 82)

Building upon these classic scholarly explorations, modern curriculum theorists Kincheloe, Slattery, and Steinberg (2000) argue that aspects of the hidden curriculum potentially have repercussions that extend far beyond the school building:

> The hidden curriculum is at the very least a subconscious communication of values, ideas, and social realities within the schooling community; at worst it is a conscious effort on the part of some teachers, politicians, and educational bureaucrats to perpetuate injustice and retain prevailing social arrangements using the subliminal programming Madison Avenue advertisers employ. (p. 324)

Beyond the theoretical discussion of a hidden curriculum, there is a practical understanding among educators that within a school, there is a very real and foundational aspect of the school's culture that functions as a form of curriculum. Let's consider some of the common dimensions of a hidden curriculum on family (Turner-Vorbeck, 2006).

School Paperwork and Forms

Paperwork and forms that are sent home with students to be completed by adults at home are generally addressed to a "parent" and are usually not flexible enough to allow for the accurate reflection of the complex caretaking networks that constitute the real-life families of our schoolchildren. This also includes the more informal papers sent home, such as requests for classroom assistance (still most often sought as "Room Mothers") and invitations to "Grandparents Day." These written documents are often the first substantial communication that family members receive from the teachers of their children, and their exclusivity reaffirms much of the societal prejudice that is already felt by othered forms of family.

Teacher Talk

Informal conversation among teachers between classes and in the teachers' lounge commonly includes concerns for children from single-parent, stepparent, adoptive, foster, and biracial families, which are widely perceived as substandard. I have sat in on many such conversations while doing research work in schools. In fact, these misconceptions about the "lower quality" of family forms that deviate from the *ideal* family (again, this is a two-parent, heterosexual, married couple, preferably of similar age, ethnicity, and religious background) seem to begin while still in teacher education programs. I have been a teacher educator for many years, and one of the most common and most difficult to displace preconceptions held by a majority of preservice teachers is the assumption of deficits in the home environment for students who are not from *ideal* families.

Dysfunctional Labels

Parents are sometimes even directly subjected to teacher prejudice on the psychological soundness of family forms when remarks are made such as, "I'll be watching for abandonment issues to surface in your child," when the child is identified as adopted. Teachers commonly are quick to blame a student's poor academic achievement or slow social development on a substandard form of family rather than to explore their own pedagogy; they are even less likely to reflect upon their own biases about forms of family and how those biases might be impacting their interaction with and expectations of students. Ways to address these biases are discussed later in this chapter.

Moral Judgments

In conservative climates, in public as well as parochial schools, students are often openly told that a gay, lesbian, and/or transgender lifestyle is immoral. These messages are often buttressed by the null curriculum on family where images of lesbian, gay, bisexual, transgender, or queer (LGBTQ) individuals, let alone families, are clearly, purposefully absent from the explicit curriculum in both visual and written forms (see also Chapter 7, this volume).

AWARENESS—REFLECTION—ACTION

The discussion in this chapter, and indeed, the entire book, leads us to the question: *What can be done?* Awareness is the place to begin, and this chapter, along with all of the other chapters in this book, is designed to help cultivate *awareness* on issues surrounding family diversity and school and culture. Following awareness is the need for *reflection* and then *action*. Each chapter in this book also provides some questions to deeply consider (either alone, in groups, or both), to begin to construct your own meanings around the issues presented in this collection. Through thoughtful reflection, courses of action become apparent. More important, through thoughtful reflection, the courses of action that become apparent to you are authentic in their origin and will hold more meaning and sustenance for you as you pursue them.

Reflective Practice

In reflective practice, self-study processes help individuals uncover information on personal dimensions related to social-psychological aspects of teaching, counseling, and advocating, such as identity, role, commitment, and socialization, allowing for even more empowerment through self-knowledge. Referring to teacher self-study through reflection, Allender (2001) states:

Intellectual and experiential knowledge are important to the ongoing development of teaching skills but preferring personal knowledge builds confidence in the power of self and self-study. When personal knowledge is in the forefront, conscious epistemological changes are feasible. Teachers can use this awareness in the classroom to better meet their own needs and those of the students. (p. 3)

Such self-study through reflection can take many shapes and forms. Among the most popular are journaling and action research.

Along with scholars who advocate for reflective practice (Darling-Hammond, 1997; Schoen, 1983; Zeichner & Liston, 1996), I have argued that education professionals need to have the resources and develop the skills with which to consider the knowledge and theories generated through academic scholarship in light of their personal, lived experiences in order to establish the relevance of such academic theories to their practices. Part of this relevance is also established by making a personal connection between their practices and their identities as teachers.

Scholars such as Dalmau and Gudjonsdotter (2002) encourage educators to go one step further and to locate the personal experience of their roles in the shared experience of their professions and to "use analytical frames of meaning to support connection-building" between their own implicit pedagogy and more formal scholarship, as well as between their own lived experiences and the sociocultural and political influences that impact the multiple forms of curriculum in schools (p. 115). This book is designed to be the launching point to help you do just that, and these words can be applied to anyone involved in the educational system.

Preservice and In-service Professional Development

In addition to self-study through reflective practice, both alone and in collaboration with other reflective practitioners, there are more formal development opportunities available to both preservice (students) and in-service (practitioners) professionals. Although it is sometimes difficult to find professional development opportunities that speak to you and your unique concerns, many are worthwhile. Let your administrators and coworkers know that you are interested in pursuing professional development opportunities related to family diversity. You will likely find others who are like-minded about this. At the very least, you will bring awareness to an important issue, stirring interest among colleagues where there may not have been any previously. Again, *awareness leads to reflection* and *reflection leads to action.*

Because of my personal, deep interest in the topic of family diversity and schooling, I have created a seminar that addresses those issues. It evolved from my teaching of multicultural education courses to preservice teachers and my being frustrated at the lack of attention to, or even mention of, family diversity among the many "multicultural" topics (race, class, gender, ability, language, age) covered in common multicultural education text-books and scholarship. The creation of this seminar is fully documented in the journal *Multicultural Education* (Turner-Vorbeck, 2005), but I will share some of the foundational principles and methods with you here. What follows are brief descriptions of the four main objectives of the seminar I created on family diversity.

Objective 1. Develop Awareness and Initial Understanding of Family Diversity

To accomplish the first objective, a very brief lecture is given to provide foundational information. The changing demographics of our nation's school population are addressed, including the fact that less than 50% of children in schools in America are represented by a two-heterosexual-parent, biological family and that the trend away from traditional, nuclear families is increasing. This demonstrates the necessity for educators to con-template how they will address and work with issues of family diversity in their schools and classrooms. A few short narratives, collected from people from nontraditional families, in which they shared some of their personal painful school experiences, are read to the participants to help put a hu-man face on the real consequences of ignorance or indifference toward family diversity. Examples of possible forms of families are introduced (e.g., foster, adopted, step, grandparent/relative, gay/lesbian, interracial) to ex-pose participants to the wide variety of forms of family with which they might not have been familiar. To complement descriptions of difference, a discussion of the unifying themes across families is provided. This notion is based upon how families function with similar goals and purposes, such as "providing for basic needs, child rearing, socializing members, establishing and maintaining cultural traditions, and delegating responsibilities and roles"(Turner-Vorbeck, 2005, p. 7).

Objective 2: Discover Participants' Opinions and Biases on Family Diversity

The second objective is achieved through a guided discussion of the assigned readings as well as discovery of the participants' own biases. The participants are asked to write down their responses to this question:

- Being honest, what are some of the personal prejudices you hold or have previously held about nontraditional (single-parent, adoptive, gay/lesbian, stepparent, multiracial, etc.) families?

Participants are then asked to move into pairs to share their responses with a partner and to work together to complete these two questions:

- How do you think those prejudices translate into the school or classroom environment?
- How, as an educator, might you create a more positive, accepting environment for children from nontraditional families?

The whole group reconvenes and answers to the question of biases held about differing forms of family are verbally volunteered, written on the board, and discussed. Responses to the second group of questions answered in pairs are then collected and discussed. Many participants are amazed at the extent to which they and their colleagues hold strong prejudicial beliefs against nontraditional forms of family.

Objective 3: Create Activities for Use in the Classroom on Family Diversity

For the third objective, small groups of three to four participants work with markers and large sheets of paper (these are provided) to create a unique activity that could allow P–12 students to express information about themselves and their families in a free and unrestricted fashion. Then the whole group gathers to share these ideas and to discuss commercially available examples of activities, materials, and lessons (these are provided), such as the film and accompanying instructor's guide, *That's a Family!* (Cohen & Chasnoff, 2000).

Objective 4. Reflect on Views of Family Diversity Through Journaling

Participants are asked to thoughtfully write answers to the questions that follow. They are asked to produce approximately two to three pages of written reflection.

- Thinking back over the discussions on family diversity, what issue(s) intrigued you most or caused you to think about something you had not considered before?
- During the class discussions, many issues concerning family diversity surfaced. What made the biggest impression on you and why?
- How do you feel that these issues have impacted your ideas about teaching?
- Do you see any of these ideas translating into your own teaching practice? How?

- Do you have any personal experiences that you can relate to this discussion?
- Describe what "family diversity" means to you now.
- What types of families do you expect to see represented by the students you will teach?

CONCLUSION

In this chapter, I draw attention to the incongruence between the multiple curricular representations of family and the actual, living, everyday families of our students and argue that curricular conceptual representations of family must be reshaped to accurately reflect and honor the many and varied ways in which people form caring groups that support and honor their members. In previous research (Turner-Vorbeck, 2005, 2006), I have documented the limited attempts on the part of classroom materials and textbook publishers to broaden conceptions and discussions of family; the damaging talk, procedures, policies, and negative biases largely held and commonly practiced in school culture; and the predominance of traditional images and portrayals of exclusively nuclear family forms in curriculum and popular culture. The other authors of this book support the notion that through continued research, education, and dialogue, the discussions about and representations of family will become more inclusive. In order to reach such goals, the building blocks of change (awareness, reflection, and action) are required. This book represents a lens through which to focus on such goals of inclusivity related to family diversity.

QUESTIONS FOR REFLECTION

1. Define *explicit curriculum, null curriculum,* and *hidden curriculum* and explain the differences between these terms.
2. What are some examples of restrictive definitions of family that you have encountered in school curriculum? In which form of curriculum did you find these representations? What about restrictive definitions of family specifically found in popular culture?
3. How could the examples you identified in question number 2 be recrafted to employ more inclusive representations of families? Give examples.
4. As an educator, what is your role in shaping students' definitions of family? As a school counselor? As a parent? As a student? Other roles?

5. What professional development opportunities related to family diversity are available to you? If none is readily available, consider developing your own.

6. How has this chapter, or any of the other chapters in this book, changed your thinking about schools, culture, and families? How do you foresee this impacting your personal or professional life?

REFERENCES

Allender, J. (2001). *Teacher self: The practice of humanistic education.* Lanham, MD: Rowman & Littlefield Publishers.

Apple, M. (1979). *Ideology and curriculum.* New York: Routledge.

Apple, M. (1982). *Education and power.* New York: Routledge.

Blumberg, A., & Blumberg, P. (1994). *The unwritten curriculum.* Thousand Oaks, CA: Corwin.

Chambers, D. (2001). *Representing the family.* London: Sage.

Cohen, H. (Producer), & Chasnoff, D. (Director). (2000). That's a family! [Motion picture]. United States: Women's Educational Media.

Coontz, S. (1992). *The way we never were: American families and the nostalgia trap.* New York: Basic Books.

Coontz, S. (1997). *The way we really are: Coming to terms with America's changing families.* New York: Basic Books.

Coontz, S. (Ed.). (1999). *American families: A multicultural reader.* New York: Routledge.

Coontz, S. (2000). Historical perspectives on family diversity. In D. Demo, K. Allen, & M. Fine (Eds.). *Handbook of family diversity* (pp. 15–28). New York: Oxford University Press.

Coontz, S. (2003). What we really miss about the 1950s. In A. Skolnick & J. Skolnick (Eds.), *Family in transition* (12th ed. pp.170–176). Boston: Allyn & Bacon.

Cortes, C. (1981). The societal curriculum: Implications for multiethnic educations. In J. Banks (Ed.), *Educations in the 80s: Multhiethnic education* (pp. 24–32). Washington, DC: National Education Association.

Cortes, C. (2000). *The children are watching: How the media teach about diversity.* New York: Teachers College Press.

Dalmau, M., & Gudjonsdotter, H. (2002). Framing professional discourse with teachers: Professional working theory. In J. Loughran & T. Russell (Eds.), *Improving teacher education practices through self-study* (pp. 102–129). London: Routledge/Falmer.

Darling-Hammond, L. (1997). *The right to learn: A blueprint for creating schools that work.* San Francisco: Jossey-Bass.

deMarrais, K.B., & LeCompte, M.D. (1999). The way schools work: A sociological analysis of education (3rd ed.) New York: Addison Wesley Longman.

Eisner, E.W. (1994). The educational imagination: On design and evaluation of school programs. (3rd. ed). New York: Macmillan

Giddens, A. (2003). The global revolution in family and personal life. In A. Skolnick & J. Skolnick (Eds.), *Family in transition* (12th ed. pp. ix–xii). Boston: Allyn & Bacon.

Giroux, H. (1981). *Ideology, culture, and the process of schooling.* London: Falmer Press.

Goodson, I. (1997). *The changing curriculum: Studies in social construction.* New York: Peter Lang.

Jackson, P. (1968). *Life in classrooms.* New York: Holt, Rinehart and Winston.

Kellner, D. (1998). Beavis and Butt-Head: No future for postmodern youth. In S.R. Steinberg & J.L. Kincheloe (Eds.), *Kinderculture: The corporate construction of childhood* (pp.85–102). Boulder, CO: Westview Press.

Kincheloe, J, Slattery, P. & Steinberg, S. (2000). *Contextualizing teaching.* New York: Addison Wesley Longman.

Kornfeld, J., & Prothro, L. (2003). Comedy, conflict, and community: Home and family in *Harry Potter.* In E. Heilman (Ed.), *Harry Potter's World: Multidisciplinary Perspectives* (pp. 187–202). New York: Routledge.

Longstreet, W. & Shane, H. (1993). *Curriculum for a new millennium.* Boston: Allyn and Bacon.

Lynch, K. (1989). *The hidden curriculum.* London: Falmer Press.

Madrid, A. (2001). Missing people and others: Joining together to expand the circle. In M. Andersen & P. Hill-Collins (Eds.), *Race, class, and gender* (pp. 23–27). Belmont, CA: Wadsworth.

Peshkin, A. (1992). The relationship between culture and curriculum: A many fitting thing. In P. W. Jackson (Ed.), *Handbook on research on curriculum* (pp. 248267). New York: Macmillan.

Portelli, J. (1993). Exposing the hidden curriculum. *Journal of Curriculum Studies, 25*(4), 343–358.

Schoen, D. (1983). *The reflective practitioner.* New York: Basic Books.

Seddon, S. (1983). The hidden curriculum: An overview. *Curriculum Perspectives, 3*(1), 1–6.

Stacey, J. (1990). *Brave new families.* Berkeley: University of California Press.

Stacey, J. (1996). *In the name of the family: Rethinking family values in the postmodern age.* Boston: Beacon Press.

Stacey, J. (2000). The handbook's tail: Toward revels or a requiem for family diversity? In D. Demo, K. Allen, & M. Fine (Eds.), *Handbook of family diversity* (pp. 424–439). New York: Oxford University Press.

Thomas, D., & Wilcox, J. (1987). The rise of family theory: A historical and critical analysis. In M. Sussman & S. Steinmetz (Eds.), *Handbook of marriage and the family* (pp. 81–102). New York: Plenum.

Turner-Vorbeck, T. (2006). Representations of family in curriculum: A poststructural analysis. In C. Cherryholmes, E. Heilman, & A. Segall (Eds.), *Social studies—The next generation: Researching social studies in the postmodern* (pp. 153–169). New York: Peter Lang.

Turner-Vorbeck, T. (2005, Winter). Expanding multicultural education to include family diversity. *Multicultural Education, 13*(2), 6–10.

Zeichner, K., & Liston, D. (1996). *Reflective teaching: An introduction.* Mahwah, NJ: Erlbaum.

About the Editors
and the Contributors

Tammy Turner-Vorbeck, Ph.D., is a visiting professor of teacher education at Wabash College whose focus includes multiculturalism/diversity, curriculum theory, and sociology of teaching. Her research explores relationships among schooling, culture, and identity, particularly family structure diversity and equity issues. Her work has appeared in *Curriculum Inquiry* and *Multicultural Education,* and she is the author of several book chapters. She speaks at educational conferences on issues of family diversity and representations of family in school curricula, and she provides workshops to preservice teachers and teachers on addressing family diversity in curricula and classrooms.

Monica Miller Marsh, Ph.D., is currently an associate professor at De-Sales University and is interested in teacher education, early childhood and elementary education, and issues of diversity. Her work has been published in journals such as *Curriculum Inquiry, International Journal of Qualitative Research in Education* and *Reflective Practice.* Her book, *The Social Fashioning of Teacher Identities,* focuses on how the identities of two first-year teachers are crafted as they move through the contexts of their teacher education programs, the elementary schools in which they teach, and the biographical aspects of their lives.

Lesley Colabucci, Ph.D., is an assistant professor of elementary and early childhood education at Millersville University of Pennsylvania, where she teaches graduate and undergraduate classes in children's literature. Her research interests include multicultural children's literature and response to literature.

Matthew D. Conley, Ph.D., is an assistant professor of education at Ohio Dominican University in Columbus, Ohio. He teaches literacy and diversity courses in the Early Childhood Teacher Preparation Program.

Elizabeth Heilman, Ph.D., is an associate professor at Michigan State University. She does research exploring the political and social imagination. Her work has appeared in journals such as *Educational Theory, Teaching Education, Youth and Society, The High School Journal,* and *Theory and Research in Social Education.* She is the editor of three books, including *Harry Potter's World: Multidisciplinary Critical Perspectives.*

Janice Kroeger, Ph.D., is an assistant professor of early childhood education in the Department of Teaching, Leadership, and Curriculum Studies at Kent State University. Her primary teaching and research interests lie in social justice for young children; home, school, and community partnerships; and identity and culture.

Ilyana Marks holds a master's degree and public school credential in school counseling and is currently working toward a master's in education leadership at Chapman University in Orange, California. She has worked with youth in group homes, homeless shelters, nonprofit organizations, public schools, and the university setting to provide supports for a path toward postsecondary education.

A. Y. "Fred" Ramirez, Ph.D., is an associate professor of education at California State University, Fullerton, where he chairs the department of secondary education's multicultural education courses, teaches a master's level course on families and schools, and is in charge of a professional development district. He received his degree from Indiana University, Bloomington, in the field of curriculum and instruction.

Lisa Rieger has been an elementary educator for 13 years with the Binghamton City School District. Presently, she is working in her district as an elementary enrichment teacher. Her areas of interest include instructional leadership, educational renewal, and the development of community and arts partnerships with schools. She is currently pursuing an administrative degree at Marywood University.

Teresa J. Rishel, Ph.D., is an assistant professor of middle childhood education at Kent State University. Her research interests include adolescent suicide, student emotional health, and teacher perceptions of caring. Other interests include social justice, equity, and multicultural awareness. She taught for 15 years in elementary and middle schools and served as an elementary principal.

Tracy Thoennes is a doctoral candidate in curriculum studies at Purdue University. Her research interests focus on issues related to the marginalization of certain student populations and the impact of poverty and homelessness upon young children's school experiences. She has 13 years of experience teaching young children in preschool programs, university laboratory schools, and elementary schools.

Index